Herbal Remedies of the Lumbee Indians

Herbal Remedies of the Lumbee Indians

ARVIS LOCKLEAR BOUGHMAN *and*
LORETTA O. OXENDINE

McFarland & Company, Inc., Publishers
Jefferson, North Carolina, and London

LIBRARY OF CONGRESS CATALOGUING-IN-PUBLICATION DATA

Boughman, Arvis Locklear, 1964–
    Herbal remedies of the Lumbee Indians / Arvis Locklear
Boughman and Loretta O. Oxendine.
      p.   cm.
    Includes bibliographical references and index.

    ISBN-13: 978-0-7864-1332-4
    softcover : 50# alkaline paper ∞

    1. Lumbee Indians—Medicine.   2. Traditional medicine
—North Carolina.   3. Medicinal plants—North Carolina.
[DNLM: 1. Phytotherapy—North Carolina.   2. Indians,
North American—history—North Carolina.   3. Medicine,
Traditional—North Carolina.   4. Plants, Medicinal—North
Carolina.   WB 925 B758h 2004]   I. Oxendine, Loretta O.
II. Title.
E99.C91B68   2004
615'.321'089973—dc22   2003022480

British Library cataloguing data are available

Cover illustration ©2004 Art Today

Manufactured in the United States of America

McFarland & Company, Inc., Publishers
  Box 611, Jefferson, North Carolina 28640
   www.mcfarlandpub.com

To Cleveland Jacobs, Lumbee basketmaker.
He was blind in physical sight, but had eyes
as sharp as an eagle's in spiritual insight.
—Loretta O. Oxendine

To my son, Micah Boughman, and
daughter, Clara-Ann Boughman.
Always keep the fire and the love burning.
—Arvis L. Boughman

For the Lumbee Nation; our blood and spirit have never died;
and in honor and memory of
Vernon Hazel Lowry Locklear and
Martinez "Mark" Godwin.
—Arvis L. Boughman and Loretta O. Oxendine

ACKNOWLEDGMENTS

We wish to thank the following people and organizations for their invaluable contributions to this work:

Amy Locklear, Dr. Stanley Knick, Glenn Ellen Starr Stilling, Joseph Bruchac, Linda Massengill, Kimberley S. Boughman, Herman Oxendine, Charles Boughman, Bruce Barton, Choogie Kingfisher, the Catawba nation, the Snowbird Cherokee, the Tuscarora Nation of North Carolina, Native American Resource Center at the University of North Carolina at Pembroke, Daystar Dial, Pete "Spotted Turtle" Clark, Hayes Alan Locklear, Henry and Leitha Chavis, Vernon Hazel Locklear, Earl Carter, Keith Brown, Mary Sue Locklear, Dr. Joseph Bell, Welton Lowry, Freddie Chavis, Rosa Lee Cooper, Sparks Cooper, Woodrow Cooper, Marilyn Cooper, Margaret Cooper, Willis Cummings, Vernon and Dorothy Boughman, Sue Lee, Conee Brayboy, Grady Locklear, Renee Hammonds, Freeman Owle, Clint Garrison, Marcus Castro, the *Fayetteville Observer*, *The State* (Columbia, S.C., newspaper), the VCR Doctor (Morganton, N.C.), Beyond Words Publishing, and the Burke County (N.C.) Public Library.

The Lumbee Nation, Ricky and Bonnie Sherrill, Eastern Band of Cherokee Indians, Ray Littleturtle, Swain County Schools, National Indian Education Association (NIEA), Tim Brayboy, Barbara Braveboy, Crystal Fedor, Frederick "Fishhound" Arch, Brandon Sutton, and Jeff Fuller.

CONTENTS

PREFACE

And God said, "Behold, I have given you every herb bearing
seed, which is upon the face of the earth, and every tree, in which
is the fruit of a tree yielding seed; to you it shall be for meat."
—Genesis 1:29

Most North Carolina Lumbee live in rural areas of Robeson and surrounding counties with access to a number of healing plants or herbs. In the past, the majority of these plants were gathered from surrounding fields, roadsides, swamps, and ditches, and the edges of forests. Many Lumbee preferred to collect plants when needed and chose the fresh and healthy looking growth. A few healers would only collect herbs during the full moon and only prepare medicine on the new moon. Others would collect the material on the west side of the plant (the direction of the setting sun). It was also the practice of many healers to leave some of the root material in the ground or soak it in water and then place the material back in the soil so the herb would return.

In Saddletree, Prospect, and many other Lumbee communities of Robeson and surrounding counties, both "town medicine" and "Indian medicine" were practiced. Folks did not have the money or time to go to town to see a doctor every time someone in the family became sick from an upset stomach, fever, burn, or other ailment. For instance, if "poppa" or "momma" (Lumbee nicknames for children) got an upset stomach, he or she would probably be told by his or her mother, aunt, uncle, or cousin to go out to the ditchbank to collect some Sassafras leaves to make into a tea. If "boosie" or "mootie" (Lumbee nicknames for children) developed a fever, he or she might be instructed to find some collard leaves to tie around his or her wrists and ankles. If "mookie" or "bubba" (Lumbee nicknames for children) had burned his or her hand on the stove, grandma might make a salve out of tobacco leaves and seeds gathered from the field. Many of the Lumbee healers learned the

1

plant remedies from their families and friends as a normal part of childhood. The "Indian medicine" really did work.

Today it is common practice to treat aches, pains, or ailments with herbal remedies, and many people swear by the results. One of the most prominent modern Lumbee "healers," not to be confused with a conjurer or rootworker, was Vernon Cooper. According to Mr. Lew Barton, Lumbee author and poet, a root worker is a person who is said to have supernatural powers to cast out spells, heal the sick, bring good fortune, and reunite estranged couples, and who has the supposed ability to bring back the spirits of deceased loved ones. Many Lumbee shunned those they believed to be rootworkers or conjurers, believing they received their power from the great evil spirit. The ancestors of the Lumbee believed this great bad spirit, called Hmbara', caused sickness, losses, disappointments, hunger, and other misfortunes.

Mr. Vernon was a resident of the Hawkeye community (a southern Hoke County Lumbee community named after a Lumbee leader called Chief Hawkeye) for most of his life and a member of the Lumbee tribe. He wove the power of Christian faith with traditional Lumbee medicine to cure both Indian and non–Indian people. He was the embodiment of a "shaman" or one which treats psychological and physical ills and understands the balance between them. Mr. Vernon, while being interviewed for *Wisdomkeepers*, a book that featured prominent Native American elders from across the country, commented:

> There's nothing happens to a person that can't be cured if you get what it takes to do it. We come out of the earth, and there's something in the earth to cure everything. In the old days, before my time, it took only a single herb to cure a person; now it takes a combination. Trouble is, you can't find most of the herbs and roots around here anymore. All these farm chemicals have killed'm off. You've got to go up in the hills to find them, and I'm getting too old for that anymore. I don't fix a tonic until I'm sure what's wrong with a person. I don't make guesses. I have to be sure, because medicine can do bad as well as good, and I don't want to hurt anybody. Whatever the Lord shows me, that's what I'm going to do. Maybe it takes some herbs. Maybe it takes some touching. But most of all it takes faith [all and Arden].

The plants and herbs gathered by the Lumbee Indian plant doctors were used to make teas, poultices, or salves. For teas, the plants were gently boiled in a pan of water until the decoction was a dark color or until half the water was lost. After being boiled from one to two hours, the teas were usually taken internally in doses from one teaspoon to one quart or more, although most doses were a swallow to a cup of liquid. The tea was generally taken hot, and the most important doses were considered to be those taken without food in the stomach before going to sleep at night and upon waking up in the morning. A decoction is a tea made from the roots and bark of a plant, but an infusion is a tea fashioned from the leaves and blossom.

Poultices were made of herbs and roots which were chopped small and boiled in water almost to a jelly. The fresh herb was crushed and bruised but the powdered or dried herb was also used on occasion. The poultice material was mixed with enough water to make a thick paste and applied to the affected area. A cloth was placed over the paste and the wound and changed as it dried. The herb was also mixed with cornmeal, Slippery Elm or Flax seed to make the paste, which was spread on a cloth and applied to the affected area. Many healers would also add a bit of bean meal, barley meal, or sweet suet. In short, a poultice is a hot herb pack applied locally. The poultice was applied to the aggrieved place to ease pain, to break sores, to cool inflammations, to dissolve hardness, or to dissipate swelling. In certain situations, the poultice would be tied and left on the affected area.

Salves and ointments were prepared by boiling the plants in water until only a small amount of liquid remained. The decoction was then strained and the liquid combined with hog fat (lard), deer fat, tallow (beef or mutton fat), or present day commercial products such as Rosebud salve or petroleum jelly.

Vernon Cooper would often taste a bit of the decoction or infusion to measure its strength. He stated that in the Lumbee belief system, the soil had varying strengths, and healing plants could be either a male or female variety. The Lumbee believed the "sex" of the plant and "strength" of the soil were the main factors that affected the potency of the cure.

The main section of this book, "Herbs and Their Applications," details how the Lumbee and some other tribes (usually in the same geographic area) used a specific herb for medicinal purposes. Following a glossary, the section titled "Ailments and Herbs Used in Treatment" serves as a cross-reference to the main body of the book by listing ailments and the associated herbs.

An appendix contains interviews with our living treasures, Lumbee tribal elders, herbalists, and healers. These interviews address an additional dimension of healing, that of faith. One theme throughout the interviews is the importance of one's own personal faith in the healing process. Faith in one's Creator or Sustainer and a confidence that he or she can be healed are the philosophical pillars of the Lumbee healing belief system. Mr. Pete "Spotted Turtle" Clark alluded to this most important facet with the phrase "mind over matter."

The authors undertook this work with the hope that placing a small part of Lumbee herbal and healing culture in print would preserve this knowledge for future generations. The herbal remedies and healing philosophy described herein were taken from personal interviews with living Lumbee tribal elders, conversations with living relatives of deceased Lumbee healers, videotapes and discussions that Paul Vestal, Mary Steedly, and Edward Croom conducted with Vernon Cooper and other Lumbee healers. A second reason this material was gathered was to prove, despite what some uninformed outside sources have indicated, that the Lumbee Indian people do have a vibrant, living Native American history and culture.

"Epta Tewa Newasin." ("Creator, we love you.")

Any attempts to use the plants named herein must be done with extreme caution. Many of them are dangerous. The Lumbee themselves would not ordinarily self-treat but instead call upon a healer, an expert in the use of plant remedies. The information contained within this book is primarily for reference and education. It is not intended to be a substitute for advice or treatment from a physician. The authors do not in any way advocate self-diagnosis or self-medication; we urge anyone with continuing symptoms, however minor, to seek medical advice. The reader should be aware that any plant substance, whether used as food or medicine, externally or internally, may cause an allergic or extremely unhealthy reaction, or death in some individuals.

HISTORY OF THE
LUMBEE INDIANS

Native American people have lived in the area now called Robeson County, in southeastern North Carolina, for thousands of years. The Lumbees are the largest Indian tribe in the United States east of the Mississippi River. They are a proud people who derive their name from their ancestors and the dark river that runs through their homeland. According to the 2000 U.S. census, more than 50,000 Lumbee live in Robeson County (and more reside outside Robeson County).

After the time of European contact, tribal movement and change became the norm rather than the exception for many southeastern U.S. tribes. At the time of contact between the native populations and European explorers, three linguistic stocks were represented in what is now the state of North Carolina. Algonquian-speaking tribes extended along the coastline as far south as the Neuse River. Inland from them were the Iroquoian tribes, the Tuscarora, Nottoway and Meherrin, east of the fall line, and the Cherokee along the ridge of the Appalachians. At the southern end of the state was a number of groups identified by John R. Swanton as Siouan-speaking, including the Waccamaw, Cape Fear, Winyaw, Keyauwee, Catawba, and Cheraw. John Lawson, English explorer, later called these Siouan-speaking tribes the Piedmont tribes because their language, folklore, dances, religious beliefs, and culture were so closely related.

The first known European contact with the Indian tribes in North Carolina occurred in 1524. In that year, Giovanni da Verrazzano, acting on behalf on Francis I of France, sailed along the Outer Banks of Cape Hatteras, thus laying claim to the area for his sovereign. But France was unable to exploit its claim because of problems at home. The Spanish under Hernando de Soto were among the first Europeans to make contact with the ancestors of many Lumbee called the Cheraw, located in what is now the southwestern corner of South Carolina, around the year 1539. The Spanish called them Xuala (Shoe-Wala), Xualla, Joara, or

5

Juada (Swanton 112, 145, 178, 183). As noted by Swanton, some of the Lumbee ancestors in 1566 were visited again by Captain Juan Pardo, a Portuguese working for the Spanish. Traveling in a northerly direction, Pardo came to the "Xuala" (Cheraw) province named by DeSoto. Pardo built a fort, which he called Fort San Juan thought to sit beside the Native American town of Joara (economic and social center for regional tribes and tribal leaders), and after leaving a small garrison of thirty soldiers, continued his explorations. One year later this fort was destroyed by the Cheraw (Swanton 112, 145, 178, 183). The remains of Fort San Juan (Berry site) were unearthed recently in the Upper Creek area of Burke County, in the central Blue Ridge Mountain foothills of North Carolina.

Prior to 1700, a Cheraw community left its homeland and settled along the Dan River in two settlements near the present day Virginia–North Carolina border. Around 1700, John Lawson found a group of Cheraw even farther east, between the Cape Fear and Yadkin rivers. By moving farther south and east, the Cheraw encountered other Siouan tribes, such as the Keyauwee Indians. These tribes were also experiencing population displacement and decline due to diseases such as smallpox (many tribes were annihilated) and increasing warfare with other tribal groups and European settlers.

Tens of thousands of native people became "prisoners of war" and shipped away as slaves to the Carribean, Europe, and West Africa. This New World form of genocide was perpetuated by many of the same individuals who had performed similar atrocities in West Africa. In an attempt to mitigate the disruptive effects of disease and warfare, some related eastern Siouan tribes such as the Cheraw and Sugaree merged for a time in the late 1600s and early 1700s with the Catawba Nation.

After living with the Catawba for approximately 12 years, however, most of the Cheraw left the Catawba Nation and migrated east towards the Great Pee Dee River near present day northeastern South Carolina to reassert their own identity and to escape from such deadly European diseases as smallpox, measles, influenza and cholera. Along the way, elements of the Keyauwee, Eno (Eno Will), Shakori (Chicora), Woccon (Waccamaw), and other eastern Siouan remnant tribes merged with the group of Cheraw to form a united community (Swanton 112, 145, 178, 183). Margaret Brown, one of the last Catawba native speakers, stated that the Croatan (now called Lumbee) were once part of the Catawba nation but left to avoid the smallpox epidemic (Speck 404-417).

Many native peoples did seek refuge in hidden swamplands and mountains. Others ran to Indian territories who gave refuge to people of all races. Some of the members of the Cheraw and related tribes found that the sloughs, pocosins, bays, swamps and lowlands of the Lumbee River area offered isolation from European encroachment and disease.

European settlement of southeastern North Carolina was first delayed, and then later made possible, by devastating diseases and wars between Indians and whites from 1711 to 1716. Another factor contributing to the isolation of the Drowning Creek, or Lumbee River, area was the fact that it was occupied by an Indian group willing to contest the land when European settlers arrived. Given the availability of cheaper and better land elsewhere in North Carolina, it is not surprising that few whites sought land in the Drowning Creek drainage area. As late as 1775, not a single road traversed the Drowning Creek area, and the nearest town was Cross Creek (now called Fayetteville), some forty miles to the north.

The European settlement of North Carolina was also influenced by two important geographical features. First, the lack of deep and wide harbors diverted European immigration to the north, into Virginia and Maryland, and to the south especially to Charleston, South Carolina. The coastal area of present day North Carolina consisted of a chain of islands or banks that were separated from the mainland by five sounds. These sounds, which represented the largest inland waters of any state, were shallow, as were the inlets, making navigation dangerous. The rivers that offered access to the deep-water ports flowed into neighboring South Carolina.

Dr. Stanley Knick, director of the Native American Resource Center and professor of Native American studies and anthropology at the University of North Carolina at Pembroke, says there is strong evidence that the Cheraw and related Siouan tribes came across a group of Native Americans who presumably called themselves Lumbee. The name "Lumbee" also follows the Siouan linguistic pattern, like the Wateree, Sugaree, and PeeDee who were already living in the area. Pottery shards, arrowheads, and other archaeological evidence prove that the Lumbee River area was inhabited by Native Americans thousands of years before the arrival of the Europeans and other native tribes (Knick 4). It has also been suggested that the word Lumbee is derived from the Eastern Siouan word "Lombe" describing the black water of the mysterious Lumbee River.

A community composed of largely Cheraw Indians was first observed on Drowning Creek (Lumbee River) in present day Robeson County in 1724. This same Cheraw community was documented in a map prepared by John Herbert in 1725. Herbert was the commissioner of Indian trade for the Wineau factory on the Black River, the closest European outpost to Drowning Creek at that time. This position allowed him to have an intimate knowledge of the location of the tribes in the area.

In 1738, the remaining Cheraw living in present day northeastern South Carolina along the Great Pee Dee River sold their land and merged with the Cheraw, Lumbee, and smaller eastern Siouan tribes already living in present day Robeson County. A small remnant of this group of Cheraw rejoined their sister tribe, the Catawba (South Carolina Indians). A few members of the devastated coastal tribes and Tuscarora also joined the Cheraw and their sister tribes. Reverend Z.R. "Zimmie" Chavis (b. July 1869, d. February 1968), a respected Lumbee minister of the gospel, stated that his great-grandfather, Ishmiel Chavis, was a chief of the Cheraw while they lived along the Great Pee Dee River, near present day Cheraw in Marlboro County, S.C., before 1738. Robert Locklear, an ancestor of one of the authors, was "king" of the Cheraw Indians in 1738. In 1753, North Carolina Royal Governor Matthew Rowan issued a proclamation identifying Drowning Creek as a frontier to Indians. Later, in 1771, information about the Cheraws of Drowning Creek was reported in the *South Carolina Gazette*.

Native American people of North Carolina learned quickly through their brief experience with the settlers that unless they behaved like their European neighbors, they could be perceived as a threat and their land could be taken away, or they would be annihilated, or they could be shipped off to a distant land. Many Cherokee Indians adopted European style clothing, spoke in English, owned plantations, and even kept slaves to avoid being identified as acting "too Indian." An unidentified Cherokee elder was heard before 1830 admonishing Cherokee children to remember that the whites were near them and unless they learned to speak the white language and write as the whites did, the Cherokee would be cheated out of their land and denied their rights. The elder further instructed the youngsters that for this reason, they needed to be diligent in their studies. Nonetheless, because gold was found on tribal land, the Cherokee were kicked out of their homes and forced on a relocation death march to lands west of the Mississippi River in 1838, known as "The Trail of Tears." The ancestors of the Lumbee, however, were fortunate that no gold was found on their land.

As early as 1725, the lower Cape Fear River received its first permanent European settlers, the Highland Scots. Scottish explorers traveling down the Cape Fear River and into present day southeastern North Carolina found a large group of Native Americans living around the Drowning Creek area. The Highland Scots (they called themselves the Macs—MacPherson, MacDonald, MacIntyre, etc.) were amazed to find that the ancestors of the Lumbee spoke in a broken form of English, held land in a common trust, practiced a form of Christianity (the Lumbee and the related Eastern Siouan tribes have always believed in one God), and grew crops in a European way to feed their families (Dial and Eliades 4). Consequently, the Indians of Robeson County were able to enjoy the freedoms the settlers cherished, such as the right to vote and bear arms, until the early 1800s.

However, in 1835, the North Carolina Constitution was amended to disenfranchise or strip the Cherokee, ancestors of the Lumbee, other Indian groups, and freed African Americans of their citizenship rights such as testifying in court, holding public office, bearing arms and voting. The majority of all remaining Native Americans were misclassified as "mulatto," "negro," "colored," "black," "issue free," or "free persons of color," and rarely listed as Indian/Native American. Later, many Native American men from the Robeson County area were conscripted or forced into slavery to work in salt mines and to build fortifications at Fort Fisher near present day Wilmington. Many who were put into the forced labor camps contracted malaria and other diseases. Some Native American men "hid out" in the swamps to avoid the disease-ridden labor compounds.

One Native American man who "hid out" was Henry Berry Lowrie, legendary outlaw and folk hero. From 1864 to 1874, Lowrie led a guerrilla war against unfair laws, illegal land seizure, forced slavery, oppressive homeguard and Confederate officials, and later, U.S. military officials. His accomplishments are remembered by the tribe and are celebrated each summer in the outdoor drama *Strike at the Wind*, performed at the N.C. Indian Cultural Center in Pembroke.

Years after the end of the Civil War, the North Carolina Constitution was finally amended to restore lost citizenship rights and classification to the remaining Cherokee, ancestors of the Lumbee, other Native American peoples, and African Americans.

In 1885, the N.C. General Assembly recognized the Indians of Robeson County as Croatan and established a separate school system for Indians. Later, in 1887, Native American leaders of Robeson County and the N.C. General Assembly established the Croatan Indian Normal School, which eventually grew to become the University of North Carolina at Pembroke. In 1933 a bill was introduced in Congress to recognize the Indians of Robeson County as Cheraw. In 1953, the N.C. General Assembly agreed to legally change the name of the Indians of Robeson County, at the urging of the tribe, to Lumbee, in honor of their ancestors and the river that ran through their homeland.

The Lumbee hold no treaty with the federal government. However, in 1956, the Congress of the United States passed the Lumbee Act, which officially acknowledged the Indians of Robeson and adjoining counties as Lumbee Indians. This bill contained language that made the Lumbee ineligible for most federal financial support and program services administered by the Bureau of Indian Affairs. This bill was passed at a time of major federal government cutbacks in assistance and services to Indians. The Lumbee have sought full federal recognition from the U.S. government for over 110 years. The Lumbee do, however, receive some federal services and assistance from the Department of Labor, Office of Indian Education, Indian housing and the Administration for Native Americans.

North Carolina now has more than 90,000 Native Americans, including seven state recognized tribes—the Lumbee, Waccamaw-Siouan, Coharie, Meherrin, Haliwa-Saponi, Sappony and Occaneechi Band of Saponi Indians—and one federally recognized tribe, the Eastern Band of Cherokee. All Native American groups in North Carolina strive to retain and rediscover what they can of their unique cultures by passing down stories and tribal knowledge to their children, conducting research, preserving the words of the elders in information storehouses such as books and CD-ROMs, holding spiritual gatherings, and sponsoring special events such as powwows and homecomings. The Lumbee homecoming is every July 4 weekend.

Herbs and Their Uses by the Lumbee

Acorus calamus *see Calamus*

Adam and Eve Root (Aplectrum hyemale); also known as Putty Root

Adam and Eve Root is actually a native orchid. The flowers bloom in May and early June once the leaves have withered and died. After blooming, the leaves reappear and live throughout the winter. The leaves are ten inches long and four inches wide with unique parallel, silver veins. The entire plant can reach a height of eighteen inches, from which yellow-purplish orchid flowers appear. Adam and Eve Root is most often found in shaded, rich, moist woods. The Lumbee healer beat the root into a powder and then boiled it for treatment of pain in the head and boils. The powder was thought by the Lumbee to help children gain weight or become "fleshy and fat." The Cherokee also fed this powder to their hogs to make them fat. The Catawba, a sister tribe of the Lumbee, used this plant to heal a wound or stop an itch.

Adam's Needle *see Bear Grass*

Adder's Tongue (American) (**Erythronium americanum**); also known as Serpent's Tongue, Dog's Tooth Violet, Yellow Snowdrop, American Dog's Tooth Violet

The American Dog's Tooth Violet or Adder's Tongue is a beautiful flower that blooms in early spring. The plant grows from a small, slender, fawn-colored corm one-half to one inch long which is buried deeply into the soil. The stem is a few inches high and bears near the ground. The leaves are oblong, dark-green, and purplish. In *The Education of Little Tree* by Forrest Carter, Little Tree, a young Cherokee boy, describes the Dog's Tooth Violet as having "long pointed yellow petals with a white tooth hanging out." Little Tree thought the white tooth looked like a tongue. Lumbee herbal experts considered the fresh leaves to have emollient and anti-scrofulous properties. For treatment of swellings, tumors, scrofulous ulcers and other skin problems such as rash, Willie French Thompson, a Lumbee healer, would make the plant into a poultice from fresh leaves for external application and recommend that the patient take the infusion at the same time. The infusion was taken internally in wine glassful doses. It was reputed to be emetic and aid in the treatment of dropsy, hiccough, and vomiting.

Agave virginica *see Rattlesnake Root*

All-heal *see Heal-all*

Allium sativum *see Garlic*

Allium vineale *see Wild Garlic*

Alnus rugosa *see Red Tag Alder*

Aloe *see Rat's Tail*

Aloe bardadensis *see Rat's Tail*

Alumroot (Heuchera americana); also known as or American Sanicle
Alumroot has a leafless stem that grows up to three feet high, arising from a dense cluster of long, stalked basal leaves. Yellowish-green blooms appear in late spring to early summer. Alum is found in moist to dry, rich soils in full sun to partial shade. This plant is considered by many herbalists to be one of the strongest astringents in the plant kingdom. A teaspoon of the chopped root, boiled in water for twenty minutes, was used by Lumbee healers as a treatment for gastroenteritis (particularly if the patient was experiencing diarrhea and dry, bilious vomiting). When combined with ¼ teaspoon of Goldenseal root and made into a tea, it was used by the Lumbee as a gargle to treat sore throats. A half-cup was drunk an hour before every meal to reportedly stimulate the healing of ulcers of the esophagus and stomach. Many healers would not suggest the tea for duodenal ulcers, though. A cup of the root tea was drunk every two hours to treat mild dysentery (for severe dysentery, an enema of Alumroot tea was suggested.) This concoction, when prescribed as a douche, was used to treat vaginitis or mild cervicitis (without dysplasia). Lumbee healers would suggest combining equal parts of the dried ground roots of Alumroot, Goldenseal, and Purple Coneflower (Echinacea angustifolia) into a tea for blood clotting and an antiseptic powder for cuts and abrasions. The Chickasaw used this plant for a wellness tonic. The Cherokee used Alumroot to treat hemorrhoids, mouth soreness, irregular menstruation, and gastrointestinal problems.

Ambrosia artemisiifolia *see Ragweed*

American Beech Tree (Fagus grandifolia Ehr); also known as Carolina Beech, Gray Beech **Warning: Large doses of the nuts have been found to be poisonous to humans and animals.**

The American or Carolina Beech is a native tree that is tall and wide. A mature tree can can reach a height of ninety to one hundred feet tall and spread from fifty to seventy feet. The growth buds on the ends of the branches have a yellow tinge, and are conical. American Beech leaves are bright green and about three inches long and turn golden in the fall. The American Beech grows best in sunny areas with deep, rich, moist, well-drained, sandy or loamy soils. This tree has a shallow root system, and the drooping branches make it difficult for anything to grow underneath. American Beech bark is very smooth, pale, and gray. The Beech tree was called "yap tukse'" in the ancient tongue of the Lumbee. The Lumbee made beech tea by boiling the bark taken from the trunk. This tea was also drunk to treat a weak back or backache. The same liquid was mixed with hog lard to form a salve rubbed on the affected area to treat bone rheumatism. The salve was also used to nurse pain from a sprain or broken limb. While uttering a prayer of thanks, many healers would only peel or scrape the bark on the north side of a tree. The Rappahanock soaked Beech bark in salt water to produce a substance to be rubbed on the skin to treat poison ivy. The Iroquois league, or the Five Nations (Cayuga, Onondaga, Mohawk, Seneca, Oneida; the Tuscarora joined in confederacy in the 1700s to become the sixth nation, which changed the name of this league to Six Nations), used Beech nut oil mixed with bear grease as a hair treatment and a mosquito repellant. The tar was thought by many healers to be stimulating and antiseptic. Some healers recommended that the tar be eaten to serve as a stimulating expectorant for bronchitis. Lumbee healers suggested that the "mast" or nuts be chewed for worms. The end of a Beech twig was also chewed up and made into a serviceable toothbrush by many Lumbee.

American Hemp *see Indian Hemp*

American Holly (Ilex vomitoria); also known as Yaupon Tree

American Holly is distinguished from other hollies by its leaves, which are finely toothed throughout their entire length. American Holly leaves are not spine-tipped. The American Holly is considered a shrub. It grows to a height of twenty-four feet. Like its cousins, it produces red, shiny, spherical berries up to a half inch in diameter. The American Holly can be found in habitats ranging from swamps to open fields. Osceola, a great chief of the Seminole tribe, was named after a ceremonial drink made from the American

Holly. This "black drink" was used widely among southeastern Native American tribes. The name Osceola is Muskogean (language family of the Creeks and Seminoles) for "black drink singer." The Seminole also used the black drink to treat someone who was experiencing nightmarish dreams, sleepwalking, or sleeptalking. Mr. Freeman Owle, Cherokee herbal expert and holy man, stated that his tribe in the past traded objects, such as flint, for the black drink with the Lumbee. The Cherokee also used the black drink in ceremonies and as a hallucinogen. In the Lumbee history and in the present day, the holy man of the tribe would prepare the leaves of the American Holly bush into "the black drink." This drink was considered to be a strong laxative, emetic (diarrhea and vomiting), and a treatment for colds or pneumonia. During this cleansing ceremony, the men of the tribe would consume "the black drink," scratch themselves with gar or other fish teeth, meditate in a sweat lodge, and bathe in the river to cleanse themselves before the busk or "green corn" and sweat lodge ceremonies. Mr. Earl Carter, Lumbee holy man, healer, elder, and keeper of the sacred fire (one who uses his or her knowledge of herbs and spirituality to keep his or her people well) states he instructs the young men that participate in "sweats" (sweat lodge ceremonies) to fast for at least one day before consuming "the black drink" or they will "lose all their cookies" (vomit).

American Mock Pennyroyal
see American Pennyroyal

American Pennyroyal
(Hedeoma pulegioides); also known as American Mock Pennyroyal, Pennyroyal; and **European Pennyroyal (Mentha pulegium)**
Warning: Large doses are poisonous. Lumbee healers never prescribed this herb to anyone who was pregnant.

American Pennyroyal belongs to the mint family. It grows six to eighteen inches in height. Small and tubular clusters of lavender or purplish flowers appear from July through October, and the whole plant has a pleasant, aromatic odor. American Pennyroyal can be found in dry woods up and down the east coast of the United States. Like all mints, it has a square stem with tiny, ovate, sparingly toothed, opposite leaves. Long ago native peoples and settlers reportedly used American Pennyroyal to induce abortion. In some cases, it was said that the mother suffered serious complications such as hemorrhaging. Lumbee healers prepared leaves in an infusion using the Pennyroyal leaves to treat colds, dizziness and headaches, and to encourage the onset of menses. One Lumbee healer stated that he suggested Pennyroyal to function as a blood purifier. A Pennyroyal tea was also prescribed as a stimulant, diaphoretic and expectorant for colds, coughs, fever, and whooping cough. Lumbee healers would boil Pennyroyal leaves and recommend that their patients put a few drops of the tea in their ears to treat earache. Many Lumbee would hold the beaten leaves in their mouths for toothache. Some healers also used a leaf poultice for treatment of headache. Lumbees also rubbed the leaves of American Pennyroyal on themselves as an insect repellent. Sometimes American Pennyroyal is confused with European Pennyroyal (Mentha pulegium) which is not a mint at all. European Pennyroyal has downy, oval leaves that are no more than a half inch long. Small, rosy lilac flowers bloom late in the summer and early autumn on the European Pennyroyal.

American Sanicle *see Alum Root*

Antennaria neglecta *see Whiteweed*

Antirrhinum majus *see Snapdragon*

Andropogon glomeratus *see Broom Grass*

Aplectrum hyemale *see Adam and Eve Root*

Apocynum cannabinum *see Indian Hemp*

Apricot Vine *see Passionflower*

Aristida stricta *see Wire Grass*

Aristolochia serpentaria *see Sampson's Snakeroot*

Artemisia absinthium *see Wormwood*

Asarum canadense *see Wild Ginger*

Asclepias rubra *see Old Timey Garlic (Garlet)*

Asclepias syriaca *see Common Milkweed*

Asclepias tuberosa *see Butterfly Bush*

Ass-ear *see Comfrey*

Asthma Weed *see Indian Tobacco*

Atlantic Manna Grass *see Blunt Manna Grass*

Ball Root (Psoralea pedunculata)
Ball Root is also known as Prairie potato. Ball Root is a semi-erect perennial with smooth stems growing to a height of about eighteen inches. The Latin name Psoralea refers to the fact that this plant has prominent flower stems. Pedunculata indicates the presence of roughly scaled glandular dots on the leaves. The three-inch leaves are oval to lance-shaped. It bears greenish-white flowers from August to September. Ball Root was called "weete woropke'" or

bald root in the native language of the Lumbee. This root was boiled to get the grease (salve) from it. Many Lumbee healers would recommend that a person with boils rub it on their flesh. The Seminole would prepare an infusion of the leaves to treat fever, headache, or constipation. The root has also been used by the Lumbee to make an aromatic tonic used to treat chronic diarrhea.

Barberry *see Yellow Root*

Bay Tree (Persea borbonia); also known as Red Bay, Sweet Bay

The Bay tree is a native, aromatic evergreen tree or shrub that can reach a height of forty feet. It has shiny, green, two- to six-inch alternate leaves and small flowers. The fruit is a black drupe, becoming ripe in late spring. It can be found in deep woods or swampy areas (bays) in the southeastern United States. The newly collected root was crushed and made into a poultice worn on a head boil (rising) to help the infection (pus) come out. This treatment was considered to be painful because it was thought to act so quickly. This plant is aromatic, and the odor of the crushed leaves is almost identical to the Magnolia Tree (Magnolia grandiflora), which is also occasionally called the bay tree. Some Lumbee used both Magnolia and Bay Tree stems interchangeably under the name "Bay" for scenting lard when hogs were slaughtered and used a Sweet Bay or Magnolia stick to stir the lard and give it a unique flavor.

Bear Grass (Yucca filamentosa); also known as Adam's Needle

Bear Grass looks a little like a small palm, but is actually related to the lilies. The leaves of Bear Grass are straplike, about an inch wide and up to two or three feet long. The leaves are basal, in that they all originate from one point, taking the form of a rosette. The margins of the leaves are decorated with long, curly threads or filaments that peel back as the leaf grows, the older leaves eventually dropping off. The individual flowers (up to several dozen) bloom on top of an erect spike, which can grow to twelve feet in height. These flowers are white and about two inches long. The plant dies after flowering and fruiting, but produces lateral buds that start new plants around the edges of the original. Bear Grass is native to southeastern United States from North Carolina to Florida and west to Tennessee and Mississippi. It grows in dry, sandy habitats in fields, on road shoulders, and in open woods. Lumbee herbal healers would tell their patients to rub the root of Bear Grass onto their bodies to treat skin irritation. Two small pieces or more were used for this medicine. The beaten root was used with or without tallow for a salve to treat sores. A tea was suggested to treat diabetes. The Catawba, a sister tribe to the Lumbee, would rub this plant on their skin and body to treat general skin disease. The Cherokee would combine Broom-sedge (Andropogon glomeratus) and Amaranth (Amaranthus spp.) to produce green corn medicine (the combination used for purification during the green corn ceremony). The Cherokee would also suggest that the crushed root be used on external injuries. Many Cherokee would also pound Bear grass roots and use the sap instead of soap to wash their blankets.

Beefsteak-Plant *see Jacob's Coat*

Beggar-Ticks *see Mark*

Bellis perennis *see Daisy*

Berberis vulgaris *see Yellow Root*

Betula lutea *see Yellow Birch Tree*

Big Red *see Indian Corn*

Bitterweed (Helenium amarum); also known as Sneezeweed
Bitter Weed is an annual herb which grows up to two feet tall. The leaves are long, alternate, and threadlike (long, thin, and spindly). The yellow flowers have six petals and bloom from late spring through early fall. The petals have two or three notches at the end. The Lumbee primarily used Bitter Weed to treat diabetes. However, one healer commented that this treatment could last a month or longer. Bitter Weed was not boiled into a tea or made into a salve. One healer would collect the whole plant and soak the material in a jar of water for approximately eight hours. This liquid was taken in the morning, afternoon, and night. One Lumbee took a half a cup full each time. The plant could be used twice. The water was replaced a second time after all the liquid had been used. This treatment was also used to nurse asthma, hay fever, and fever. The Koasati tribe would take a sweatbath using Bitter Weed to treat dropsy and swelling. A poultice of roots was applied to sprains by the Nanticoke tribe.

Black Cohosh (Cimicifuga racemosa); also known as Black Snakeroot, Rattleweed
Black Cohosh is a perennial herb that grows on a long stem from three to eight feet in height. A lengthy spire of white flowers bloom from June until September. The leaves have toothed edges and are large. "Black" in the name of this plant refers to the black root and not the white flowers. Some Lumbee placed the root of this plant in alcoholic sprits (sometimes moonshine whiskey) and used this liquid (tincture) to treat rheumatism. This preparation was also thought to perform as a tonic, diuretic, and an emmenagogue. A poultice was made by some tribes to treat snakebite. The tea is used to treat colds, coughs, constipa-

tion, rheumatism, fatigue, hives, or backache. The root has a coarse texture. The word "cohosh" is taken from the Algonquian word for "rough." This plant was used by the Cherokee for an analgesic (pain reliever) and ingredient in cough medicine.

Black Gum Tree (Nyssa sylvatica); also known as Sour Gum

Black Gum is a large tree found near swamps and stream edges. It is a native North American tree that reaches sixty to eighty feet in height when mature. It prefers full sun to partial shade. Black Gum leaves are alternate, glossy green, and two to five inches long. The fruits are oval and have dark blue drupes about a half inch long with large, ribbed pits. In the ancient Lumbee tongue, the Black Gum was called "yab be be," or immoveable tree. Many Lumbee families would cut Black Gum branches to serve as a toothbrush. They would strip the bark from a section of a small branch. The end of this branch was then chewed until the end was compressed or ragged like toothbrush bristles. With the flattened end, the gums and teeth were massaged. This stick was sometimes left in the mouth an hour for chewing and occasional rubbing. Some Lumbee healers would scrape the bark from the roots of the Black Gum tree and boil it to make a tea to treat colic, cramps, or worms. The inner bark was made into a tea to

treat milky urine and diarrhea. Some local healers would also boil the branches of the Black Gum with Gall of the Earth to obtain a tonic used to treat high blood pressure.

Blackhaw (Viburnum prunifolium); also known as Nannyberry

In early autumn, many nature enthusiasts stop to enjoy the fruits of the Blackhaw. This tree or shrub is a member of the honeysuckle family and can be found near streams and in woods. The Blackhaw can be a tree or shrub that grows to thirty feet in height. The bark of older trees is cracked into plates and is usually gray to brownish-red in color. The lightly toothed leaves grow in opposite pairs. The mature bluish-black fruits follow the umbellate, small, white flowers. Blackhaw was called "webusa'p" in the Lumbee traditional language. Some Lumbee healers made a Blackhaw tea from the roots to treat stomach trouble. The bark of the Blackhaw was known as "Cramp bark" and was viewed by many Lumbee as a tonic and diaphoretic. An extract of boiled Blackhaw had traditionally been employed as a uterine tonic (a substance that aided in childbirth by stimulating the muscles in the womb) and as a medicine to prevent abortion and miscarriage. Modern scientists have found that a Blackhaw bark decoction possesses an agent that could act as a uterine sedative (an agent that relaxes uterine muscles and hence alleviates menstrual cramps). A decoction (½ oz. to a pint of water) was also given in a tablespoon dose by some Lumbee healers as a nerve sedative or anti-spasmodic for asthma. The Delaware used the rootbark and leaves in a tonic to strengthen the female reproductive system.

Black Snakeroot *see also Black Cohosh*

Black Snakeroot (Euphorbia corollata)

Black Snakeroot is a perennial herb that can grow to three feet in height. It has thick, deep reaching roots with a multi-branched stem above. The stem contains a milky juice. The one to three inch leaves are alternately arranged except being whorled at the base. The small flowers appear to be a green cup with pink, white, or greenish petal-like extensions growing from the center. For a dog suffering from the bite of a poisonous snake, the Lumbee healer would suggest that the owner drench the dog with the root in sweet milk. The roots of this plant were often crushed in the milk, and the mixture was given to the dog.

Black Walnut Tree (Juglans nigra)

The Black Walnut is a large native tree with an open crown of dark green, aromatic foliage. Mature trees can range in height from seventy to ninety feet. The two- to five-inch leaves are pinnately com-pound, finely saw-toothed, and broadly lance-shaped. These leaves turn yellow in autumn. The bark is dark brown and deeply furrowed into scaly ridges. One elder reported that when he was little, his father went to catch some fish. The elder said, "My father put Walnut bark in the water. It was a deep hole in a branch of the river, and there at the edge of the branch he put the Walnut bark in the hole, and stirred it up by using a pole. In a little while, the fish began floating to the top of the water." He was able to get "a right smart" (many fish) by spearing them. Modern science has found that walnuts contain Omega-3 (fatty acid). This compound is thought to prevent plaque buildup in arteries (prevent heart attacks). The Lumbee also used Black Walnut bark and nut husks to make a dark brown or black dye for cloth and basket weaving material. The walnut also provided edible nuts that could be eaten alone or used in puddings, pies, and cakes. The Comanche tribe pulverized the leaves and rubbed this on the skin to treat ringworm.

Black Willow Tree *see Wild Willow Tree*

Blackberry *see Dewberry*

Blackwort *see Comfrey*

Blazing Star *see White Bloodroot*

Bloodroot (Sanguinaria canadensis); also known as Indian Paint

Bloodroot is a low growing (about twelve inches) perennial herb that has a reddish rhizome (stem that's underground) from which eight- to ten-petaled, round-lobed, flowers bloom. Each bloom is surrounded by a single leaf that grows bigger after the flower blooms. Bloodroot can be found on wet banks and in moist woods. Bloodroot was called "puccoon" in the Algonquian language. Captain John Smith recorded notes about Bloodroot, stating how the Native American peoples in the area of Jamestown, Virginia, used it for pain in their joints, blood vessel spasms, swelling, and body aches, and as a red dye for their hair, baskets, and clothes. Bloodroot leaves a reddish-pink color when boiled and is moderately acidic. So, some tribes used this root as a treatment for skin cancers, fungal growths, and ringworm. Mr. Vernon Cooper, Lumbee healer, used asafetida (plant resin), Sweet Gum tree resin, and Bloodroot in an ounce or two of liquor to treat shortness of breath. Mr. Cooper recommended a Coca-Cola chaser while holding one's nose. According to Mr. Vernon's nephew, Woodrow Cooper, Mr. Vernon used Bloodroot in many medicines. The Lumbee also drank a tea from the dried, crushed herb to treat rheumatism and asthma.

Blooming Sally see Fireweed

Blue-Eyed Grass see Purge Grass

Blunt Manna Grass (Glyceria obtusa); also known as Water-root, Atlantic Manna Grass, Wild Evergreen Grass

Blunt Manna Grass can be found in wet soil and sometimes in shallow water. It is a perennial herb that has four to seven green or tan flowered spikelets $\frac{1}{6}$ to $\frac{1}{3}$ inch long. Its stiff, smooth, and unbranched stem is upright but can often lie sideways at the base. Blunt Manna Grass can grow up to four feet in height. The leaves are elongated, flat, or folded, up to $\frac{1}{3}$ of an inch wide, and are rough on the upper surface and smooth on the lower surface. The fruit is broadly elliptical smooth grains that are eaten by waterfowl. The evergreen grasslike leaves were gathered in moist areas or in little water. Blunt Manna Grass was called "isda warup wii' ti" or backache medicine in the traditional language of the Lumbee. One Lumbee healer boiled the whole plant into a tea to treat backache. Some Lumbee healers would crush Blunt Manna Grass in water and let it stand for one day. It was considered beneficial if the tea was left in the sun to become sour, then taken. Some healers suggested that their clients drink the liquid three times a day. This plant was used mainly as an analgesic and orthopedic agent for back and muscle ailments.

Boneset (Eupatorium perfoliatum)

Boneset is a perennial herb that can reach a height of five feet. It has a stout, hairy stem that bears opposite pointed leaves united at the base so as to seem perforated by the stem. These leaves are finely toothed, and rough above and downy and resinous below. The whitish flat-topped flowerheads bloom from July through October at the top of the stem. Some of Boneset's purported uses were as a tonic, sudorific, stimulant, emetic, purgative, antiseptic, diuretic, and febrifuge. Many Native American tribes used Boneset for its reported ability to promote perspiration and stimulate the bowels. The Lumbee made a infusion from the leaves and flowers and used it in treatment of colds, sore throat, and flu. The infusion of one ounce of dried herb with one pint of boiling water was taken in one to two cup doses, hot or cold. It was given hot as a tonic and as a treatment for colds. Mr. Vernon Cooper, Lumbee healer, also used Boneset as an ingredient in a stimulating tonic tea (a mild laxative) prepared for elderly patients. The ingredients were Rabbit Tobacco, Horehound, Stargrass and Pine tops. For a cold, he simply combined Boneset and Horehound to make a tea. A Lumbee healer known as Will D. stated that he suggested a tea made of Big Boneset, Little Boneset (these are, according to Lumbee herbal lore, the male and female varieties of Boneset), Goldenrod, and Rabbit Tobacco to treat a cold. The Waccamaw-Siouan tribe, sister tribe to the Lumbee, used the twigs and leaves of the Boneset to reduce fever and increase the appetite. Eupatorium purpureum, or Joe Pye weed, is a closely related plant. This purple-flowered plant was named after the Native American healer Joe Pye from the New England area, who used this plant as a treatment for typhus. The Abnaki tribe used Boneset to help "mend bones."

Bourtree *see Elderberry*

Brassica oleracea *see Collards*

Brassica oleracea capitata *see Cabbage*

Broom Grass (Andropogon glomeratus); also known as Broom Straw, Broomsedge
Broom Grass might first be noticed as tall blue-green grass with a large, whitish, hairy top, growing along ditchbanks. Broom Grass stands erect to seven feet tall with tufted stems and folded or flat leaf blades. Broom Grass was called "wi'tisura'k" or root grass in the Lumbee traditional language. Lumbee healers would soak the roots in water for one day to make a tea to treat jaundice. The healer would pull the Broom Grass up by the roots, and use the grass and roots to boil into a tea for treatment of frostbite, or bowel problems such as diarrhea. Some Lumbee healers would also mix the tea with tallow to rub onto sores. Broomsedge was also commonly used as an analgesic, antidiarrheal, and febrifuge. Many Lumbee also used this tallow and

Broomsedge mixture to treat pain and irritation from hemorrhoids, skin ailments, and orthopedic ailments. Mr. Earl Carter, Lumbee healer, states that the Lumbee would also use Broom Grass in burial rituals. In *The Education of Little Tree* by Forrest Carter, a young Cherokee boy called Little Tree explains, "If you lay a broom sedge straw crosswise on a watermelon and it just lays there, the watermelon is green. But if the broom sedge straw turns ... lengthwise, then you have a ripe watermelon." The Catawba, a sister tribe to the Lumbee, would also use Broom Grass as an analgesic (pain reliever) to treat backache. Broom Grass roots surrender a yellow dye when boiled. The Catawba and Lumbee of long ago used Broom Grass, harvested in the fall, to serve as roofing and bedding material. Broom Grass' name also indicates another purpose among the Lumbee. Some Lumbee women in the present day still use twine or modern day tape to tie around a bundle of Broom Grass or Wire Grass to fashion into a broom. Most Lumbee women used these brooms to sweep inside and outside their homes. An old Lumbee belief stated that if the woman did not sweep away the children's footprints in the dirt before night, the "little people" or "boogers" (known as Yeha'suri' in the Lumbee traditional language) might come during the night to make their children sick or steal them away.

Broom Straw *see Broom Grass*

Broomsedge *see Broom Grass*

Bugle Plant (Sarracenia purpurea); also known as Indian Jug, Frog Bonnets, Sidesaddle Flower

The Bugle Plant is a native evergreen perennial herb that grows from a rhizome. The Bugle Plant's two- to twelve-inch leaves grow in a basal rosette (circular). The tubular maroon flowers bloom in the spring. Moist, open areas in the eastern United States are the most likely spot to find this rare plant. Lumbee healers fashioned a tea from the rhizome of the Bugle Plant for treatment of gravel (kidney stones). The Algonquian tribes also made a decoction from the roots to treat urinary disorders. The Cree tribe (Walter Pinchbeck [Cree] was a prominent member of the Lumbee community) used a decoction of the Bugle Plant to prevent women from getting sick after childbirth.

Bunny Ears *see Mullein*

Burr Tremor *see Sycamore Tree*

Butterfly Bush (Asclepias tuberosa); also known as Pleurisy Root, Butterfly Root, Butterfly Weed

Warning: The seeds, roots, flowers, stems and leaves of the Butterfly bush have been found to be poisonous if taken in large doses.

The surprising spatters of brilliant orange color along roadsides and fields during the heat of midsummer are called the Butterfly Bush. The Butterfly Bush is a two foot tall, herbaceous perennial that dies back in winter and re-sprouts from its underground tuber each spring. The brilliant orange flowers are followed by green pods that open to release silky parachute-like seeds. The Butterfly bush is a native plant that occurs naturally in open woods and fields throughout the U.S. east of the Rocky Mountains. Butterfly Bush is an appropriate name because monarchs and swallowtails are especially attracted to the small, clustered, orange flowers. In the Lumbee ancient tongue, the Butterfly Bush was called "tupenune," or butterfly medicine. The Lumbee healer would cut a handful of roots to finger length and wash and boil the plant material for about 10 to 15 minutes. The local healer prepared the liquid to treat stomach discomfort and dysentery. Pleurisy root is also an appropriate name for this plant because many Native American tribes made a tea from the root to treat severe respiratory ailments and promote perspiration. A root tea was also prepared to treat heart trouble. The seeds and roots were considered by many healers to act as a heal-ing agent for sores and wounds when beat into a powder and mixed into a paste. The seeds and roots were also thought to be a gentle laxative.

Butterfly Root *see Butterfly Bush*

Butterfly Weed *see Butterfly Bush*

Butternut Tree (Juglans cinerea)

The Butternut Tree is sometimes called the White Walnut. This indigenous tree has stout branches, a broad, open crown, a short, straight trunk and a fruit with a sticky husk. The Butternut grows to a height of forty to seventy feet. Its gray bark is relatively smooth. The leaves are large and pinnate, divided into eleven to nineteen pointed and toothed leaflets. The flowers are small and green in the early spring. The three- to five-inch fruit appears in drooping clusters and is narrow, long pointed, and egg shaped. This fruit has two ridges and has rust-colored sticky hairs and a thick husk. Inside the husk is the shell of the butternut. The shell itself is light brown, thick, and rough with eight ridges containing a very oily edible seed (butternut). Dried Butternut inner bark was used by some Lumbee healers, like rhubarb, as a mild cathartic. In fact, some healers would suggest that Butternut bark be used as a habitual laxative (also for dysentery). The expressed oil of the Butternut fruit was used to treat tapeworm. The Cherokee would make pills from the inner bark of the Butternut to treat toothache. The Iroquois confederacy tribes would use a compound decoction to treat urinary pain and use the nutmeal with bear grease as a hair treatment. Many Native tribes used Butternut wood for plates, bowls, and utensils and the bark was boiled down to make a brown dye to color splints for baskets and cloth.

Button Snakeroot *see White Bloodroot*

Cabbage (Brassica oleracea capitata)

Most individuals have tasted cabbage in coleslaw, salads, or in other preparations. Cabbage has tightly clustered leaves with a few loose leaves at the base. Eventually, the middle of the plant forms a green, leafy ball. Cabbage is similar in appearance to lettuce except it has a thicker, firmer leaf. The Lumbee and other tribes used raw cabbage leaves to treat engorged breasts and sore nipples. Some Lumbee mothers, to dry up their milk supply or treat sore and milk-engorged breasts, would wash and paste raw cabbage leaves to their breasts (later many would place them inside their bras). Some Lumbee healers would at times advise expectant mothers to use the cabbage leaves for a brief time to "unplug" their milk ducts.

Calamus (Acorus calamus);

also known as Flag, Sweet Flag **Warning: Blue Flag (Iris versicolor), when not in bloom, can be mistaken for Calamus. The rhizomes of Blue Flag are extremely poisonous.**

Calamus is a grasslike, rhizome forming perennial that can reach six feet in height. The leaves and other parts of this plant resemble the Iris. Flag lives in wet areas such as swamps, lakes, stream edges, and ditches. It often shares habitats with the Cattail. The plants have creeping roots that can grow almost six feet long in older plants. Calamus rarely flowers, but when this occurs, the blooms are one to two inches long, green to brown and covered with many rounded spikes. Many Native peoples would hunt for muskrat around Calamus plants because muskrat were quite fond of eating these roots. Mr. Vernon Cooper, a Lumbee healer, said many Lumbee grew Flag around their wellhouses and used this plant to treat colic. Mr. Cooper stated, "But we also used that peppermint weed." Lumbee healers believed that Calamus possessed stimulant and stomachic virtues. A tea was made from the leaves and stems to treat colic, worms, yellowish urine, and dropsy. This tea was also used as a diaphoretic. The root was chewed by many Lumbee to treat colds, headache, stomachache, upset stomach and sore throat. Many Lumbee would also drink the hot root tea to doctor a cold. The root was boiled in water and given to a child to drink to treat colic or a cold. Sometimes Calamus was combined in a decoction with Red Sassafras (Sassafras albidum), Pipsissewa (Pip) (Chimaphila umbellata), and Garlic (Allium sativum) for a shotgun heart remedy (heart treatment).

Pipsissewa was combined with other plants when infection was believed, by the local healer, to be the fundamental cause of a malady. The Calamus was thought to assist in treating heartburn. Sassafras was employed by many healers to free the blood from any impurities, and the Garlic was specifically suggested to treat heart issues.

The Abnaki would use Calamus to ease stomach discomfort and the Algonquian tribes would use this plant for a cold remedy.

Carduus repandus *see Thistle*

Carolina Beech *see American Beech Tree*

Carolina Jessamine *see Yellow Jessamine*

Carolina Vetch (Vicia caroliniana)
Carolina Vetch is a native climbing perennial herb that grows to three feet. The flowers bloom at the top of the erect stalk and are tipped with purple. The dark green leaves are oblong and lanceolate with an alternate arrangement. Carolina Vetch fruit is a legume or bean. This species is related to the plant that produces the Fava bean. Some Lumbee healers would prepare the Carolina Vetch plant into a decoction to treat dyspepsia or back pains. This decoction was also rubbed on the abdomen for stomach and intestinal cramps. In instances of muscle pain, the Cherokee holy man would make scratches over the place of the patient's complaint and rub a Carolina Vetch infusion in that location. An infusion of Carolina Vetch was also taken by Cherokee stickball players to give them "wind"—endurance and stamina—during the contest.

Carpweed *see Ragweed*

Carya illinoensis *see Pecan Tree*

Carya ovata *see Hickory Tree*

Castor (Ricinus communis); also known as Castor Bean, Castor Oil Plant
Warning: At high doses the Castor Plant is deadly poisonous.
Castor is a nonnative, tall, stout herb with large, alternately arranged, palmate leaves. It has small flowers and the fruit (bean) is covered with spines that are red. Castor oil has been used as a laxative since before the time of the ancient Egyptians. A byproduct of the Castor bean is used to make the deadly gas Ricin (WMD). The Lumbee put two seeds from a house plant (also used to drive away burrowing moles) in the food of a hog or a dog to treat intestinal worms. Many healers believed that if more than three seeds were used, it could harm or take the life of the beast. The Cahuilla tribe crushed the seeds and used this greasy substance to rub on sores.

Castor Bean *see Castor*

Castor Oil Plant *see Castor*

Catmint (Nepeta cataria); also known as Catnip

Catmint is a member of the mint family. It is a gray-green, aromatic perennial that grows to three feet and exhibits a square stem, fuzzy leaves, and twin-lipped flowers, like most members of the mint family. The oblong, pointed leaves have scalloped edges and gray or whitish hairs on the lower side. The flowers are white with purple spots and grow in spikes from June to September. The flowering tops were the part utilized by the Lumbee healer in medicine and were harvested when the plant was in full bloom in August. This treatment was prepared by pouring water over the plant, allowing it to sit for a day. Lumbee healers believed that Catmint produced free perspiration and used it to treat colds. "Catnip" tea was also considered by the Lumbee to be a valuable drink to treat fever because of its purported action, inducing sleep and producing perspiration without increasing the "heat of the system." The following ingredients were mixed by the Lumbee to make a cough syrup—Catmint, Mullein root, Wild Plum bark, Wild Cherry bark, American Holly bark, green Pine needles, Life Everlasting leaves (Rabbit Tobacco), and Sourwood bark. The compound was boiled for ten or fifteen minutes until it was reduced to a thickness described as "cooks until it strings." It was next strained through a cloth to make it clear. Sugar was sometimes added to make the compound easier to swallow. The syrup was to be taken at regular intervals. Catmint or "Catnip" tea has also been prescribed by Lumbee healers for intestinal cramps, infant colic, and gas pains. Lumbee healer Mr. Vernon Cooper, would recommend Catnip tea, on occasion, to treat "bad nerves" or "stomach trouble." Lumbee babies were said to be fond of the sweetened liquid. This tea was considered by many healers to be a treatment for babies with "slick stomach" (which included diarrhea, vomiting, and upset stomach). Some healers suggested the juice from the leaves be used to stimulate menstrual flow. A poultice from the leaves was suggested for use on boils. An old Lumbee remedy for toothache was chewing Catnip leaves. A tea was made with Heal-all and Fevergrass and applied to cuts. Catmint secretes an oil that inspires excitement in cats. This oil is secreted by the plant to ward off insects, but also acts to bring the kitten out in many cats. Cats usually learn the more they destroy the plant, the more pleasurable oil is released.

Catnip *see Catmint*

Cattail (Typha latifolia)

The Cattail is a tall, native, perennial herb. The cattail stalk arises from a white, fleshy rhizome. Alternate leaves tightly clasp the base. These leaves are long, upright, flat on the inside, and rounded on the outside. Flowers are borne on compact terminal spikes familiar to most people as the "cat's tail." The Cattail is found in slow flowing, quiet water in shallow marshes, swamps, and lake edges. The sticky juice found between the leaves was thought by many healers to be antiseptic if rubbed on the skin. The young shoots were peeled and eaten raw for food. The top (cattail itself) was broken and used for pillow stuffing. Ms. Lucie Mae Hammonds Locklear, a Lumbee elder, compared this stuffing to the softness of rabbit fur. The roots can be peeled, dried and pounded into flour to make a type of bread. The Algonquian tribes used a poultice of crushed roots to treat a wound. The Cheyenne made a decoction from the dried pulverized root and the basal leaves to treat abdominal cramps. The Mescalero Apache made a "pollen medicine" out of the tops of the Cattail. This "medicine" is used in a ceremony when a girl reaches womanhood.

Ceanothus americanus *see Red Shank*

Cedar Tree (Juniperus virginiana); also known as Red Cedar

Red Cedar is the most widespread evergreen conifer in the United States. It grows up to forty to fifty feet in height when mature. This aromatic tree is symmetrical and pyramidal in shape and has reddish-brown bark. The two-foot trunk is noticeably tapered, becoming fluted at the base. It occurs most frequently in dry, shallow soils in open areas, such as fields or meadows. The Lumbee called Red Cedar "tcu wese'" or red wood tree in the traditional language. Tea from Cedar branches has been used by some Lumbee healers as a treatment for whooping cough, but Mr. Vernon Cooper and other healers did not recommend it. Mr. Cooper said Cedar has been known to "cause other problems such as lung infection." The Rappahannock used an infusion of the berries with wild ginger to treat asthma. The Cree used the needles as a diuretic. The Dakota, Omaha, Pawnee, and Ponca burned the twigs and inhaled the smoke for head colds while the patient and fumigant were enclosed in a blanket. The Comanche regarded Red Cedar as a depurative. The Creek used the fumes for neck cramps, and the steam from heated cedar liquid to promote delivery. The Chickasaw heated Red Cedar limbs with Elder in hot water and applied the liquid topically for a headache. The Chippewa made a decoction of the twigs or made an herbal steam to treat rheumatism. The Dakota used Red Cedar for cholera. The Pawnee used Red Cedar smoke for bad dreams and nervousness. The Ojibwa took bruised leaves and berries for a headache. To the Cherokee, Cedar wood was sacred. They believed the blood of a wicked medicine man colored the wood. The Cherokees only burned this wood on ceremonial occasions when they thought the smoke would chase off evil spirits. In *The Education of Little Tree* by Forrest Carter, Little Tree, a young Cherokee boy, shares how he and his grandfather would use the green "spring boughs from the cedar tree to sleep on" when they were sleeping outside. He claimed, "If you don't, red bugs will eat you up…. They are all over the leaves and bushes…. They will crawl on you and bury up in your skin, causing rashes of bumps to break out all over you."

Celtis laevigata *see Sugarberry*

Celtis occidentalis *see Sugarberry*

Cercis canadensis *see Red Bud*

Chenopodium ambrosioides *see Jerusalem Oak*

Chickasaw Plum *see Wild Plum*

Chigger Weed *see Queen Anne's Lace*

Chimaphila umbellata *see Pipsissewa*

Chinaberry (**Melia azedarach**) Chinaberry is a nonnative, deciduous tree with alternate, toothed, and pointed leaves. The lilac-colored flowers are small but numerous. The fruit is a yellowish and wrinkled drupe that doesn't fall off the bush until winter. The berry "flesh" was considered poisonous to people by most Lumbee healers. Chinaberry is found in weedy or disturbed areas such as roadsides. The Lumbee boiled the Chinaberry seed with sugar to treat a child with a severe cold.

The healer also made a root and bark tea to treat worms, ringworm, and tetter. Crushed leaves were also used by the Lumbee to drive out house insects. Mr. James Hammonds, a Lumbee elder from the Saddletree community, stated that his father used Chinaberry to treat worms in mules. The ripe berries, just picked off the tree, were put in the animal's feed bin. If the animal did not eat them, many healers suggested that no food be given until a large part of the fruit was eaten. This remedy was used on chickens, mules, horses, and other animals. Vernon Hazel Locklear, a Lumbee elder, stated, "When the children had worms, stomach worms, my mother would take the berries from a Chinaberry tree and boil that and made a medicine." Mr. Vernon Cooper stated that he prescribed the fresh mashed fruit as an animal laxative. To the Ponca and Omaha, the seeds were a good luck charm. One of the authors and other Lumbee artisans make beautiful Chinaberry necklaces from the dyed seeds of this plant.

Chokecherry *see Wild Cherry Tree*

Cimicifuga racemosa *see Black Cohosh*

Cirsium repandum *see Thistle*

Cladina subtneuis *see Moss*

Cladrastis lutea *see Graybeard*

Clotburs *see Sheepburr*

Coat Ticklers (Eragrostis spectabilis); also known as Tickle Coats, Purple Love Grass, Tumble Grass, Petticoat Climber

Coat Ticklers is a small, native, erect, perennial bunchgrass that grows from eight to twenty inches in height. The blades range from four to sixteen inches long and are approximately ⅓ inch wide. The tiny, widely spaced violet flowerheads give the appearance of a pink-purple haze over pastures, hayfields, roadsides, and dry, sandy areas from Maine to Minnesota and south to Mexico in mid to late summer. A handful of the grains that form at the top of the plant and attached stalks were heated in water until the liquid turned yellow. To prevent plant remains from getting caught in the throat, the Lumbee healer would strain the tea several times. A cupful was taken internally. One Lumbee individual claimed that drinking a tea made of the Coat Ticklers plant had helped treat her kidney problem when she was younger. She stated that she had painful urination with blood in the urine, and Coat Ticklers tea help treat what she called "the gravels" (kidney stones).

Cockleburr *see Sheepburr*

Colicroot *see Star Grass*

Collards (Brassica oleracea); also known as Winter Cabbage

Collards belong to the "Acephala" or "no head" cabbage family, referring to the fact that the Collard leaves do not form a ball or head. Collards are a green, leafy vegetable with the large leaves borne in rosette fashion. Collards can grow to a height of three or more feet. This plant was thought to be best—sweetest and most effective—when collected after the first frost. It is a common plant in gardens in the southeastern United States. The Lumbee called the Collard "wa ya yu ha hare'" or winter cabbage in the native tongue. The leaves were made into a tea by many Lumbee and drunk to treat jaundice. Ms. Zelma Lowry and Mrs. Delois Lowry, Lumbees from the Prospect community, report that soaking collard leaves in water and plastering them to the chest was a Lumbee treatment for fever. Tying the leaves around the wrists and ankles was thought to have a similar effect. The Rappahannock pasted the green leaves to their temples to treat a headache and wore the leaves under their hats to protect against strong sun.

Coltsfoot (Tussilago farfara); also known as Coughwort, Son Before the Father

Coltsfoot is a perennial herb that grows to forty inches in height. It has a creeping rhizome and long runners. Both the flower and leaf buds grow on the rhizome. In the early spring, the erect, unbranched, woolly stems, covered with reddish-brown scales, grow from the flower buds, terminating in a pale yellow flowerhead (Dandelion-like). The early spring flowers become a white, downy sphere when the long-stalked, heart-shaped, and mildly toothed basal leaves began to sprout. Coltsfoot does not open its leaves until the flowers have bloomed (thus the name Son Before the Father). Many individuals think the leaves form the shape of a horse's hoof Coltsfoot. The extracts of Coltsfoot leaves and flowers have long been used in Lumbee and other Native American tribes for cough syrups, asthma teas, and herbal smoking mixtures for asthmatics. The Iroquois confederacy used a decoction of the roots to fabricate a cough medicine and treat tuberculosis (consumption). The mucilage in the plant was purported to soothe inflamed mucous membranes. Some tribes would burn Coltsfoot leaves and use the ashes as a salt substitute.

Comfrey (Symphytum officinale); also known as Healing Herb, Ass-ear, Blackwort

Warning: Do not confuse this plant when not in bloom with a Foxglove, a deadly poisonous plant.

Comfrey is a perennial that grows to three feet in height. Oval, dark green leaves grow on an erect, hairy stem that branches at the top. Purplish to pale yellow flowers arise as a rosette from the ground, have a rough texture, and bloom in clusters from May through September. Comfrey has been used by many Lumbee as a demulcent, mild astringent, and expectorant. This tea was considered by many Lumbee to be a gentle treatment in cases of diarrhea and dysentery. A decoction was made by boiling one-half to one ounce of crushed root to one quart of water or milk, which was taken in one to two cupful doses, frequently. Many Lumbee healers thought the root was more effectual than the leaves and stems in the case of cough. The local healer, in cases of bronchial disorders, intestinal problems, or internal hemorrhage, recommended a strong decoction or tea made from the root. A teaspoon of Witch Hazel extract was added to the Comfrey root tea, purportedly to heighten its effects. Comfrey leaves have been used externally in a poultice for severe cuts and as a healing agent for burns, bruises, or swelling. Ms. Gertrude Allen, Lumbee, states that her father, who was considered a community expert on healing plants, would often recommend Comfrey to ease swelling and treat heart problems. Comfrey leaves can be boiled to yield a yellowish-orange dye.

Common Lousewort *see Wood Betony*

Common Milkweed (Asclepias syriaca)

Common Milkweed is a herbaceous, perennial plant which can reach seventy inches in height. The stem has a milky juice. The leaf arrangement is opposite and each leaf, which grows to about ten inches long, is entire. Milkweed flowers are dull pink to greenish purple. The flowers first appear in early summer and continue into late summer. The fruit is a pod filled with tiny seeds, each with a tuft of silky hairs which become airborne. The mostly likely place to find Common Milkweed is in fields, along fencerows, and in waste places in the eastern and Midwestern United States. Monarch butterflies lay their eggs on Milkweed, which is the only plant the larvae eat. Toxic glycosides from the plant make the adult butterflies poisonous to birds and other predators. The plant was rubbed on the skin where a snakebite occurred. In the past, a Lumbee who had been bitten by a poisonous snake would chew the root, swallowing a sufficient quantity, and apply the rest to the wound. Ms. Mary Bell, a Lumbee healer, combined Milkweed, Fig leaves, Bayberry bark, Peppermint, Wild Cherry bark, and brown sugar (honey was said to make the concoction bitter) to nurse bronchitis. Lumbee herbal experts also believed that Milkweed could act as a sudorfic, diuretic, emmenagogue, and cathartic. For colds, some healers recommended this plant to treat pleurisy. A root tea or powder was used as an expectorant and cathartic in large doses. The Iroquois confederacy used the dried, pulverized root to act as a contraceptive or give women temporary sterility.

Cornus florida *see Dogwood Tree*

Coughwort *see Coltsfoot*

Crataegus spp. *see Hawthorn*

Cucurbita pepo *see Pumpkin*

Cultivated Tobacco (Nicotiana tabacum)
Cultivated Tobacco is a tall, erect annual plant that can grow up to eight feet high. The leaves are large (growing up to one foot wide and more than a foot long), alternate, ovate, and lanceolate. The stalk is knobby, green, thick and fibrous. The light pink to creamy yellow flowers are tubular in shape and grow in organized panicles at the top of the plant. When the flower bloomed, many Lumbee and other tobacco growing families would "top the tobacco"—snap or pick these flowers off—and also pick off the stunted leaves or "sucker" it. They would do this because it was believed that not topping and suckering would stunt the plant's growth. Cultivated Tobacco was called "I'pa" in the traditional language of the Lumbee. Many Lumbee families depended on growing tobacco and selling it in late summer or early fall at huge local markets or warehouses to support their families in the late nineteenth and the twentieth centuries. Cecil and Josephine Locklear grew great

amounts of tobacco in the Saddletree community. In the summer, it was not unusual to see huge fields of tobacco in Robeson, Hoke, Scotland and surrounding counties. Lumbee wives and mothers would also use the Cultivated tobacco seeds (from the tops) and leaves to make a salve. They would use this salve as a pediculicide (lice killer), and a treatment for rheumatism, bug bites, and swelling and pain of contusions and wounds. Many healers would also suggest this salve for use as an analgesic (external pain reliever) and as a treatment of bee stings and spider bites. The Lumbee also make a tea out of Cultivated Tobacco seeds as a horse tonic. An old Lumbee treatment for hiccoughs was to paste a wet Tobacco leaf onto the stomach. The Cherokee would use Cultivated Tobacco in rituals and the crushed plant to treat boils and insect bites.

Daisy (Bellis perennis)
Caution: Some individuals suffer from hay fever and other allergies from exposure to Daisies.

The Daisy is a perennial, stemless, herbaceous plant. Its leaves are ovate. The flowers have yellow centers which radiate numerous white petals. Many Lumbee would toss some young leaves or white petals in an early spring salad for an interesting contrast. A leaf tea was drunk as a purported spring tonic, expectorant, and as an aid to circulation. The leaves were moistened, crushed, and used as a poultice for bruises. The Lumbee used a Daisy flower infusion in a bath to revive winter-dulled skin and for relief from eczema.

Dandelion (Taraxacum officinale); also known as Lawn Weed

The Dandelion is a short-stemmed perennial herb. It has a rosette of "lion's tooth" leaves, and has a slender hollow stalk bearing a yellow flowerhead made up of two hundred or more florets. Dandelions can be found in meadows, on roadsides, and on lawns. These flowers open up in the morning and close in afternoon. When the flower matures, the yellowhead turns into a downy sphere of silk tufted seeds that give way to the wind. The Dandelion has a long taproot that arises from a short rhizome. It produces a bitter, milky white sap. This poor, lowly "weed" actually was used for many purposes among the Lumbee and other tribes. Although the Dandelion is a nonnative herb, Native American tribes such as the Mohegans quickly found a use for this common flower. The Mohegans boiled a tonic tea from Dandelion leaves, and other tribes fashioned a tea from the roots to treat indigestion. The Aleuts used the Dandelion to treat sore throat and stomachache. Ms. Mary Sue Locklear, a Lumbee healer, would recommend the milky sap from the Dandelion to treat warts and would also recommend bathing the wart. Ms. Mary Bell, a Lumbee healer, made a tea or extract of Fig tree leaves and Dandelion greens. She considered the Fig tree to be a "cureall" tree. The fruit and leaves of the Fig tree were also boiled with Dandelion flowers into a tea that was used as a cough syrup. Ms. Mary Locklear commented that Dandelion is "a very valuable weed." She used a Dandelion tea to treat diabetes, and a Goldenseal and Dandelion tea for an immune system enhancer. The very young Dandelion leaves were tossed into a salad by many Lumbee. In *The Education of Little Tree* by Forrest Carter, Little Tree, a young Cherokee boy, states that his grandmother mixed dandelion "with fireweed greens, poke salat (Poke), and Nettles" to make a salad. An infusion of the bitter leaves was considered diuretic. This infusion was thought by many Lumbee healers to aid in treatment of kidney infection, constipation and jaundice. A wine, made from the blossoms, was drunk by many Lumbee to increase the appetite. Some tribes boiled the flowers to make a yellow dye and the roots to make a dark red dye.

Dangleberry *see He-huck-leberry*

Datura stramonium *see Jimson*

Daucus carota *see Queen Anne's Lace*

Devil's Shoestring
(Tephrosia virginiana); also known as Goat's Rue, Rabbit's Pea

Devil's Shoestring is a herbaceous perennial that can reach a height of two feet. Its leaves are alternate and pinnate, and each leaf is divided into fifteen to twenty-five leaflets. Most of the plant is covered in short, downy hairs. The flowers are irregularly shaped and are whitish to light yellow with a pink keel. The flowers bloom in late spring to early summer. This plant has lengthy, strong, whitish roots. Devil's Shoestring is native to the southeastern and central United States and is most often found in woods and meadows in well-drained soils. Lumbee healers paired this plant with Queen's Delight (Stillingia sylvatica) root for feminine trouble (irregular secretion and disease). Two to three of the roots were boiled in two pints of water for two hours for treatment of kidney difficulty and gonorrhea (clap). Occasionally, Sumac (Rhus typhina) was added to treat this disease. Mr. Vernon Cooper, a Lumbee healer, used the Devil's Shoestring as a tonic or dried the leaves to be used in a tea to treat a weak back, with a combination of other plants including Sampson snakeroot and Lion's Tongue. Many Lumbee rubbed Devil's Shoestring juice on the hook and line to encourage fish to bite. The Cherokee used the Devil's Shoestring as a shampoo, with the belief that it would make their hair as dense and strong as the Devil's Shoestring plant. Cherokee stickball players would also rub a decoction of Devil's Shoestring on their limbs to toughen or strengthen them before a contest. Some Cherokee would prepare a Devil's Shoestring tea for their children to make them strong. The Catawba, a sister tribe to the Lumbee, would use this plant to treat rheumatism or put Devil's Shoestring in their shoes to treat pain or fever in the body.

Dewberry (Rubus hispidus) and Wild Blackberry (Rubus allegheniensis)

Caution: Modern herbalists only use Dewberry leaves that have been thoroughly dried. They believe fresh leaves possess dangerous toxins.

The Dewberry and Blackberry are members of the Rose family. The thorny stems of the Wild Blackberry and the smaller thorned Dewberry give clues about their lineage. Both the Dewberry and Blackberry exhibit one-half inch flowers from May to June. The Dewberry is most often found in low woods, swamps, and pocosins. The Wild Blackberry is most often found in disturbed areas and open fields. The Dewberry is a trailing shrub that has stems that trail on the ground. It differs from other blackberries by having flower stalks less than one inch long and flower petals less than one-half inch long. The Wild Blackberry, conversely, grows on branches sprouting off three to four foot (or longer) thorny stems (a thornbush). The fruits of the Dewberry are slightly larger than the Wild Blackberry. These half-inch fruits begin as small, green berries and mature to red, then fully ripe black drupelets. The Blackberry was called "wi ya'ro" (Blackberry), and Dewberry was called "wi ya' re haktco," or blackberry on the ground, in the traditional tongue of the Lumbee. The Lumbee boiled the roots and leaves of the Blackberry and Dewberry into a tea and drank a cupful three times a day to treat diarrhea in children and adults. A tea was also made by the Lumbee to regulate urination and act as a blood and skin tonic. Their general use among the Lumbee was as an anthelmintic, antidiarrheal, febrifuge, and tonic. Mr. Vernon Cooper, a Lumbee healer, remarked that he recommended Dewberry for treatment of diarrhea and other medicinal purposes such as glaze on the lungs (asthma). In *The Education of Little Tree* by Forrest Carter, Little Tree, a young Cherokee boy, explains that "after a warm spell in April there comes a sudden cold snap called Blackberry Winter.... This is to make the blackberries bloom...."

Diamondback Rattlesnake Root *see Sampson's Snakeroot*

Dioscorea villosa *see Wild Yam*

Diospyros virginiana *see*
Persimmon

Dog-Fennel (Eupatorium
capillifolium)
Dog-Fennel is a native perennial
herb that can reach the height of
six feet. The leaves are alternate
and one to three inches long. Several hairy stems protrude from the
crown and small white flowers
bloom, forming a panicle in the
fall of the year. Dog-Fennel is
common to pastures and old fields
in the southeast and midatlantic
states. Many Lumbee healers suggested that a root tea of Dog-Fennel be taken to treat a fever. The
stems and leaves were boiled down
in water. One Lumbee healer
stated that some rootworkers or
conjurers would put a drop or two
of this tea to an individual's drink
or food to make the unsuspecting
person "do what they wanted
them to" (obey every command of
the rootworker). One Lumbee
herbalist shared that these evil-
doers (rootworkers or conjurers)
used Dog-Fennel for this purpose
with caution because the taste of
this herb was considered to be
very bitter. One particular healer
suggested to men that they smear
the decoction on the penis, to supposedly keep a stiff erection.

Dog's Tooth Violet *see*
Adder's Tongue

Dogwood Tree (Cornus
florida)
The Dogwood is a small, native,
flowering tree with a short trunk
and spreading, nearly horizontal
branches. This tree can reach a
height of thirty feet and a diameter of eight inches. The green,
nearly hairless leaves have slightly
wavy edges but are not toothed
and have six to seven long, curved
veins on each side of the midvein.
The leaves turn bright red in autumn. Dogwood bark is rough and
is dark reddish-brown in color.
The flowers bloom around mid–
April and are $\frac{3}{16}$ of an inch wide
with four large yellowish-green
petals. The small, red, berrylike
fruit is from $\frac{3}{8}$ to $\frac{5}{8}$ of an inch
long. Several of these fruits can be
found at the end of a long stalk in
late August to early September.
Mr. Vernon Cooper, a Lumbee
healer, would eat raw Dogwood
berries to treat chills. He believed
their virtue lay in their extreme
bitterness. Lumbee healers would
fabricate an extract of the bark to
nurse sore and aching muscles.
Ms. Annie Mae Oxendine, a Lumbee healer, would cut the root bark
from the Dogwood tree and make
it into a ball six to nine inches in
diameter and boil it in water for an
hour or longer. She said this tea
made a powerful laxative. She also
recommend that an aspirin be
taken with this tea. She exercised
caution in recommending how
often to drink this tea because she
believed it would "scrape you
out," and too much could cause
severe abdominal pain (grippe).
To treat malarial fever, some healers would boil a tea from "sap
bark" of the stem and combine it

with the twigs and buds. A table-spoonful taken three times a day was recommended. Mr. Vernon Cooper would combine the bark from the Dogwood, Cherry, Magnolia, and Poplar trees to boil a tea to treat malarial fever. Some southeastern tribes would use Dogwood root to make a red dye. The Lumbee called the Dogwood "ta siyup re," or the dog tree, in their native tongue.

Double Tansy *see Red Myrtle*

Echinacea angustifolia *see Purple Coneflower*

Elderberry (Sambucus nigra); also known as Bourtree, Pipe Tree

Warning: The leaves, bark and roots of some elders, including American elder, contain poisonous alkaloids and should not be used internally.

The Elderberry is a nonnative large shrub or small tree that grows up to thirty feet tall. The saw-toothed, elliptical leaves are alternately arranged and are pinnately compound. Elderberry bark is light gray or brown with raised dots. The fragrant, flattopped flowers are a half inch wide and bloom in late spring. The fruit is a juicy and slightly sweet purplish-black berry. Medicinally, Elderberry has been used for many common ailments among the Lumbee. A syrup from the berry juice was once thought to be a treatment for coughs. Many Lum-bee cold sufferers comforted themselves with a hot drink of mulled Elderberry wine. A handful of the fresh roots or leaves and stems were boiled in a quart of water for two hours. Swollen feet were soaked in the decoction. Sores and swellings were also bathed in the liquid. A tea made from the flowers was prescribed by Lumbee healers as a mild laxative, diuretic, and perspiration producer. Elderberry flower water, a mild astringent, was used as a skin lotion. The Cherokee used this plant as a salve to act as a burn dressing. They would also use the leaves as a wash to prevent infection. Sometimes the Elderberry flower water was sold in old-fashioned pharmacies. Elderberry berries can be boiled to make a lilac or purple dye.

Elephantopus Carolinianus *see Wood's Mullein*

Elephant's Foot *see Wood's Mullein*

Epilobium angustifolium *see Fireweed*

Eragrostis spectabilis *see Coat Ticklers*

Erythronium americanum *see Adder's Tongue*

Eupatorium capillifolium *see Dog-Fennel*

Eupatorium perfoliatum *see Boneset*

Euphorbia corollata *see Black Snakeroot*

Euphorbia maculata *see Milkweed*

Euphrasia officinalis *see Eyebright*

Eyebane *see Milkweed*

Eyebright (Euphrasia officinalis)

Eyebright is a nonnative annual herb that grows in meadows, pastures, and other grassy areas. It can grow to eight inches in height. It has a square, leafy stem and is branched near the base. This small, downy herb bears lanceolate, oppositely arranged leaves at the base of this plant and alternately arranged leaves above. Each leaf displays four or five teeth on each side. The flowers are small and are either white, red, or yellow, often tinged with purple. Some Lumbee healers recommended Eyebright to treat diseases of the sight, weakness of the eyes, ophthalmia, etc., combining it often with Goldenseal in a lotion. Many healers used the Eyebright-Goldenseal combination for general disorders of the eyes. The juice was obtained from a recently gathered plant (crushed). It was also used in an infusion combined in milk, but the simple infusion in water was the more common application. When the patient was in much pain, it was considered desirable to use a warm infusion more frequently to treat inflamed eyes. When the healer considered the patient's problem to be an ordinary one, the cold application was usually used.

Eyeroot *see Goldenseal*

Fagus grandifolia Ehr. *see American Beech Tree*

False Aloe *see Rattlesnake Root*

False Heartleaf *see Wild Ginger*

False Solomon's Seal (Smilacina racemosa); also known as "False Spikenard"

False Solomon's Seal is a tall, herbaceous perennial growing from thick, whitish, branching rhizomes. The leafy, arching stems grow about three feet tall, and the leaves are smooth-edged, broad, and elliptical, coming out alternately from the stem in two rows. False Solomon's Seal flowers bloom from April to June and are small, densely clustered, white, and strongly perfumed. This plant grows in rich woods, thickets, and moist clearings. The fruit begins as a red berry and changes between August and October to a green, brown, or mottled striped berry with fine red dots at maturity. The berries are small ($\frac{1}{16}$ inch in diameter) and densely clustered. In the past, the Lumbee chewed the fresh berries from False Solomon's Seal to freshen breath and treat bleeding gums. In other tribes the young greens, ripe berries, and rhizomes were eaten. The rhizomes were cooked after a long soaking to purge the disagreeable taste. The cooked rhizomes were also employed in a poultice to treat external wounds.

Fennel (Foeniculum vulgare)

Fennel is an aromatic biennial with soft, feathery, almost hairlike foliage. The plant grows to about two feet tall. In the second season, fennel produces flowering stems that show flattopped umbels of little golden flowers. An umbel is an umbrella-shaped cluster of flowers in which the individual flower radiates from a common point on the main stalk. Fennel has an elongated, white, carrotlike root. The Lumbee chewed the seeds as a digestive aid, and the healer would also suggest the seeds to relieve gas in adults and colic in children. Fennel seeds are commonly sold as a spice or flavoring. Some healers would take extract from the root and add it to the seed infusion to make a detoxifying and diuretic tea. Many healers also made a tea from Fennel seeds to be used as an eyewash. The Hopi used the Fennel plant as a tobacco substitute.

Fever Grass (Heterotheca graminifolia); also known as Silk Grass, Silver Grass

Fever Grass is a perennial herb that can grow from fifteen to thirty inches in height. Its parallel veined, grasslike leaves are four to fourteen inches long. The yellow flowers bloom in daisylike heads from late summer to early fall. This native plant can be found along roadsides and in dry woods and old fields in the eastern United States. Many Lumbee would crush the leaves of Fever Grass and boil them into a tea for fever. They would taste the tea to judge the strength.

Field Cat's Foot see Whiteweed

Field Thistle (Sonchus asper); also known as Spiny Leaved Sow Thistle

The Field Thistle is spread mostly by the wind because the seeds are equipped with a small parachute of hair that carry them over long distances. Its stem branches near the top, while its leaves, which have small prickles, clasp the stem. Field Thistles contain a bitter, milky juice and the flowers are about one inch broad and golden yellow. This plant is a creeping rooted annual that grows from sixteen inches to five feet tall. The Iroquois confederacy used a compound with Field Thistle to soothe crying or upset babies. Lumbee healers washed the fresh root and cut it into pieces one-fourth to one-half inch long which were strung like beads on a string. The necklace was put around the neck of a baby who was running a fever thought to be caused by teething difficulty. The necklace was left in place for two weeks and was then replaced with a fresh one for two more weeks.

Fire Root (Pteridium aquilinum)

Fire Root is a perennial fern with long roots. Its spores are located on the underside of its fronds. It has stiff, erect leaves that can grow to forty inches and a smooth, rigid stem. The rhizome of Fire Root was sliced into pieces approximately the size of the patient's thumbnail and submerged in water. This nonboiled fluid was employed to soak the painful or injured area to reduce discomfort. The Iroquois confederacy tribes used the Fire-root to make a decoction to treat diarrhea and a tonic to treat "weak blood." Modern science has found that Fire Root juice has antimicrobial effects against certain kinds of bacteria, but also contains possible carcinogenic agents.

Fireweed (Epilobium angustifolium); also known as Blooming Sally, Willow Herb

Anyone who has driven past a recent forest fire may have seen bright magenta flowers. This plant is called Fireweed. Fireweed is native to North America and Europe. It thrives in burned over or disturbed land. Fireweed is an erect perennial with unbranched stems growing up to eight feet. The leaves are lance shaped, alternate, and look similar to those of a Willow tree (thus the name Willow Herb). The Lumbee called Fireweed "sura ki'p," or grass fire, in the traditional language. Lumbee healers have used Fireweed to serve as an astringent, alterative, tonic, cathartic, and emetic. The dried leaves were boiled into a tea to serve as a demulcent (soothing mucous membranes), an astringent, and as a treatment for kidney problems. In the form of an oil, extract, or infusion, it was used for treatment of dysentery. The fresh roots and leaves were made into a tea by some Lumbee healers to treat asthma, whooping cough, and hiccoughs. Many Lumbee ate the young shoots or cooked the middle of the stem to make a soup. Some Lumbee have used the young Fireweed flower stalks and leaves as ingredients in salads.

Flag *see Calamus*

Flax (Linum usitatissimum)
Warning: Immature seedpods can cause poisoning.

Flax is an nonnative annual with a one- to three-foot-high slender stem that branches at the top. Alternate, pale green, small leaves grow on the stem and branches. The light blue flowers appear at the end of each branch from February through September. The Lumbee made the seeds into a tea and used them to treat gravel, which is a burning sensation during urination or actual kidney stones. The Lumbee chewed the seeds frequently and many healers believed the Flax reduced the risk for heart disease. There are three components of Flax seed oil which modern science thinks may benefit general health. These ingredients are Omega-3 fatty acid (heart), fiber (digestive tract), and lignans (hormonal aid). The Flax seeds were soaked overnight to soften the hard shell then ground fine and used as a flour in recipes. An extract from the seeds was used in salves and ointments. The Cherokee also used a tea from the seeds to treat gravel (kidney stones) and burning urination. Flax has been found to be one of the first plants that man did not use solely for food. The Egyptians used cloth spun from the fibers of this plant to wrap the bodies of the pharaohs (mummies), and the cloth also became the material for religious garments for Greek and Hebrew priests.

Foeniculum vulgare *see Fennel*

Fragaria vesca *see Wild Strawberry*

Fringe Tree *see Graybeard*

Frog Bonnets *see Bugle Plant*

Gallberry (Ilex glabra); also known as Inkberry
Gallberry is an open, evergreen shrub that reaches a height of ten feet. The evergreen, leathery leaves are alternately arranged and serrated on the upper half. The leaf is shiny and dark green above and lighter and dull underneath. Small greenish white flowers form on the top of the plant. The Lumbee healer would give children the fresh fruits of the "Inkberry" to induce vomiting after they had swallowed a poison. However, because of the strong emetic action, Lumbee herbal experts also considered the fruits to be somewhat poisonous themselves.

Gall of the Earth (Prenanthes Trifoliolata); also known as Lion's foot

Gall of the earth is a native plant that has a stem and leaves without bloom. The lower leaves are thin and usually separated into three segments. This plant also has a smooth, purplish, waxy, reddish stem. Some of the whitish, dangling flowers have a cinnamon-brown material underneath the bloom. The entire plant is from one to four feet in height. Gall of the Earth can be found in woods and thickets in the southeastern United States. Mr. Vernon Cooper, Lumbee healer, would prepare the Gall of the Earth in a tonic combined with Black Gum to treat high blood pressure. The roots have been used to treat stomachache. Many Lumbee would eat the leaves in a cooked salad.

Garlic (Allium sativum)
The leaves of the Garlic plant are long, narrow, and flat, like grass. Garlic bulbs (the only part eaten) consist of numerous bulblets, known as cloves, grouped together in a thin sack. The flowers at the end of the stalk are whitish and are grouped together in a globular head. It is evident by looking at this plant that Garlic is closely related to the onion. Many Lumbee healers have adopted the plant for its culinary and medicinal qualities. They use Cultivated Garlic (Allium satvium), a nonnative plant, and Wild Garlic (Allium vineale), a native plant, in similar fashion. Garlic is marketed in modern herbal markets as a medicinal aid. Modern science has shown recently that garlic

is one of the best sources of the mineral selenium. This mineral reportedly promotes antioxidant activity. The fresh bulbs were cooked and eaten by the Lumbee to treat asthma, colds, coughs, and worms. A fresh poultice of the mashed plant has been used to treat hornet stings, snakebite, and scorpion stings. The bulb was pressed against the gum to treat toothache. A tea from the Garlic root was made by some healers to treat hypertension (high blood pressure) or hypotension (low blood pressure). This tea was also thought by some healers to inhibit the production of harmful bacteria in the colon. Garlic oil was suggested by some healers to treat earaches. The Cherokee used Garlic as a stomachache and cough treatment.

Gaultheria procumbens *see Wintergreen*

Gaylussacia dumosa *see Ground Huckleberry*

Gaylussacia frondosa *see He-Huckleberry*

Gelsemium sempervirens *see Yellow Jessamine*

Glyceria obtusa *see Blunt Manna Grass*

Goat's Rue *see Devil's Shoestring*

Goldenrod (Solidago virgaurea); also known as Solidago canadensis
Goldenrod can be found in woods and dry, open fields in the eastern United States. It is a perennial herb with five-inch, smooth edged, green leaves. Goldenrod can grow from twenty to forty inches tall. Tiny yellow flowers form clusters on the upper end of curving branches from July to September. At one time, Goldenrod was blamed for hay fever. Many individuals suffer with this allergy during mid to late summer. However, it was found that Goldenrod pollen was carried by bees and not through the air. The real cause of this summer/autumn discomfort was found to be the pollen that comes from Ragweed's unremarkable flowers. Ragweed (Ambrosia artemisiifolia) blooms at the same time as the Goldenrod. Historically, Goldenrod has been used topically for wound healing. In fact, the name Solidago means "to make whole" in Latin. Some Lumbee healers recommended that a tea of the leaves be used to treat intestinal disorders and a tea of the leaves and flowering tops be used specifically for colic. Mr. Hayes Alan Locklear, Lumbee healer and historian, said many Lumbee made a tea from the flowers to treat bladder, kidney, or urinary disorders, and dropsy (edema). Some local healers have also employed Goldenrod as an aromatic, stimulant, and carminative. Other healers, in later years, would put Goldenrod tea, made from the entire plant, in a spray bottle to spray inside the mouth for treatment of oral maladies. Lumbee healers thought Goldenrod taken in the form of a tea was a great value

in treating Diphtheria. Boiled Goldenrod flowers yield an orange-yellow dye.

Goldenseal (Hydrastis canadensis); also known as Eyeroot, Ground Raspberry, Yellow Indian Paint

Goldenseal is a perennial bush native to the damp meadows and moist fields of eastern North America. It has a rough, wrinkled root. A small, solitary, white flower appears in May and June, and the berries are small and resemble raspberries. The stem is hairy, eight to twenty inches tall, and sprouts with dark green, five-lobed, leaves. Lumbee herbal experts considered Goldenseal to be a tonic remedy that stimulated the immune response. They also believed that this plant was antimicrobial. Cat Lowry, a Lumbee midwife and healer, suggested that her patients use Goldenseal to treat internal bleeding or to strengthen any tonic or tea. Another healer stated the belief that Goldenseal could be used as a treatment for any disease. Lumbee herbal experts believed that Goldenseal, taken with any herb, increased the properties for the specific organs that were being treated. The roots and rhizomes not only supplied many Native American tribes with paint, but were also utilized in a root scrapings tea to treat mouth ulcers, cancer, indigestion, tuberculosis, and dropsy (edema). A wash was made from the entire plant to treat inflamed eyes, and a poultice or salve was used as an antiseptic or to stop bleeding. One Lumbee lady shared that when she had a problem with ants in her kitchen cabinets, she would place a small amount of Goldenseal in each one of them. The Iroquois confederacy tribes used Goldenseal in a compound infusion to treat earaches.

Gourd (Lagenaria siceraria)

The Gourd is an annual climbing vine that can grow to thirty feet or more. It has heart-shaped alternately arranged leaves, and tubular, white flowers. The Gourd is a relative of the squashes and exhibits a greenish fruit that grows to different shapes and sizes. However, a common type has a long thin neck with a large round end. Eventually, the green gourd turns tan and hardens. One Lumbee healer said he would soak the Gourd leaves in vinegar and bind the leaves to the sides of the head to treat fever. Gourds were also used as bird houses, swimming floats, liquid and seed containers, and masks that were worn in dances. Small Gourds are also worn around the wrists and ankles in Lumbee traditional dances such as the Smoke Stomp, and Canoe (etc.). Many Lumbee would use the crushed, flaky inside of the Gourd sprinkled on the water as "vivarium" or an agent to encourage the fish to bite. Arthur Lowery, a Lumbee elder from the Saddletree community, stated, "When the wind blows lightly out of the east, the fish will bite." One of the authors recalls that his grandfather,

Loy Locklear, would throw grass up in the air to see if the wind was blowing lightly enough out of the east to be favorable for catching fish. The Cherokee soaked Gourd seeds and used the liquid to treat boils. The Seminole would burn the seeds to "smoke the body" treat insanity, treat headaches and treat body pains. One author's family continues the Lumbee artistic tradition of making beautiful works of art from carving and painting the gourd.

Graybeard (Cladrastis lutea); also known as Yellow Wood, Fringe Tree

Graybeard is a native tree that grows from six to twenty-four feet in height when mature in the midwestern, southeastern, and northeastern United States. The leaves are opposite, smooth, oblong, and oval in shape. In May and June when the leaves are only partially developed, the fragrant, white flowers, from whose fringelike petals the tree derives its name, appear in dense panicles. The fruit is an oval purple drupe. Scrapings of the roots were boiled by some Lumbee to make a wash to treat poison ivy. Mr. Earl Carter, Lumbee healer, relates a story about a physician who asked his advice about a patient who had been clearing some brush and got poison ivy on his face and in his throat. Nothing had seemed to work to treat the problem. Mr. Earl told the doctor to use more poison ivy. The doctor thought Mr. Earl had lost his mind,

but the Lumbee healer told him to boil it and make a tea out of it (homeopathy). The bark of Graybeard was prepared to be used as an astringent. Some Lumbee healers would boil the bark in water to obtain an extract used to nurse external wounds. The mashed bark was also employed to fashion a poultice to treat open wounds for severe cuts and as a healing agent for burns, bruises, or swelling. The Choctaw also used the Fringe Tree as an astringent. They employed a poultice to help close wounds out of crushed bark of the Graybeard, and boiled a bark tea to help clean external injuries.

Gray Beech see American Beech Tree

Ground Cedar see Rheumatism Plant

Ground Huckleberry (Gaylussacia dumosa)

Ground Huckleberry or Dwarf Huckleberry is a native, small, deciduous, erect, and multibranched shrub which grows from twelve to thirty inches in height. Many stems ascend from the base, forming a low, dense, rounded crown. The twigs have short and curly hairs. The small, deciduous leaves are simple, leathery, and elliptical. The pinkish bell-shaped tubular flowers are borne on a raceme at the end of the branchlets. The fruit is a blue, fleshy berry with ten nutlets, each carrying one seed. Lumbee healer Mr. Vernon Cooper would prepare Ground

Huckleberry into a tonic to treat "neuritis" (later stages of diabetes) or "sugar in the bone" (severe diabetes) in combination with Wild Cherry bark and St. John the Worker. A decoction using all parts of the plants was recommended. A handful of twigs and leaves, approximately as long as the length of the patient's third finger to the base of his or her palm, was boiled in a pint of water until only a third to a half of the liquid remained. Adults were given a full tablespoon of the liquid. Teenagers were given one-half to three-fourths of a tablespoon and children under ten were usually given a teaspoon and adults were given a full tablespoon. In preparing a tonic for diabetes, Mr. Vernon combined the male and female varieties (small and larger plants) of the Ground Huckleberry so that treatment could be used by either men or women.

Ground Raspberry *see Goldenseal*

Gum Tree *see Sweet Gum*

Hackberry *see Sugarberry*

Hamamelis virginiana *see Witch Hazel*

Hawthorn (Crataegus spp.); also known as May Blossom

Hawthorns are large shrubs or small trees which have dark brown bark, flaking in scales. A unique feature of the trunk are the sharp protruding spines. The white, or occasionally red, foul-smelling flowers are located toward the end of the leaf branches in round clusters. These small, roselike flowers are abundant. Hawthorn haws (fruits) are pear-shaped and about the size of a blueberry. This tree is usually found in partially shaded wooded areas. The Lumbee used an infusion of Hawthorn leaves, flowers, and haws (dried fruits) as a cardiac and circulatory tonic. Some Lumbee healers recommended Hawthorn to treat heart disease they deduced had been caused by kidney problems, arterial spasms, irregular heartbeat, or thickening of the heart walls. Mr. Welton Lowry, Lumbee elder, states he takes Hawthorn on a regular basis for his heart. The Lumbee thought that Hawthorn controlled both high and low blood pressure by dilating the blood vessels and improving the pumping action of the heart. Some Lumbee used the leaves as a substitute for tobacco and tea. The roasted seeds were ground into a type of coffee. Local healers also used a bark tea to promote good circulation and prevent current spasms. Reportedly, the berries were eaten by some Lumbee to increase the appetite.

He-Huckleberry (Gaylussacia frondosa); also known as Dangleberry

This native plant is a perennial, deciduous shrub that grows to six feet tall. It has pinkish, bell shaped flowers. The leaves appear whitish-green and are alternate. The fruit is a blue, fleshy berry (blueberry). Mr. Vernon Cooper, a Lumbee healer, prepared the leaves and fruit of "He-Huckle-berry" into a tonic to treat the early stages of diabetes. The tops were gathered from May to September and the roots the remainder of the year. The tea was recommended for treatment of diabetes of the blood or kidneys. Mr. Vernon believed that diabetes of the kidneys caused a lot of fluid buildup in various parts of the body.

Heal-all (Prunella vulgaris);
also known as All-heal

Heal-all is a low growing mint that could be easily overlooked in a grassy field. If one takes a closer look, one sees the beautiful purples and blues of the intricate flower. Heal-all grows from one to two feet in height. It is mainly found around the edges of fields. A few are found in dry areas of the woods. Heal-all flowers bloom from July to August. Some Lumbee healers have used this herb to treat epilepsy, convulsions, and an obstructed liver. A tea was brewed by Lumbee healers to treat contagious fevers. It was also used as an astringent and often prescribed as a gargle to treat sore throat and to clean wounds. It was also suggested for internal and external wounds. For treatment of internal wounds and mouth ulcers, many Lumbee healers would prepare a tea. A poultice was advised for external wounds and sores. Lumbee healer Mr. Vernon Cooper stated, "Heal-all was an ingredient in my grandmother's cancer salve along with Cat Tongue leaves, Fever Grass, Sampson snakeroot, Eyebright, Sweet Gum tar, Heartleaf, and sheep tallow." The Algonquian tribes would fashion an infusion of Heal-all leaves as a treatment of fever. The Blackfoot tribe would also make an infusion of this plant to burst boils and to apply to neck sores. The Blackfoot and other Plains area tribes would also apply this infusion to back and saddle sores on their horses.

Healing Herb see Comfrey

Heartleaf (Hexastylis arifolia); also known as Little Brown Jug, Pitcher Leaf Plant

Heartleaf is similar to Wild Ginger (Asarum canadenses). This plant is evergreen and herbaceous. Heartleaf has basal leaves only. These leaves can be as wide as forty inches and each heart-shaped leaf is entire. The flowers have three regular parts that can grow up to one inch. The name Little Brown Jug fits because the mid to late spring flowers look similar to small, reddish-brown jugs. These flowers are often hidden by leaves. Heartleaf is most often found in shady places such as deciduous forests. Mr. Vernon Cooper, a Lumbee healer, would recommend Heartleaf for flavor in tonics and to treat heart trouble. He stated, "They have a mighty good odor. I used them when I was suffering so much with my heart." Ms. Lucie Mae Hammonds Lock-lear, a Lumbee elder, said it was her belief that the Creator made the Heartleaf in the shape of a heart so that "man would know how he [should] use it." She would make a "pad" out of several of the leaves and press it to her chest to purportedly kill the pain or "take the fever out." Ms. Locklear did not believe Heartleaf would help someone who had a heart defect. Ms. Vernon Hazel Locklear said her grandmother, Ms. Rhoda Jane Lowry, would send her out to the woods to collect Heartleaf so she could make it into a tea for her grandfather, Mr. Orlin Lowry. A tea from the leaves has also been used to regulate the bowels, to treat colds, stomach cramps, and lung trouble, and as a flavoring in foods. The Catawba, a sister tribe of the Lumbee, would prepare an infusion of the leaves to treat stomach pains or backaches.

Hedeoma pulegioides *see American Pennyroyal*

Helenium amarum *see Bitter Weed*

Heterotheca graminfolia *see Fever Grass*

Heuchera americana *see Alumroot*

Hexastylis arifolia *see Heartleaf*

Hickory Tree (**Carya ovata**); also known as Shagbark Hickory
Hickory Trees can reach a height of one hundred fifty feet with a canopy spread of over fifty feet.

Most Hickory trees, however, only reach eighty feet in height. The Hickory is a close relative to the Pecan tree. Hickory nuts are light tan and are enclosed in a brown hull. The leaves are alternately arranged and turn yellow in the fall. The bark of the mature "Hickory" is gray and broken up into long, flat plates. Some Lumbee healers would soak the bark of the Hickory tree for one day and then boil it to make a tea for rheumatism. A stronger dose was thought by some healers to have diaphoretic or emetic properties. The word Hickory is a derivative of the Algonquian word "pawcohiccora," which was used to describe the meal (similar to cornmeal) made from crushing and grinding the Hickory nuts. The Iroquois confederacy tribes would combine the nutmeal with bear grease for a hair treatment or mosquito repellant. These tribes would also manufacture a bark decoction and poultice to treat arthritis. To treat a headache, the Chippewa would boil the small Hickory shoots and use the rising steam as an inhalant. The Delaware would use the Hickory to treat gynecological disorders or diseases.

Hog apple *see Mayapple*

Holly Bush (**Ilex opaca**); also known as Sharp leaf tree
The Holly is a native, large shrub or small tree than can grow as tall as fifty feet. Its thorn tipped evergreen leaves are alternate, simple and elliptical. However, the lustrous leaves can range from yellow

to olive green. The fruit is a berry-like dull red drupe that grows grows to the size of a Dogwood berry and matures in October. The Holly Bush can be found from open areas to woods in the southern half of the United States. The Holly produces dull white, four lobed flowers. Lumbee herbal experts viewed Holly leaves as a diaphoretic, and an infusion of fresh leaves was prepared to treat measles, pleurisy, and smallpox. Lumbee healers also prepared the leaves to treat intermittent fevers. The berries purportedly possessed totally different qualities from the leaves. Lumbee healers considered the berries to be violently emetic and purgative. Some supposedly experienced severe vomiting soon after they swallowed the berries. However, some healers boiled the red berries until they became a thick, "stewlike" soup. This soup was given to people with a "slick stomach" or to stop diarrhea. The stew was given in doses of one-half teaspoon (more for adults) three times a day. A decoction was made from the stems and leaves of Holly combined with Pine (Pinus spp.) and Rabbit Tobacco (Gnaphalium obtusifolium) to treat colds, flu, and pneumonia. For treatment of the swelling of extremities due to edema (dropsy), Lumbee healers would sometimes tell individuals to strike their legs with a branch of the sharp leaves until fluid ran out of their body. The Catawba, a sister tribe of the Lumbee, would use an infusion of the leaves to treat sores. The Cherokee made a dye from the berries and also used them to treat colic in babies. To treat sore eyes, the Choctaw used a Holly Bush leaf infusion.

Honeysuckle (Lonicera perclymenum); also known as Woodbine

Caution: The black berries are poisonous.

Honeysuckle is a slow growing, irregular, variegated vine that blooms from summer to fall bearing fragrant clusters of tubelike flowers that vary in color from cream to orange-red (Trumpet vine) depending on the specific species. Ms. Lucie Mae Hammonds Locklear, a Lumbee elder, used the syrup made from the flowers of the honeysuckle to treat coughs. It was her belief that the syrup would cause individuals to cough up the phlegm. She also commented that this elixir was made by creating a strong infusion of the flowers by cooking them at a low boil to a consistency of honey. It was also used by some healers for the treatment of asthma and as a diuretic. In *The Education of Little Tree* by Forrest Carter, Little Tree, a young Cherokee boy, tells how his grandmother would "always put honeysuckle in her lye soap" to make the soap smell sweet.

Horehound (Marrubium vulgare)

Horehound or White Horehound is a nonnative, perennial herbaceous plant that flourishes in waste places and by roadsides. Horehound is a bushy plant, growing up to three feet tall. It produces numerous annual, quadrangular, branching stems which are a foot or more in height. The inch-long leaves are wrinkled, opposite, and are covered by white, felted hairs which give them a woolly appearance. The whitish flowers bloom from June to September on round clusters. The leaves have a unique musty smell which is diminished after drying. This Horehound is not the Horehound of cultivation (Eupatorium rotundifolium). It is a mint. Horehound has been used to flavor candy and tea for many years. A handful of the tops (stems and leaves) were boiled for two hours in a quart of water. The tea was used alone or combined with Pine (Pinus spp.) and Rabbit Tobacco (Gnaphalium obtusifolium) or with Pine and Goldenrod (Solidago spp.) to treat colds and flu. This was a very popular remedy among the Lumbee. Mr. Vernon Cooper, Lumbee healer, used Horehound as an ingredient in a stimulating tea he suggested to some elderly people. He would combine the Horehound with Rabbit Tobacco, Boneset, Stargrass, and pine tops. One modern herbal expert stated he would combine Horehound, Wild Cherry bark, Eucalyptus (nonnative plant), and Mullein. He suggested to his clients, to treat a severe sinus headache, supplementing the tea by inhaling the vapors of the simmering herb mixture.

Horsemint *see Spotted Horsemint*

Hydrastis canadensis *see Goldenseal*

Hypericum hypericoides *see Saint John the Worker*

Ilex glabra *see Gallberry*

Ilex opaca *see Holly Bush*

Ilex vomitoria *see American Holly*

Impatiens spp. *see Wild Touch-Me-Not*

Indian Apple *see Mayapple*

Indian Corn (Zea mays); also known as Big Red
Corn or Indian Corn is a native, vigorous annual grass that varies greatly in size according to species and growth conditions. The drooping, green leaf blades can be thirty inches long or more. When near maturity, a flowering white to red (depending on species) tassel forms at the top. Its fruit is arranged in longitudinal rows of kernels covered by a husk or a sheath. At the top of the husk, there protrudes a long yellow to red (brown when fruit is mature) silky tassel. There is one distinct species of Indian Corn unique to the Lumbee called Big Red, named for its dark red ears. It is not unusual for the stalk in the Big Red corn to grow to eleven or more feet in height. Ms. Angelina Okuda-Jacobs mentions the Big Red corn, grown by Jesse James Locklear and others, in her mas-

ter's thesis titled *Planting Health, Culture and Sovereignty: Traditional Horticulture of the Lumbee Nation of North Carolina*. A Lumbee legend tells how the Yehasuri (little people) changed some of the red corn to a multi-colored grain. Corn was called "ku's" in the native language of the Lumbee. Lumbee healers made an emollient poultice from the leaves of the Indian Corn. Mr. James Hammonds, a Lumbee Indian from the Saddletree community, said that when he was young he had the mad itch (scabies). Mr. James stated he went to the doctor in town, but that didn't help. Finally, he went to a local healer who told him to rub his skin vigorously with cornmeal. Local healers, to allay nausea and vomiting, suggested an infusion of parched corn, and some Lumbee healers, to treat gravel (kidney or bladder stones), prescribed a tea made from the silks. The leaf infusion from this plant was made with Pine (Pinus spp.), Rabbit Tobacco (Gnaphalium obtusifolium), and Mullein (Verbascum thapsus) for colds and the grippe (described as a severe cold that makes the bones ache). A tea to break a fever was made with Poplar (Liriodendron tulipifera) leaves added to the corn blade decoction. The shucks from around the ear of the corn were made into a tea that many Lumbee considered tasty. This shuck milk was also used by local healers to treat measles. John Lawson, in his history of his explorations of North Carolina in 1701, wrote that a white North Carolina planter had an ugly ulcer on his leg. The planter feared that the infection might cause his death. Having tried every remedy known to him and his white physician, the planter decided to see an Eastern Siouan (ancestor tribes of the Lumbee) healer. After looking the patient over, the healer mixed into a poultice "nothing but the rotten grains of Indian Corn [purportedly akin to modern age penicillin], beaten into a powder, and applied it with the soft down of a turkey." According to Lawson, this application healed the ulcer, and the patient enjoyed a healthy life until he died by drowning. Corn was a staple food for Native Americans of the southeast. Some Lumbee still prefer the old way of preparing corn into hominy, meal, or mush by using a hollowed out log and a beating/grinding stick. The ancient Lumbee and other southeastern tribes would also use the corn husks to wrap the meal or bread to keep it fresh. Mrs. Penny Lowry, a Lumbee tribal member from Pembroke, N.C., said many Lumbee would boil a tea from dried corn husks to treat kidney problems. In the past, the Lumbee made mattress filling and floor mats out of corn husks. In *The Education of Little Tree* by Forrest Carter, a story of a small Cherokee boy and his Cherokee grandparents, Little Tree tells of another use for Indian Corn. Little Tree's grandfather made corn whiskey for a living. Many Lumbee also made "moonshine" during the depression years. One Lumbee told how a disreputable man down the road would put potash (Oak ashes) or bird droppings in the whiskey to give it a good bead. Little Tree explained how his grandfather (Wales) took pride in his trade and only used a red Indian Corn, which gave the whiskey a light red tint. Like the some Lumbee, a few Cherokee would sell moonshine whiskey and use it to help treat medical ailments. The Cherokee would also use the parched grains of corn in an infusion to give stickball players "long wind" or stamina in the game. The Mohegan tribe used dried cobs to fashion a wash for poison ivy.

Indian Elm *see Slippery Elm*

Indian Hemp (Apocynum cannabinum); also known as American hemp

There is an old misconception that the Lumbee and other Native American tribes in precontact European times smoked (in pipes) a plant that is known today as marijuana. In truth, however, those plants are not native to the North or South American continents (Cannabis sativa is Eurasian and Cannabis indica is from India). There is, however, a plant called Indian Hemp which is indigenous to the Americas that was used for medicinal and utilitarian purposes by many Native American tribes. The roots of Indian Hemp were also widely used as a treatment of kidney and urinary ailments. Some Lumbee healers would beat the root into a powder and boil it into a decoction and recommend that their patients drink it for a treatment of rheumatism, asthma, or whooping cough. Other healers also suggested that this decoction be taken as a diuretic. But there is no evidence that any of the Native American tribes smoked the leaves of Indian Hemp. Native Americans did manufacture an Indian Hemp twine by harvesting the stems in October, just as the leaves were starting to turn. The plant was first split open from bottom to top with a sharp stick. Second, the woody outer skin was pulled off after rubbing the stems. Then the fibrous parts just under the skin were bundled together and hung by the tops in the wind to dry. When dry, the fibers were brittle. These fibers were made into twine by twisting and rolling them with the hand on the bare thigh. This twine could be kept many years in a cool, dry place. Indian hemp was used for making fishing lines and nets because it kept its strength under water without shrinking. It was also used to make rope, deer nets, slings for hunting small game, nooses for snaring game birds, hide stretchers, garments, quilts, and moccasins, and so forth.

Indian Jug *see Bugle Plant*

Indian Paint *see Bloodroot*

Indian Pink (Spigelia marilandica)
**Warning: Can be fatal if taken
internally.**

Indian Pink is a beautiful wild-
flower that grows up to two feet
tall from perennial roots. There
are four to seven pairs of oval, opposite leaves which can grow to
two inches long. Each leaf is
pointed at the tip. The stem of the
Indian Pink may bear two to
twelve colorful, tubular flowers.
The corolla is bright red externally, opening at the tip into five
starlike, sharp-pointed lobes
which are yellow inside. Indian
Pink can be found in rich soils at
the edges of woods and woodland
clearings from the Piedmont to the
coastal plain of North Carolina
southward to the Gulf Coast to
Texas. This plant's root was made
into a tea by some Lumbee healers to treat intestinal worms, especially roundworms. The Creek
tribe would also use the Indian
Pink plant in a decoction to treat
worms.

Indian Tobacco (Lobelia
inflata)and **Wild Tobacco**
(Nicotiana rustica); also
known as Asthma Weed, Puke-
weed
**Warning: Indian Tobacco has
been declared poisonous by the
U.S. Food and Drug Administration**

Indian Tobacco is an annual or
biennial herb indigenous to the
eastern United States. This plant
grows to six feet in height, has an
erect, hairy, angular stem, and
contains a milky sap. The thin,
light green leaves are alternate,
hairy, ovate, and bluntly serrate.
Numerous small, two-lipped, blue
flowers grow in spikelike racemes
from July to November. The fruit
is a two-celled capsule filled with
small, brown seeds. Indian or Wild
Tobacco was called "nieye umpa
re,"—the people's tobacco—in the
native language of the Lumbee. It
is a well known fact that tobacco
was originally a Native American
plant "discovered" by Europeans.
However, most people do not
know that these plants are actually
three separate species. The Lumbee and other Native American
tribes used Indian Tobacco and
Wild Tobacco as a part of their religious ceremonies. In such a con-
text, tobacco was literally a sacred
plant. Legends tell that is was a gift
from the Creator. But traditional
ceremonial use of tobacco bears
little resemblance to the habitual
smoking seen in today's society.
The leaves of Indian and Wild Tobacco were used by the Lumbee
and other tribes in the past to treat
asthma and other lung ailments.
Mr. Earl Carter, Lumbee healer,
performs a special ceremony when
gathering the leaves or other material from plants. First, he stops to
say a short prayer. Then he pulls
out a small pinch of dried tobacco
and to offers it to the plant. Then,
he thanks the plant, collects the
material, and places the bits and
pieces in a wooden peach basket.

Modern scientific research has studied the effects of Indian Tobacco (Lobelia inflata) on treating asthma (also how it purportedly works as an expectorant). These scientists have found that this species contains lobeline. The agent lobeline is an ingredient of some cough medicines today, and is also found in some over-the-counter preparations marketed to break the smoking habit.

Inkberry *see Poke or Gallberry*

Ironweed (Sida rhombifolia);
also known as Teaweed

Ironweed is a perennial herb that can reach a height of five feet. The stems are hairy and have strong internal fibers. The leaves are long, alternate, and toothed. The cream to pale yellow flowers bloom from spring to fall on top of an elongated stalk. Ironweed is a native plant to southeastern United States. Ironweed roots were gathered after the first frost and parts above ground were gathered in the spring, summer, and fall. Seven four inch long sections of the Devil's Shoestring (Tephrosia virginiana) root were boiled four hours with two or more Ironweed plants (two feet tall) to nurse a weak back. Three swallows were taken in the morning, noon and bedtime. To treat pimples, a bath was prepared mixing the above decoction with salt. When the horses or mules appeared too skinny (showing their ribs), some Lumbee would parch Ironweed and mix it with the feed to make them fat (slick them up).

Jacob's Coat (Perilla frutescens); also known as Beefsteak-Plant, Perilla

Jacob's Coat is an erect herb that has distinctive green or purplish-green leaves with toothed margins. Its leaves are opposite and oval and have a mint odor when crushed. The small flowers occur in terminal clusters that range in color from white to whitish purple. This is primarily a plant of pastures, hayfields, fencerows, and roadsides. Jacob's Coat was combined with Cherry (Prunus serotina) and Poplar (Liriodendron tulipifera) bark to treat fevers. Jacob's Coat was also planted around Lumbee homes and areas where animals were kept to fend off fleas and flies. Some healers also advised hanging a bouquet of dried tomato leaves in all rooms of the house to keep out bothersome bugs.

Jerusalem Oak (Chenopodium ambrosioides)

Warning: This plant itself is deadly poison. If taken internally, it will kill you.

Jerusalem Oak is an erect annual or perennial. Its leaves are alternate, simple, and irregularly toothed. The small, greenish flowers form an elongated, dense, and terminal cluster. The flowers have no petals. Its fruits are small and green with black seeds. It is found in disturbed areas of cultivated fields and waste places. The Lumbee called the Jerusalem Oak "witside we," or healing medicine, in the traditional language. Mr. Vernon Cooper, a Lumbee healer, said that he suggested the Jerusalem Oak to treat snakebite. The whole plant was beaten to a mash and bound as a poultice to the part of the body of man or beast to draw out poison. Mr. Cooper warned, "It is in itself a poison; if drunk it will kill you." Some Lumbee were also apprehensive about telling tales at night because they believed it could cause "trouble from the snakes." Often when a Lumbee man was preparing for a hunting trip or other venture and was not planning to return home until late at night or for several days, he would leave a day or short time earlier than the departure time he announced to his family. His family understood, of course, that he was only trying to confuse the snakes, which might lie in wait for him if they knew where and when he was going. Although healers believed that Jerusalem Oak itself was a poison, the fresh or dried seeds were eaten by some Lumbee, with honey, as a treatment for worms.

Jimson (Datura stramonium); also known as Jimsonweed
Warning: Do not take Jimson internally. It is deadly poisonous.

Jimson is a member of the deadly nightshade (poisonous potato) family. Jimsonweed is an annual herb growing up to four feet tall with a foul odor. The foul-smelling flower usually opens after dusk and closes by mid-morning. Unevenly toothed oval leaves are about eight inches long. The corollas are up to six inches long and have five teeth that are often tinged with purple or lavender around the margins. Large, white, trumpet-shaped flowers bloom March through November. Jimson was called "i'tube'" or immoveable rock in the ancient tongue of the Lumbee. The leaves and roots were boiled and made into an ointment that was applied to tick bites or external cancers. Heartleaf (Hexastylis arifolia) was added by some healers to the decoction to make the odor more pleasant. The Delaware made a poultice of crushed leaves and applied it to fresh wounds. They also pounded the seeds and mixed the paste with tallow to treat hemorrhoids. The Rappahannock used an infusion from the green leaves and a salve to treat wounds and inflammations. The Waccamaw-Siouan, a sister tribe of the Lumbee, called Jimson "Dr. Jimmy Weed." They used Jimson to treat typhoid fever and to increase the appetite.

Jimsonweed *see Jimson*

Judas Tree *see Red Bud Tree*

Juglans cinerea *see Butternut Tree*

Juglans nigra *see Black Walnut Tree*

Juniperus virginiana *see Cedar*

Kalmia carolina *see Wicky*

Lactuca canadensis *see Wild Lettuce*

Lagenaria siceraria *see Gourd*

Lambkill *see Wicky*

Laurus sassafras *see Sassafras Tree*

Lawn Weed *see Dandelion*

Lemon Balm (Melissa officinalis); also known as Melissa, Sweet Balm

Lemon Balm is a perennial plant with upright and hairy, branching stems that can reach three feet in height. Its foliage has a distinctive lemony fragrance when bruised. The leaves are light green, egg shaped, crinkled, slightly hairy, and are strongly toothed on the margins. Lemon balm grows in full sunlight along roadsides, waste places, and disturbed land throughout the United States. Lumbee herbal experts, to treat feverish colds and headaches, relieve menstrual cramps, and to calm a nervous stomach, used Lemon Balm tea or an infusion from the leaves. A tincture from the fresh leaves was sometimes suggested. This dose was 5 to 10 drops in water. The tinture was considered to be more potent than an infusion. The extract from the leaves was considered, by modern Lumbee herbal experts, to have antiviral quality, and this extract has also been used by many Lumbee to clean wounds. Lemon Balm is diluted in sterile water by modern herbalists to manufacture a wash used to treat eczema. The crushed leaves were used on wounds and insect bites. Lemon Balm was also used for making teas and cool drinks, and as a flavoring in salads, soups, and egg dishes by many Lumbee. Today, Lemon Balm is used commercially in many perfumes and cosmetics.

Lepidium virginicum *see Pepper Grass*

Liatris regimentis *see White Bloodroot*

Life Everlasting *see* Rabbit Tobacco

Linum Usitatissimum *see Flax*

Lion's Foot *see Gall of the Earth*

Lion's Tongue *see Pipsissewa*

Liquidambar styraciflua *see Sweet Gum Tree*

Liriodendron tulipifera *see Poplar Tree*

Little Brown Jug *see Heartleaf*

Lobelia inflata *see Indian Tobacco and Wild Tobacco*

Loblolly Pine (North Carolina Pine) *see Pine Tree*

Longleaf Pine *see Pine Tree*

Lonicera periclymenum
see Honeysuckle

Lycopodium flabelliforme
see Rheumatism Plant

Magnolia grandiflora *see*
Magnolia Tree

Magnolia Tree (Magnolia
grandiflora)
The Magnolia is a native evergreen tree with a straight trunk
and conical crown. Its extremely
large and fragrant, white flowers
make this tree distinctive. The
Magnolia grows from sixty to
eighty feet in height when mature.
Its two- to three-inch shiny green
leaves are oblong or elliptical,
thick, and firm with edges turned
over. The bark of the Magnolia
tree was combined with Cherry,
Dogwood, and Poplar barks in
boiling water to prepare a tea to
nurse malarial fever. Some Lumbee healers would recommend
that their patients sniff a warm tea
made from Magnolia bark tea up
their noses for treatment of sinus
trouble, stomachache, or abdominal cramps. This plant is very aromatic and the odor of the crushed
leaves is almost identical to that of
the Bay. Some Lumbee used both
Magnolia (M. grandiflora) and
Bay tree (P. borbonia) stems interchangeably under the name
"bay" for scenting lard when hogs
were slaughtered, and used a
Sweet Bay or Magnolia stick to stir
the lard to give it a unique flavor.

Mandrake *see Mayapple*

Mark (Bidens frondosa); also
known as Beggar-Ticks, Stick-
Tight
Mark is an erect annual that grows
to three and one-half feet in height.
It has a purplish, smooth, and slender stem except at the upper node.
The leaves are ovate, lanceolate,
serrated, and divided into three to
five leaflets. Mark has a prickly fruit
that facilitates seed dispersal by
sticking to the fur or clothing of
any person or animal that acciden-
tally brushes by it. This plant can
be found in pastures and hayfields,
and on roadsides. Aunt Cat Lowry,
a Lumbee healer, would boil the
fresh leaves and stems for half an
hour. A rag was then submerged in
the liquid and held to the sides of
the forehead to treat headache.
Back spasm or pain was treated in
the same fashion before bedtime.
The Seminole tribe used a sister
plant of the Mark in an infusion to
treat sun poisoning, eye disease,
headache, and high fever.

Marrubium vulgare *see*
Horehound

Mayapple (Podophyllum pell-
tatum); also known as Mandrake, Hog Apple, Indian Apple
**Warning: All parts except the
ripe fruits are poisonous.**
Mayapple is a perennial herb that
comes up in the woods each spring.
Each plant has two large, deeply divided, umbrella-like leaves. At the
crotch, there is a single nodding six-
to nine-petaled flower from which a
large, lemonlike berry forms. It is
said that many tribes recognized the

Mayapple's toxic qualities. It is said they sometimes ate the roots and shoots to commit suicide. However, modern science has found the rhizomes of the Mayapple contain potent anti-cancer substances, and a derivative of one of these substances is used in present day medicine to treat human cancers. Lumbee herbal experts also knew that the joints of the roots were poison. It was thought best to use only the rhizomes. The Lumbee ate the fully ripe fruits raw in moderation. The powdered rhizomes, root tendrils, were thought to have a potent laxative effect. Many Lumbee healers thought it best to gather the root in late fall and let it dry in the shade. The root was then beaten into a powder and diluted in water. The powdered root was also used on ulcers or sores. A drop of the fresh root juice in the ear was also thought by some Lumbee to treat certain types of deafness. Mayapple was also used by Lumbee healers as an anthelmintic, antirheumatic, aphrodisiac, cathartic, emetic, hydragogue, insecticide, laxative, purgative, stengthener, and tonic.

May Blossom *see Hawthorn*

Maypop *see Passionflower*

Melia azedarach *see Chinaberry*

Melissa *see Lemon Balm*

Melissa officinalis *see Lemon Balm*

Mentha labiatae *see American Pennyroyal*

Mentha piperita officinalis *see Peppermint*

Mentha Spicata *see Spearmint*

Merker Tree *see* **Red Myrtle**

Milkweed (Euphorbia maculata); also known as Spotted Spurge, Eyebane

Milkweed is a perennial herb that reaches a height of two feet. It has milky juice within the stalk. The dark green, opposite leaves usually have a red dot in the center. It grows in fields and open places in the eastern United States. The recently collected plant was mashed and the milky sap or inside gummy substance was rubbed on wounds by many Lumbee. The "milk" was also used to treat acne and poison ivy. This gummy sap was washed off after approximately two minutes. Ms. Mary Bell, a Lumbee healer, would combine Milkweed, Fig leaves, Bayberry bark, Peppermint, Wild Cherry bark, and brown sugar (honey was said to make the concoction bitter) to nurse bronchitis.

Mistletoe (Phoradendron serotinum)

Mistletoe is distributed throughout warmer parts of North America. It is most abundant on Apple trees, Poplars, Lindens, and Hawthorns. Mistletoe is considered a parasite, because it reduces the vigor and even threatens the survival of many shade trees. The Mistletoe has a green stem with thick leaves that are nearly oval in shape. Small, sticky, whitish berries are produced from October to December. Evergreen clumps of Mistletoe are readily observed high up in the branches of deciduous trees in winter after the leaves have fallen. Mistletoe was called "yop ha waruwakure" or everlasting bush in the traditional tongue of the Lumbee. A Mistletoe tea using the leaves, berries, and branches was suggested by some healers as a treatment for high blood pressure. This tea has also been suggested to treat kidney stones in men. Many Lumbee would also bathe their heads in Mistletoe ooze to treat a headache.

Mitchella repens *see Partridge Berry*

Monarda punctata *see Spotted Horsemint*

Moss (Cladina subtenuis); also known as Reindeer Moss

Moss is a light gray-green lichen which grows close to the ground. It is found in sandy soils in the southeastern United States. The Lumbee healers would submerge the plant in water and boil it for ten to thirty minutes. A poultice and wash was made from the extract and applied to sores. Lumbee herbal lore stated the belief that this remedy would "take out the fever" so the wound could drain and heal.

Mountain Birch *see Wintergreen*

Mule Tail *see Mullein*

Mullein (Verbascum thapsus); also known as Bunny's Ears, Mule Tail

Mullein (rhymes with sullen) is regularly found in old fields, disturbed areas, vacant lots, wood edges, and in the middle of trails. This biennial plant grows up to eight feet tall. A rosette of leaves appears on the ground the first year; a tall spike of flowers rises the next year. Leaves and stems are both velvety. Mullein is usually found in full sun. The yellow, five-petaled, unstalked flowers appear in densely packed spikes, and bloom at random from spring until fall. The flowers are fragrant and leaves were once stuffed in shoes or moccasins of many Lumbee to keep their feet warm in the winter. In the past, some Lumbee mothers also used the big Mullein leaves as diapers for their babies. Some Lumbee healers thought that Mullein had demulcent, emollient, and astringent properties. A poultice or salve was made from the leaves to treat swollen, sore or aching muscles or hemorrhoids. Some Lumbee today will bathe their legs in root infusion to treat dropsy. A root or leaf tea was prepared by Lumbee healers to treat female trouble. Mullein flowers, often soaked in oil for a time, were used to bathe sores. Smoking Mullein leaves was an old Lumbee remedy for treatment of asthma and colds. Mullein was combined with Rosinweed (Silphium compsoitum) and boiled to make a decoction used to bathe areas affected by swelling. Some healers combined the leaf or mashed root with Red Shank (Ceanothus americanus) and Red Oak (Quercus spp.) covered with vinegar to make a poultice to treat the pain of a sprain or swelling. To relieve pain from an attack of gout, many Lumbee would soak their feet in an infusion made from the leaves. One individual that used this treatment stated that stewed Mullein leaves and flowers have an awful smell. Reportedly, the leaves were also used to treat wounds. To "take the fever out" (cool or stop the pain), Mullein root was crushed and put on boils and sores. To treat colds, a tea was made by stewing Mullein leaves with Pine (Pinus spp.), Rabbit Tobacco (Gnaphalium obtusifolium), and Corn (Zea mays). Mullein leaves and stalks can be boiled to make an orange-yellow dye.

Myrica cerifera *see Red Myrtle*

Nannyberry *see Black Haw*

Nepeta cataria *see Catmint*

Nettle (Urtica dioica)
Caution: The fresh plant can cause a reaction from the histamines located in the thorns.

The Nettle is a nonnative, erect perennial that ranges in height from twenty-four to seventy inches. It has coarsely toothed, opposite, narrow, heart-shaped leaves and small greenish flowers which bloom in axillary clusters. The Nettle's most distinctive feature is the small, stinging hairs on the stalk. In *The Education of Little Tree* by Forrest Carter, Little Tree, a young Cherokee boy, says, "Nettles make the best greens, but have little tiny hairs on them that sting you all over when you're picking. Me and Grandpa many times failed to notice a nettle patch, but Granma would find it and we would pick them. Grandpa said he had never knowed [*sic*] anything in life that, being pleasurable, didn't have a d--- catch to it—somewheres." The Cherokee also used Nettles to treat an upset stomach. Only well-dried leaves were used by the Lumbee with applications of this plant. Lumbee healers used the well-dried leaves in a tea, and suggested this plant as a treatment for those suffering from asthma. In tincture form, approximately 20 ml of material to a mug of hot water was used to treat the pain associated with urinary tract infections. The Cree used a decoction of the Nettle to keep blood flowing after childbirth. The Iroquois confederacy tribes used a Nettle compound and dried snake blood to make a "witching medicine."

New Jersey Tea *see Red Shank*

Nicotiana rustica *see Indian Tobacco and Wild Tobacco*

Nicotiana tabacum *see Cultivated Tobacco*

Nyssa sylvatica *see* ***Black Gum Tree***

Oak Tree (Quercus alba); also known as White Oak Tree
The Oaks have thick, light gray bark, and are deciduous. These common, large trees reach a height of more than one hundred fifteen feet. The White Oaks have bright green, lobed leaves. The acorns (fruits), which are adored by squirrels, are light brown when mature. In the traditional tongue of the Lumbee, the White Oak was called "yap ta ktcere," or white tree. White Oak acorns were also a food staple for many Native American tribes who crushed them in water, boiled them, dried them to make a flour, or ate them raw. The Lumbee would often parch the acorns to rid them of some of their astringent quality due to the high tannin content. However, Ms. Mary Bell, a Lumbee healer, stated that she picked up acorns soon after they hit the ground and boiled these nuts into a tea. This tea was used to bathe insect and spider bites. Other tribes used this astringency to boil an acorn tea for treating bleeding hemorrhoids and diarrhea. The Lumbee believed that the magical, capricious little people (Yeha'suri) who lived in the forest would eat acorns and the fungi that grew around Oak trees. In remedies used by the Lumbee, a variety of the White and Red Oak groups were used. One healer believed that the Red Oaks were more po-tent than the White Oak group. The oaks were thought to be very powerful medicine and the amount taken was considered vital. Most healers used only the "sap layer" or inner bark (phloem), although some used the exterior bark and branches. Oak bark and wood was not only used in medicine, but also in the preparation of soap and foods. David Lowry, a Lumbee elder from the Saddletree community, related how his mother and grandmother would use the lye obtained from burned Oak ashes (pot ash lye). This lye was mixed with lard to make soap or boiled with corn to make "Big Hominy" ("to crack the corn"). Hominy was known as "kuspi seratere" in the Lumbee traditional language. Modern science has discovered the benefits of handwashing with soap in fighting infectious diseases. A handful of the sap layer sliced very thin, combined with Wild Cherry (Prunus serotina) and Poplar (Liriodendron tulipifera) was boiled in a quart of water until only three pints remained to treat bladder and kidney issues. The dose was a tablespoon taken three times a day. Oak tea was often prescribed for diarrhea, which was treated with two doses of one tablespoon each. Sores were also bathed in this decoction. For suspected viral infections, many latter-day Lumbee healers would fashion a decoction from three pieces of the inner bark four inches long combined with two cups of water. This combina-

tion was boiled down until only one cup of liquid was left. One healer recommended that the patient only take a small amount because too large a dose, it was thought, could cause constipation. To stop menstrual flow, a sap layer tea was manufactured. To increase the strength of a particular medicine, Red and White Oak branches were combined with other plants. For example, Mullein (Verbascum thapsus) leaves and the root from Red Shank (Ceanothus americanus) were combined with the sap layer of the Oak in a poultice used to treat sprains and swelling. In *The Education of Little Tree* by Forrest Carter, Little Tree, a young Cherokee boy, said his grandmother "ground them (acorns) up into a meal that was yellow-gold and mixed hickor'nuts [Hickory nuts] and walnuts in the meal and made bread fritters." The Cherokee would also use Oak bark to treat indigestion and diarrhea. They also chewed the bark to treat mouth sores.

Old Timey Garlic (Garlet)
(Asclepias rubra); also known as Red Milkweed

Old Timey Garlic is a perennial, herbaceous plant that grows from one to four feet in height. It has lanceolate, oppositely arranged leaves. Red flowers bloom in mid-summer and the seeds have long, silky hairs. Old Timey Garlic is a close relative to Butterfly Bush/Root (Asclepias tuberosa). Both plants are members of the Milk-

weed family, named for the abundant, sticky, white sap found in the stem of these plants. Old Timey Garlic was called "wiita's wiit ut'" or milk grass in the Lumbee traditional language. Some Lumbee healers would recommend Old Timey Garlic as a blood purifier. It was combined by the healer with Possum Haw (Viburnum nudum) for treatment of diabetes. A piece of the root, the length of two of the patient's thumbnails, was boiled for three hours in four to six pints of water.

Onion (Allium cepa)

A nonnative perennial herb that grows from a bulb, this plant can reach a height of four feet and it has four to six cylindrical leaves. The greenish-white flowers bloom in June or July and grow in globular, solitary umbels, one-half to one inch across, in a long, hollow stalk. One healer stated that she put sliced onions in a pot of water and covered them with sugar and let this sit overnight. She commented that the patient would then drink the juice to treat a cold. Another treatment for cold and respiratory ailments was taking a bath in warm or hot cooked onions two to three times per day. Ms. Leitha Chavis, Lumbee elder, states that her grandmother, Aggie Brewer, would make an onion poultice to treat a fever. The Mohegan tribe made a syrup from chopped and boiled onions to treat colds. A native herb of North Carolina related to the onion is the

Ramp or Wild Leek (Allium tric-occum). This plant is similar in appearance and function to the Onion, but is primarily found in the Appalachian region, north to Maine, and west to Iowa. The Cherokee used the Ramp in ancient medicine in a spring tonic tea and a poultice to treat bee stings. Some Cherokee would make a decoction of the Ramp to treat coughs and colds. Frederick "Fishhound" Arch (Eastern Band of Cherokee) preferred to gather ramps around early February when the shoots were less than 1½" inches high. The Cherokee and many communities in western North Carolina and Tennessee continue to hold Ramp festivals to celebrate the taste and heritage of this herb. Modern science has also found that the Ramp contains the fatty acid prostaglandin A1. This compound has been found effective, by scientists, in treating hypertension and arteriosclerosis. The Menominee called the Ramp "pikuate sika-kushia," or skunk plant. In fact, the Menominee referred to an area on the southern shore of Lake Michigan as "Cicaga Wini" or skunk place because of the abundance of Ramps. The white settlers later applied this name to their settlement now known as Chicago.

Oswego Tea *see Spotted Horsemint*

Oxydendrum arboreum *see Sourwood Tree*

Panicum spp. *see Star Grass*

Partridge Berry (Mitchella repens); also known as Squaw Vine, Turkey Vine

Partridge Berry gives color to the forest floor in the winter. Red fruits and evergreen leaves can be found in some places in North American, offering a creeping, green carpet during the coldest of months. This plant has shiny, opposite leaves with white outlines along the veins. The five-fringed petals bloom from May through July. The flowers are only half an inch wide. Partridge Berry was a popular treatment among the Lumbee to ease menstrual pains and prevent miscarriages. Many Native American women from various tribes drank a tea from the leaves of the Partridge Berry to help ease childbirth. A leaf lotion was used to relieve breast soreness for nursing mothers. Modern science has found two medicinal properties of this plant—tannin and saponin. The Abnaki used the Partridge Berry for inflammations.

Passiflora incarnata *see Passionflower*

Passionflower (Passiflora incarnata); also known as Apricot Vine, Maypop

The Passionflower is a native North American plant. It is a woody, hairy, climbing vine that can reach up to thirty feet long. Its alternate, serrated leaves have three to five lobes and taper in sharp points. White to pale lavender, flamboyant, two-inch flowers bloom from June to September. The fruit is an edible, many-seeded berry (Maypop) that can be almost as large as a chicken egg. A tea from the entire plant including the flower was used in Lumbee herbal medicine as a sedative and a painkiller. Some Lumbee healers thought this tea could ease dysmenorrhea (painful menstruation). Lumbee healers have also used the tea from the Passionflower for many years to act as a sedative and analgesic (painkiller). Today this tea is sold commercially in drug stores and supermarkets and is used in many "over the counter" herbal medicines. The Iroquois confederacy tribes made a social drink from the crushed fruit of the Passionflower (Maypop). They strained the juice and added cornmeal to thicken it.

Peach Tree (Prunus persica)

The Peach is a deciduous tree with leaves that are alternate, simple, long-pointed, and toothed on the margins. The fruit is fleshy and varies from white to dark maroon with a large, rough pit or stone. The Peach was called "turiiye'" or sweet fruit in the traditional language of the Lumbee. Many Lumbee healers suggested that their patients eat the seeds (cracked out of the peach pits) to treat "knots" or bruises from trauma to a part of the body. Lumbee herbal lore suggested that tea from any part of the peach could act as a purgative or febrifuge. Lumbee healers thought the leaves and bark had a demulcent, sedative, diuretic, and expectorant action. A tea of ½ ounce of the bark or 1 ounce of the dried leaves was put into a pint of boiling water to make a tea. This tea was thought by many healers to ease irritation or congestion of the gastric system. Many healers have also used the tea to treat whooping cough, ordinary coughs, and chronic bronchitis. The local healer usually suggested a dose from a teaspoonful to one or two cupfuls as required. The fresh leaves, applied outwardly to the body as a poultice, were suggested to expel worms. An infusion of the dried leaves was also recommended for the same purpose. Many Lumbee healers would apply the milk or cream of the kernels to the forehead to help a sick individual rest. An old Lumbee treatment for sore throat was to swab the mouth as far back as possible with a rag soaked in peach bark tea wrapped around a Peach tree stick. Ms. Leitha Chavis, a Lumbee elder, states that when she was young, children would run around barefooted through the woods and fields. They would sometimes get an infection between their toes. They called this the foot itch or ground itch. Her grandmother would gather Peach twigs and boil them into a tea to treat this foot itch. The Delaware tribe used Peach leaves in an infusion to prevent children from vomiting.

Pecan Tree (Carya illinoensis)

The Pecan is a large, deciduous tree closely related to the Hickory Trees. In fact, it is a member of the Hickory tree family (Carya). Its shape looks somewhat like an upright vase. The leaves are oddly pinnately compound, and the male flowers produce catkins. Pecan pollen is a common allergen. The fruit is two to ten individual nuts found in terminal clusters. A green, fleshy shuck surrounds the ovoid one- to two-inch nut. Pecan shells stored for long periods of time may contain aflotoxin, a dangerous poison. Today, Pecan oil is an ingredient in many essential oils and cosmetics. The name "Pecan" comes from the Siouan family word "pacene," which means "nut so hard as to require a stone to crack it." The Lumbee would use the Pecan nut as food and occasionally fashion a bark tea to treat dyspepsia (upset stomach). Other tribes used this Pecan bark tea to treat blood ailments, flu, fever, hepatitis, stomachache, and malaria. The Kiowa used a decoction from the bark to treat tuberculosis, and the Comanche used pulverized Pecan leaves for ringworm.

Pedicularis canadensis *see Wood Betony*

Pennyroyal *see American Pennyroyal*

Pepper Grass (Lepidium virginicum); also known as Poor Man's Pepper

Pepper Grass is a native annual herb that can reach twenty inches in height. The upper leaves are serrated and lobed, but the lower ones are without teeth or lobes. The small, white flowers bloom from late spring to early summer. The fruit or seed is oval and flat. Pepper Grass can be found in fields, on roadsides, and in disturbed areas of the eastern United States. Mr. Vernon Cooper, a Lumbee healer, said the entire Pepper Grass plant was collected in the spring and mixed with Five Finger Grass (identity unknown) to fabricate a tea. Mr. Cooper would recommend this tea to treat "courage" (sex drive) in elderly people. Mr. Frederick "Fishhound" Arch, Cherokee elder, states the Cherokee would use Ginseng for the same purpose. Ms. Leitha Chavis, Lumbee elder, stated that her grandmother, Aggie Brewer, would collect the top of Pepper Weed (Pepper Grass) to make a tea to treat gravel (kidney stones). Ms. Leitha recalls, "That tea was hot. I've heard that's why they sometimes call it the Pepper seed." Some other Lumbee would use a tea made from Pepper Grass leaves to treat poison ivy and rash. A Lumbee healer simply known as "Van" said that Pepper Grass (or red pepper), cornmeal, salt, and one's own urine mixed together could be used for treatment of pain in the joint. He believed the "plaster" would "move anything," but the "plaster" had to be changed once every twenty-four hours. Pepper Grass seeds and leaves have also been used in the past by some Native Americans to flavor soups and other foods that were served warm.

Peppermint (Mentha piperita officinalis)

Peppermint is a nonnative, hybrid,

perennial plant that exhibits a one- to three-foot, erect, square, reddish-purple tinged, branching stem. Its leaves are not quite as green as that of Spearmint. The whorled clusters of little reddish-violet flowers sprout from the top leaves. This plant is also found in damp or wet areas and woods. However, Spearmint and Peppermint are widely cultivated by the Lumbee and other peoples. Some Lumbee boiled or chewed raw leaves to treat indigestion, a sick stomach and colds. An infusion of the leaves was used to treat flatulent colic and general sickness. Menthol is a modern day derivative of Peppermint and is a common ingredient in many over the counter treatments for respiratory ailments or aching muscles. Some Lumbee healers boiled the leaves down to a syrup to make into a salve to treat chronic rheumatism. Many Lumbee also used Peppermint as a diaphoretic, emmenagogue, insect repellent, and diuretic for urinary disorders.

Perilla *see Jacob's Coat*

Perilla frutescens *see Jacob's Coat*

Persea borbonia *see Bay Tree*

Persimmon Tree (Diospyros virginiana); also known as Possum Fruit Tree

Persimmon or Possum Fruit Tree is a common tree native in the southeastern United Sates. It averages from thirty to fifty feet in height with a width from twenty to thirty-five feet. It prefers sun to light shade and grows best in moist, well-drained soil, but is very tolerant of dry or sandy soil. The leaf is 2.5 to 5.5 inches long. The leaf is alternate and simple, and has a dark green color that turns yellow or orange to mauve in the fall. The fruit is one to two inches in length and attracts birds, caterpillars and other wildlife. Persimmon was called "edre'" or possum fruit tree in the ancient language of the Lumbee. Many Lumbee enjoy the fruit raw or cooked in pies, jams, jellies, or puddings. "Persimmon" was originally an Algonquian Native American language family word (the Cree word "pasiminan" means "dried fruit"). Lumbee healers boiled Persimmon bark into a syrup and utilized it to wash a baby's mouth to treat thrush. An infusion of the green fruit was fashioned to treat diarrhea, dysentery, and uterine hemorrhages. Many Lumbee chewed Persimmon bark to treat heartburn. Lumbee healers would also utilize a bark tea of Persimmon, Alder, White Walnut and Wild Cherry to treat toothache. A boiled bark tea or cold water poured over the bark was drunk for treatment of bile and liver disorders. An old Lumbee treatment for sore or chapped hands or lips is a salve or ointment made from Persimmon bark. The Persimmon has been utilized by the Lumbee as an astringent, an intoxicant, and a styptic. It has also been utilized to aid in treatment of cancer, gastro-intestinal disturbances, hemorrhage, hemorrhoids, mouth ailments, skin ailments, stomatitus, throat ailments, and venereal ailments. The Cherokee chewed Persimmon bark for heartburn and fashioned a wash to treat hemorrhoids.

Petticoat Climber *see Coat Ticklers*

Phoradendron serotinum *see Mistletoe*

Phytolacca americana *see Poke*

Pigeonberry *see Poke*

Pine Tree—Longleaf Pine (Pinus palustris), Shortleaf Pine (Pinus echinata), Loblolly Pine (Pinus taeda), and Virginia Pine (Pinus virginiana)

Pine trees are evergreen and their needles range from very long and feathery, as found in the Longleaf Pine, or short and stubby, as seen in the Shortleaf Pine. The Longleaf Pine bark eventually develops plates, whereas other species develop deeply furrowed, scaly, gray bark. All pines are conifers or cone producers. These imbedded seed cones range from 1½ inches to 2½ inches in the Virginia Pine to six to ten inches long for the Longleaf Pine, and the shape varies from egg shaped for the Virginia and Longleaf Pine to almost conical in some other species. The Lumbee used all available species of pine to treat various ailments. One healer preferred to use the Longleaf Pine (Pinus palustris). The Lumbee called the Longleaf Pine "tcuwe nu re'" or fat (rich) pine in the native language. The Pine was extremely important to the Lumbee for medicine. However, this tree was also important to the livelihood of many families. In the late 19th and early 20th centuries, many Lumbee men and families migrated to areas in Florida, Alabama, and Georgia (specifically around Claxton) to make a living collecting rosin from the Yellow Pine tree. During this time, this rosin was the only source of "naval stores" or tar, pitch, and turpentine. Turpentine was used in many prescription medicines in the 19th and early 20th centuries. The last five inches of the twig, needles, and bud at the end of the twig are called the "tops." Flu, colds and other respiratory ailments were treated using the tops. Vernon Hazel Locklear, a Lumbee elder, recalls, "I remember we children had colds a lot in the wintertime and my mother would go in the woods and she would get some pine tops, a little limb out of the pine tree. She would bring it home and there was a wood that had a lot of fat in it and she would sit that piece of wood on fire and that would drip off of the pine top. It would make a tea and we drank that for colds." Sometimes the healer would suggest Pine by itself to treat respiratory problems, but in many cases the tops were used with other plants. These combinations included: Mullein (Verbascum thapsus), Rabbit Tobacco (Gnaphalium obtusifolium), and Corn (Zea mays); or Goldenrod (Solidago spp.), Wild Horehound (Marrubium vulgare), and Rabbit Tobacco. Also, Holly (Ilex opaca), Sweet Bay (Persea borbonia or Magnolia grandiflora), and Rabbit Tobacco were used in a combination to treat various respiratory ailments. Some healers would boil the tops in a quart of water for two to three hours to make a tea. One individual added a little moonshine whiskey and honey to the tea after it was made. The tea was taken hot two or three times a day. The most important dose was considered the one taken before bedtime. Many blankets were put on the patient to encourage perspiration if the patient was thought to have a fever. Pine rosin was chewed by the Lumbee to nurse stomach discomfort, and the fresh pine needles were also chewed to treat a stomachache. Pine rosin was called "tcetpa hitcuwe'" or chewed pine in the Lumbee traditional language. Some Lumbee healers took the white rosin scratched from the tree and coated it with wheat flour to be taken as a pill to treat kidney problems. Diabetes and arthritis were often treated with brown resin. One of the authors and other Lumbee artisans still fashion baskets made out of Longleaf Pine needles. Some Lumbee put Pine needles on their gardens to protect the young plants from frostbite and add some acidity to the soil. The

Cheyenne used a species of Pine known as Sweet Pine for purification and to strengthen medicines.

Pinus echinata *see Pine Tree*

Pinus palustris *see Pine Tree*

Pinus taeda *see Pine Tree*

Pinus virginiana *see Pine Tree*

Pipe Tree *see Elderberry*

Pipsissewa (Chimaphila umbellata); also known as Rat's Vein, Lion's Tongue, Wild Rat's Bane, Ratsy Vein
Pipsissewa has green-edged evergreen leaves with white-lined centers. These leaves lie at the base of tall flower stalks. Pipsissewa bears downward-opening, white flowers in early summer. "Pip," or Ratsy Vein, as many Lumbee called this plant, was commonly found in dry woods, especially in somewhat open areas. Pip was called "kiup siwi" or fireflower in the native language of the Lumbee. "Pipsissewa" is an Algonquin Indian word, referring to the plant's reported ability to break up bladder or kidney stones. The entire plant was collected in a bunch approximately one-half inch in diameter and was boiled in a quart of water. The Lumbee healer would usually prescribe a tablespoon of the liquid to be used three times a day for a livestock tonic. Pop M., a Lumbee healer, mixed Lion's

Tongue (Pipsissewa) with corn meal to feed it to all of his animals to treat all their diseases. He would parch the Lion's Tongue root until it was brittle and then he mixed it with the cornmeal. Mr. James Hammonds, a Lumbee elder from the Saddletree community, commented, "My father would also give Rat's Vane [Ratsy Vein] to our mules. They stayed healthy and they were the slickest, prettiest mules you would ever want to see." Lumbee healers used Pipsissewa in a tea to function as a diaphoretic, diuretic, and astringent. Some Lumbee healers also used "Pip" to strengthen the stomach and treat pain. Pipsissewa tea was also suggested for treatment of female ailments, backache, and fever. Hayes Alan Locklear, Lumbee historian and herbalist, states that "Ratsy Vein" was used to treat high blood pressure. Lumbee healers recommended it in poultice or salve forms as an external treatment for cancer, rheumatism, dropsy, and urinary problems. Lumbee healers also made a wash from the tops and the roots to aid in treatment of rheumatism, scrofula, external cancer, and ulcer. A salve was made combining the extract with hog's lard to treat tetter and ringworm. A poultice was manufactured from the leaves for treatment of pain. A tea was prepared from the leaves to aid in treatment of colds, fevers, and to cause a baby to vomit.

Pitcher Leaf Plant *see Heartleaf*

Platanus occidentalis *see Sycamore Tree*

Plantago virginica *see White Plantain*

Pleurisy Root *see Butterfly bush*

Poke (Phytolacca americana); also known as Pokeberry, Inkberry, Pigeonberry, Pokeroot **Warning: Modern science has found that this plant possesses some poisonous properties. The most is found in the roots, with lesser amounts in the fruit, stems, and leaves. A Lumbee healer commented that a cup of tea made from root caused bloody vomiting and diarrhea. Poke leaves have been found to possess more than 10 percent oxalate, a compound that has been found to inhibit use of calcium in the body.**

Poke is a common native plant of the eastern United States. Poke is a foul smelling, perennial weed that can reach a height of nine feet. It has a large, white root; a green, red, or purple stem; leaves up to one-foot long; and white flowers in a drooping raceme. The fruit is a purplish-black berry. Poke is mainly found in full sunlight in damp fields, or open woods. The young leaves were collected in early spring and boiled in water. Cooked greens were also eaten by many Lumbee to build the blood. This "mess of greens" was also taken as a to treat boils (risings), other "diseases of the blood," and as a spring tonic. Open wounds were treated by the juice of the fruit being rubbed on the skin or a fresh root being applied to the affliction. A salve was made from the Pokeweed to treat cancers and ulcerous sores. Dried, crushed roots were used on old sores, and a root tea was used to treat eczema. The root was prepared to treat cramps (muscle spasms) in men and women. The roots and berries were used by the Lumbee as a poultice for rheumatism, nervous fevers, and swelling. To deworm chickens, the root was covered with water and placed in the feed bowl. The Waccamaw-Siouan, sister tribe to the Lumbee, used the roasted and split Poke root to treat sore feet. Many Lumbee ate a large poke leaf to treat worms. A cold tea of the powdered root was fashioned to treat kidney trouble. Mr. Vernon Cooper, a Lumbee healer, suggested Pokeberry wine to his clients as a treatment for diarrhea or "slick stomach." The berry wine was also employed to treat arthritis. Mr. Cooper recommended that his patients take only one spoonful. To make Poke wine, a quart jar was filled just below the jar line with ripe berries. Cold water was added until it was one-half to one inch over the berries. The jar lid was screwed on and the juice inside was allowed to "work" for two to three weeks. The wine was strained and stored for later use. Some healers recommended their patients take a teaspoon or swallow at each meal. Many heal-ers thought that a bigger dose would make their patients drunk. The Lumbee called the Poke berry "si ka warete wire" in the native language. In *The Education of Little Tree* by Forrest Carter, Little Tree, a young Cherokee boy in the story, states, "Poke salat berries, however, are poison and they will knock you deader than last year's corn stalk. Any berries you see the birds don't eat, you had better not eat." However, the Cherokee did use a poke berry infusion to treat arthritis and a cold infusion of the powdered root to address kidney disorders.

Pokeberry *see Poke*

Pokeroot *see Poke*

Polygonatum biflorum *see Solomon's Seal*

Podophyllum peltatum *see Mayapple*

Polypodium Fern (Polypodium polypodioides); also known as Resurrection Fern
Polypodium Fern is a nonnative, perennial, evergreen fern. It has spores on the lower surface of its fronds which look like golden dots. This long-stalked fern has pinnately divided green leaves that grow up to twelve inches tall. The Lumbee harvested the roots, leaves, and stems of this fern. The root is purported to have a licorice flavor that is a thousand times sweeter than sugar. The Polypodium Fern is often found growing close to Oak trees. Some

herbalists of the nineteenth century believed that the plant absorbed the vigor of this great tree. Other individuals believed that anyone who carried the fern would become invisible. Polypodium was called "tapasi moso here," or plant that grows on a rough branch, in the native language of the Lumbee. The Lumbee submerged the roots, stems and leaves in water and boiled this combination until only a little liquid was left. The liquid was combined with Vaseline Petroleum Jelly (a modern day application), tallow, or Rosebud Salve (also a commercial product) and warmed until the different ingredients mixed together. The salve that was obtained was rubbed on the sore or external wound. Polypodium leaves were not collected in drought or when no rain had fallen in quite some time. It was said that the plant's appearance completely changed during these dry times. Only the succulent green leaves were used. The dead looking wrinkled leaves were not gathered.

Polypodium polypodiodes
see Polypodium Fern

Poor Man's Pepper see Pepper Grass

Poplar Tree (Liriodendron tulipifera); also known as Tulip Tree

The Poplar is one of the tallest and is considered by many people to be the most beautiful of the eastern hardwoods. Poplar trees have a long, straight trunk and large, showy flowers that resemble lilies or tulips. The squarish leaves are five to eight inches long and wide with a broad tip and base. One leaf is large enough that a serviceable water container can be fashioned from it. The leaf is shiny dark above and paler underneath, and turns yellow in the fall. The thick bark is dark gray and deeply furrowed. The cup-shaped flowers are 1½ to 2 inches long and wide and have six rounded, green petals that turn orange at the base. The Poplar was called "yap suke'" or red tree in the traditional language of the Lumbee. Will D., a Lumbee healer, would put the chips or bark of the Poplar tree in a bucket of water and let it soak for one week. He would suggest that his patients drink what was in the bucket to increase appetite. Mr. Will would also make a tea from the bark to treat indigestion in adults and worms in children. Other Lumbee healers took scrapings of the bark and boiled them to make a tea given to children to treat stomach worms. A tea was also prepared for dyspepsia, dysentery or rheumatism. A decoction of the bark was used to bathe snakebite and was also prepared as a cough syrup. Three fresh Poplar leaves were bound to a sore or wound to "draw the fever out" (eliminate swelling, pain, and soreness). To treat fever, many healers would make a decoction by combining Willow (Salix nigra) bark or Corn (Zea mays) and Poplar leaves and buds.

This tea was made with four buds or Poplar tops of the Poplar sixteen to eighteen inches long. The combination was boiled in a quart of water until about a third of the brew was evaporated. A tablespoon was prescribed three times a day to treat a fever. According to one healer, the strength of the tea was reduced for people below the age of twenty by preparing less of the plant. Poplar leaves were combined with Jacob's Coat (Perilla frutescens) and Cherry bark (Prunus serotina) for another fever treatment.

Possum Fruit Tree see Persimmon Tree

Possum Haw (Viburnum nudum); also known as Swamp Haw

Possum Haw is a native, deciduous, small tree or shrub that grows up to twenty-feet in height. It has simple lanceolate leaves. The five-petaled flowers are small and white. The fruit is a drupe which is initially pink but turns a dark blue-black at maturity. It is a common tree found in low woods, pocosins, bogs, and swamps throughout the southeastern United States. Possum Haws are eaten by many different birds and mammals. The Abnaki and the Algonquian tribes also used the "Haw" for food. The Lumbee called Possum Haw "turo hita'" or sour fruit in the traditional language. Possum Haw was used to treat individuals exhibiting symptoms of diabetes (adult onset).

Possum Haw roots were considered at their most effective if gathered in early autumn. The Lumbee combined one to two handfuls of the dried or fresh root and a half a quart of water. This combination was simmered for a half day or until about one pint was left. One healer recommended taking the decoction at the morning and afternoon meals and at night during the first four days. Afterwards, it was suggested the patient take a half an ounce in the morning and at night.

Prenanthes trifoliata see Gall of the Earth

Prunus americana see Wild Plum

Prunus angustifolia see Wild Plum

Prunus persica see Peach Tree

Prunus serotina see Wild Cherry Tree

Prunus virginiana see Wild Cherry Tree

Psoralea pedunculata see Ball Root

Pteridium aquilinum see Fire Root

Pukeweed see Indian Tobacco

Pumpkin (Cucurbita pepo)

The Pumpkin is a vine with tendrils and a creeping, prickly stem that reaches thirty feet in length. The triangular, dull green leaves can reach one foot wide and are rough in texture. The bright yellow flowers are funnel shaped and are followed by the fruit (the pumpkin). The Lumbee would chew the seeds fresh or dried and swallow them to treat kidney problems. The Pumpkin seeds were called "wa'tap hanu'" in the Lumbee traditional language. To help ease urinary discomfort, the Menominee would make a tea from powdered squash and pumpkin seeds.

Purge Grass (Sisyrinchium spp.); also known as Blue-Eyed Grass

Purge Grass reaches a height of ten to twelve inches. This grass is topped off with an abundance of lavender-blue flowers in mid-summer. Purge Grass will most often be found in the full sunlight to partial shade in meadows or fields. The roots of Purge Grass were gathered all year and used fresh or dried. If not used immediately, the roots were stored in an airtight container in the dark. The exposure to air was thought to weaken the effectiveness of the remedy. One healer removed the dead, black roots because he believed they caused gripping lower abdominal pain, thought to be a common side effect of the tea. The roots of eight to ten plants were boiled in ten to twelve ounces of water until one-fourth of the liquid was gone. One healer recommended that his patient take two doses of Purge Grass tea. The first

one was to be taken in the morning and the other at night. Caution was observed not to take an overdose, as the laxative effect was thought by many healers to be a very drastic one.

Purple Coneflower (Echinacea angustifolia)

Purple Coneflowers have a single, long stalked, light purple flowerhead with petals seated around a high cone. This native perennial herb grows to about two feet in height. Its leaves are long and lanceolate with veins running along their length. This plant grows in open, sunny areas of North America. The Purple Coneflower has been used to enhance the immune system and restore general good health among the Lumbee for many years. Inhaling the burning plant was recommended by some Lumbee healers as a headache remedy. The Blackfoot chewed Purple Coneflower roots to numb the mouth if they developed a toothache. The Cheyenne used the leaves and roots in a tea or chewed the roots to nurse a sore mouth, gums, or throat. The dried rhizome and roots have been prescribed by many other tribes as an aid for snakebite and other poisonous bites and stings. Modern herbalists claim that the Coneflower possesses an antibiotic, antiseptic, and a sweat-producing agent. An extract from the rhizome has been popularized by modern herbalists as a cure-all for many things, including blood poisoning, and has been used to treat AIDS. Its more popular name is Echinacea. Holy men from many Native American tribes also held the Coneflower in high regard. One medicine man would wash his hands with Coneflower juice before plunging them into scalding water. Another gentleman stated that he would use the root of this plant before placing a red-hot coal in his mouth.

Purple Love Grass *see Coat Tickle's*

Pussytoes *see Whiteweed*

Putty Root *see Adam and Eve Root*

Queen Anne's Lace (Daucus carota); also known as Wild Carrot, Chigger Weed

Warning: Do not confuse Queen Anne's lace with the poisonous Water Hemlock (Cicuta maculata), Poison Hemlock (Conium maculatum). The red or purple flower in the center distinguishes Queen Anne's Lace.

Queen Anne's Lace root is small, spindle shaped, whitish, slender and hard. It has a strong, aromatic smell. The stems of Queen Anne's Lace are erect and branched, reaching about two feet in height. The leaves and stems are clothed with stout, coarse hairs. Queen Anne's Lace is in bloom from June to August with densely clustered flowers with flattened, white heads. Many Lumbee used the seeds as a way to treat in-

testinal worms, stomach discomfort and flatulence. An extract from the root has also been used by many Lumbee medicinally as a diuretic and as a treatment for kidney stones. Scientists have shown that the root is filled with vitamin C, vitamin A, and carotene. Some Lumbee also viewed the root as a treatment for high blood pressure and for killing bacteria. For colds and pneumonia in Lumbee children, the stems and leaves were covered in water and boiled until the leaves turned brown. A cloth was then soaked in the extraction and applied to the young child's chest. The leaves were eaten by many Lumbee to help them gain strength. A tea was made from scrapings of the root and taken to reduce swelling. Many tribes made an interesting coffeelike beverage from the roasted herb. Mr. Earl Carter, a Lumbee healer, suggests that his patients drink the juice from a grated cultivated or Wild Carrot to treat abdominal cramps, heartburn, and stomach acidity. To expel worms, some Lumbee healers would suggest drinking carrot juice while abstaining from solids. Many Lumbee made a carrot soup to treat diarrhea and tonsillitis. A modern scientific study was recently conducted concerning pain in cancer patients. They discovered that placing them on a cultivated carrot diet appeared to be helpful in pain management. The Iroquois confederacy tribes used Queen Anne's Lace root in a decoction to treat blood disorder in men and to treat pimples, paleness, urine stoppage, and loss of appetite. Queen Anne's Lace flowers and stalks can be boiled to make a yellow dye.

Queen's Delight (Stillingia syllvatica)

Warning: Queen Delight has been found by scientists to contain a skin irritant and carcinogens (cancer or tumor causing substances).

Queen's Delight is a native plant of the southern United States. It is a perennial herb that grows up to four feet. It has one- to three-inch elliptical, finely toothed, alternate leaves. The leaves appear to have no stalk. Tiny, nonpetaled, yellow flowers appear in terminal spikes and bloom from March to August. Mr. Vernon Cooper, a Lumbee healer, would suggest that his patients use the Queen's Delight to treat "female-type infections and discharge" (cysts, venereal disease, yeast infections). One Lumbee healer would cut six fresh pieces of Queen's Delight root into two-inch sections and mix it with Devil's Shoestring and slowly boil it in water for six hours to treat female disorders. If the difficulty was thought to be severe or lie deep, the healer recommended that the patient drink the tea and use this decoction as a douche. The douche alone was recommended if the healer believed the problem was not severe. The suggested dosage for the tea and the douche was morning, afternoon, and at bedtime.

Quercus alba see Oak Tree

Quercus maxima see Red Oak Tree

Rabbit Tobacco (Gnaphalium obtusifolium); also known as Life Everlasting or Catfoot

Rabbit Tobacco grows from one to three feet in height. Its stem is covered with white, woolly hairs. The leaves are long, thin, and lanceolate. Tiny, creamy to yellow white flowers bloom in late summer to early fall. Disturbed areas and fields in the eastern United States are likely areas to spy this common native plant. Rabbit Tobacco was known as "dupu hawa umpa" in the native language of the Lumbee. To treat colds, some Lumbee healers would boil Rabbit Tobacco with Mullein (Verbascum thapsus), Corn (Zea mays) fodder, and Pine tops (Pinus spp.). Another combination for treatment of colds was Rabbit Tobacco, Goldenrod (Solidago spp.), and Wild Horehound (Marrubium vulgare). Rabbit Tobacco, Tag Alder (Alnus serrulata), and Purge Grass (Sisyrinchium spp.) were also used to treat colds. A handful of the above material was boiled in a quart of water until it became a dark brown color. One-half to one cup was suggested as a dosage by one healer. To treat colds and cough in children and adults, Rabbit Tobacco leaves were chewed. Holly (Ilex opaca) leaves and Pine tops added to the

Rabbit Tobacco were combined in an infusion to treat flu, colds, and pneumonia. A few Lumbee healers fashioned a decoction of Rabbit Tobacco to doctor neuritis (sugar of the bone). As a rule, the brown lower leaves were the only parts gathered in the spring and summer. The leaves and stems were collected after the first frost of fall or in winter (to be dried and saved). Some healers believed that the green leaves could cause a person to become ill. The infusion was drunk hot, as with most medicinal teas, and was said to cause profuse sweating. For treatment of asthma, many Lumbee healers would suggest that their patients stuff their pillows with Rabbit Tobacco to prevent asthmatic attacks. Some healers recommended that leaves be replaced once a year. Hayes Alan Locklear, Lumbee herbalist and historian, states that the Lumbee used Rabbit Tobacco in a tea to treat colds and flu. An old Lumbee treatment for earache was to blow the smoke from Rabbit Tobacco into the afflicted ear. Rabbit Tobacco was one of the most used plants among the Lumbee. The Cherokee would use Rabbit Tobacco with Carolina Vetch to treat rheumatism, muscle twitch, or muscular cramps.

Rabbit's Pea *see Devil's Shoestring*

Ragweed (Ambrosia artemisiifolia); also known as Carpweed

Ragweed is a native, branching, annual plant that grows up to three feet tall. The hairy stems are green to light pinkish red. The leaves grow up to six inches long and four inches across. Its leaves are broadly lanceolate in shape, being as wide at the base as they are at the tip. The leaves are opposite or alternately arranged along the stems. The small flowers are initially green, but later turn yellowish green and brown as they mature. Ragweed can be found in sunny areas. It is such a common plant because the seeds can germinate even if they have been out of the soil for up to five years. The flowers, stem, and leaves were harvested in the autumn. After the plant material was dried, two handfuls were covered and boiled. The dosage was a tablespoon taken at each meal. This Ragweed tea was used to treat diabetes. The Cherokee used the juice from Ragweed leaves to nurse infected toes and prepared a tea to treat fever or pneumonia.

Raspberry (Rubus idaeus)

Raspberry is a nonnative (although closely related to the native plant Rubus strigosus found in the Pacific states), thorny, erect, perennial shrub that grows to more than six feet in height. It is a close relative of the Blackberry. Its leaves are alternate and compound. The leaves are white and dropping, measuring eight to twelve millimeters across. The fruits appear in dense red druplets approximately one centimeter across. Mr. Earl Carter, Lumbee healer, stated that Raspberry was the herb that he most often uses, recommends, and suggests for treatment of a variety of ailments. Raspberry leaves have been used as an astringent and stimulant. The leaves have been combined with powdered Slippery Elm bark to create a poultice for cleansing wounds, burns and to promote healing. The Lumbee used a Raspberry leaf tea as a gargle for the treatment of mouth and throat discomforts. The tea has also been recommended to treat diarrhea, discomforts of pregnancy (i.e., morning sickness), and poor milk production in lactating women.

Rat's Tail (Aloe barbadensis);
also known as Aloe

Rat's Tail—or Aloe, which is its more popular name—is a nonnative clump-forming shrub-like plant with green, ten to twenty inch long, succulent leaves forming a rosette. The leaves appear more like plump, toothed points than leaves. Aloe has yellow flowers. This plant varies from a height of six inches to six or more feet. Rat's Tail has become a popular houseplant across the United States, and has become a readily available treatment for the pain of a burn. The succulent leaves were cut open and the fresh juice was applied to injured skin. The Lumbee gathered the leaves from this potted houseplant fresh year round. Today Aloe is used in many commercial lotions and over the counter wound treatments.

Rat's Vein (Ratsy Vein) *see Pipsissewa*

Rattlesnake Root (Agave virginica); also known as False Aloe

Warning: Lumbee herbal experts considered this to be a strong medicine.

Rattlesnake Root is a perennial plant. The broad, linear, and fibrous leaves grow upward from the base to form a massive rosette. The leaves are gray and smooth on both sides and have prickly edges. After ten years or more, the plant produces a flower stalk which bears large yellowish-green flowers on many horizontal branches. The fruit is a three-celled capsule. After flowering and fruiting, the plant dies. The Lumbee called Rattlesnake Root "'ya' sua wiiti-iwa," or rattlesnake medicine, in the traditional language. Many Lumbee would chew Rattlesnake root for obstinate diarrhea. The chewed root was also used to treat snakebites, liver problems, and worms.

Rattleweed *see Black Cohosh*

Red Bay *see Bay Tree*

Red Bud (Cercis canadensis);
also known as Judas Tree

Red Bud is a small to medium sized tree that occasionally reaches forty feet in height. The branches form a spreading, flattened, rounded crown. The leaves are simple and heart shaped appearing after magenta flowers (red buds) bloom in early spring. The Kiowa tribe would use the slender stems for fuel during the winter months, and celebrated the appearance of the Red Bud flower as a sign of spring. Red Bud is found most often in moist east coast woodlands west to Nebraska. The Red Bud was called "yap pete'" or flat tree seed in the traditional language of the Lumbee. A tea was fabricated from the scrapings of bark or roots and used as a wash lotion to bathe parts affected by rheumatic pain. Many Lumbee children also ate the blossoms of the Red Bud as a treat. Some healers also believed this tree also had antiemetic, astringent, and febrifuge properties. The Micmac tribe would use the water-soaked roots and powdered mussel shell in a poultice to treat swelling.

Red Cedar Tree *see Cedar Tree*

Red Elm Tree *see Slippery Elm Tree*

Red Milkweed *see Old Timey Garlic (Garlet)*

Red Myrtle (Myrica cerifera); also known as Double Tansy, Wax Myrtle, Merker Tree

The Red Myrtle grows in thickets near swamps and marshes near the southeastern Atlantic coast. This shrub grows from three to eight feet in height. Red Myrtle's shiny leaves are lanceolate, dotted on both sides, and fragrant when rubbed. Red Myrtle leaves were used for improving the flavor of other herbs. Many healers suggested the use of Double Tansy to treat problems related to the digestive system (mouth, esophagus, and stomach). To treat itching, some Lumbee would bathe in a leaf infusion. Stomach ulcers were treated by chewing a piece of the root recently taken from the ground. Ms. Lucy Mae Hammonds Locklear, a Lumbee elder, boiled the leaves from this tree, which she called the Merker tree, into a tea to treat whooping cough. The Choctaw would use Red Myrtle leaves and stems in an infusion to nurse a fever and sore throat.

Red Oak Tree (Quercus maxima); also known as Turkey Oak Tree

The Red Oak is a deciduous tree that can reach one hundred feet in height. Red Oak earned its name from its reddish brown twigs and buds. Red Oak leaves are also red tinged and the leaf blade is ovate to elliptical. Red Oak leaves also turn red before dropping in the fall. The Red Oak acorn is one inch long and reddish-brown with fuzzy scales that cover a third of the nut. Red Oak bark is shiny and gray or dark gray with shallow fissures. The Red Oak was called "watka' hure" in the Lumbee traditional language. A handful of Red Oak bark was boiled until the water became a deep red. This wash was created by Lumbee healers to rub on the skin affected by poison oak. The Lumbee also used the Red Oak in an external wash to bathe or aid in the treatment of chills and fevers. A tea from the Red Oak was used by many

Lumbee healers to aid the system, especially after a long intermittent fever. The bark was also used as an astringent, a tonic, and an antiseptic. This tea was also drank to serve as an emetic, and to treat indigestion, chronic dysentery, asthma, and debility of the system. The bark was also used externally and applied to sore, chapped skin. Many Lumbee would chew the bark to treat mouth sores, drink this bark tea for relief from asthma, and drink a decoction of Red Oak inner bark for a lost voice.

Red Sassafras Tree *see Sassafras Tree*

Red Shank (Ceanothus americanus); also known as New Jersey Tea

Red Shank is a low, shrubby, deciduous perennial that can reach a height of three feet. Its two- to four-inch toothed leaves are alternate and simple. The whitish flowers grow in dense round panicles. Its has slender, greenish brown twigs and red roots. Lumbee healers used Red Shank root to increase the potency of herbal preparations. A poultice made from Red Shank root, inner bark of the Red Oak (Quercus maxima), and Mullein leaves (Verbascum thapsus) were used to treat inflammation and sprains. The Chippewa used a decoction of the roots for constipation and shortness of breath.

Red Tag Alder (Alnus rugosa)

Red Tag Alder grows in a low and clump-forming shrub. Sometimes this plant can grow into a small tree, reaching twelve feet in height. The dull green leaves form in three rows, two to four inches long, in an elliptical or ovate shape. The leaves are broadest near or below the middle and are irregularly saw-toothed and wavy lobed. The Latin species name "rugosa" refers to the network of sunken veins prominent on the lower leaf surface. The tiny, clustered flowers form in early spring before the leaves. Red Tag Adler thrives in wet soils in swamps and along streams and lakes. The bark is gray and smooth. The Lumbee called Red Tag Alder "yap si wi suka' re" or red tree blossom in the traditional language. Some Lumbee kept Red Tag Alder in their houses for good omen or luck. A handful of bark peeled from a tree that was knotty and gnarly was boiled down by Lumbee healers to make a strong tea of a deep red color to reduce swellings and sprains, cough, and skin eruptions. Aunt Cat Lowry, a Lumbee midwife and an herbal expert, would recommend a tea made from the Red Tag Alder to nurse the pains of the mother related to the birthing process. Many healers thought an ingredient in this tea cleared milky urine. For drooping eyes, some healers would rub and blow decoction of bark into the eyes or suggest a bark tea for general pain and heart trouble. A hot berry tea was often prescribed to treat fever. Drinking a cold tea from Red Tag Alder bark scrapings was suggested by one healer to help the kidneys act. Lumbee mothers would often give their babies this bark tea to treat "thrash" (thrush), a mouth soreness. Sugar was added to the tea by many Lumbee mothers and given to a baby for hives or toothache (teething). A cold bark tea was prescribed by Lumbee healers to purify blood and bring down high blood pressure. For the decoction, one ounce of bark in one pint of boiling water was used in 1½ to 2 cup full doses.

Reindeer Moss *see Moss*

Resurrection Fern *see Polypodium Fern*

Rheumatism Plant (Lycopodium flabelliforme); also known as Running Pine, Ground Cedar

Rheumatism Plant is a clubmoss rather than a conifer and reproduces by means of spores released from candelabra-shaped cases. A single plant may cover several square yards with dense, shining green, cedarlike foliage. The six-inch, upright stalks arise from long, horizontal stems that lie beneath the top layer of humus. It has been said that Native Americans of long ago must have suffered greatly from rheumatism because there appear to be more herbal treatments for rheumatism than any other ailment in Native American communities. Lumbee healers thought it best to gather the Rheumatism plant when the

"candles" (cones) were present, but it was gathered at all times of the year. Two to three handfuls of the entire plant were covered with water and boiled. A cloth was soaked in the tea and applied as a wet compress to the painful areas.

Rhus typhina *see Sumac*

Ricinus communis *see Castor*

Rosinweed (Silphium compositum)

Rosinweed is a tall, erect perennial herb that can reach twelve feet in height (most mature plants average about six feet) arising from a basal cluster of leaves. It exhibits four- to twelve-inch-long toothed and lobed leaves. The numerous eight-petaled yellow flowers bloom in daisylike tops from spring to fall. This native plant can be most often found in old fields, woodlands, roadsides, and sandy soils in the southeastern United States. Many Lumbee healers would boil the root of the Rosinweed and Mullein (Verbascum thapsus) together for three hours. The inflamed area was soaked in the decoction. The Cherokee used Rosinweed to build strength in females preparing for childbirth.

Rotting Logs or Wood (any variety)

Ms. Angeline Locklear, a Lumbee from the Saddletree Indian community, said she would find nine or ten wood lice—little gray plated bugs found under rotting logs and vegetation—and tie them in a cloth bundle. This bundle was then tied around a baby's neck to treat teething pain.

Rubus allegheniensis *see Dewberry and Wild Blackberry*

Rubus hispidus *see Dewberry and Wild Blackberry*

Rubus idaeus *see Raspberry*

Rue (Ruta graveolens)
Rue is an evergreen, perennial, herbaceous plant. Its alternate leaves are bluish-green, and this plant produces clusters of small, yellowish flowers. The stems and leaves are dotted with tiny oil glands that look like dark, translucent dots. These glands produce pungent, bitter, and powerful essential oils. The oil is so powerful that simply touching the leaves may cause skin blistering or irritation. Mr. Vernon Cooper, a Lumbee healer, recommended squeezing a teaspoon of oil from the thick, long leaves to treat worms. Mr. Cooper said he treated himself with Rue, and taking it was almost as bad as having worms. Mr. Cooper said, "I've never tasted nothing like it."

Running Pine *see Rheumatism Plant*

Ruta graveolens *see Rue*

Sage (Salvia officinalis); also known as Sage Spice
Sage is a perennial, herbaceous to shrubby herb that grows up to two feet in height. The leaves are stalked, oppositely arranged, and are oblong to lanceolate in shape. These leathery textured leaves are covered in a fine down. The blue flowers, which appear in June and July, occur as whorls in a spike at the end of stems. Even though Sage is native to the Balkans and Mediterranean region, it has become one of the most important healing plants among the Lumbee. Ms. Barbara Locklear, a Lumbee elder, described how Mr. Earl Carter, a Lumbee healer, visited her hospital room when she was critically ill. She stated that Mr. Earl did a smudging (smearing) around the hospital room from the ashes of Sage and Sweet Grass to cleanse and repel evil influence. Ms. Locklear stated that after the smudging, it was necessary to provide a lengthy explanation to the medical staff at the hospital. Ms. Lucie Mae Hammonds Locklear, a Lumbee elder, related a folk belief of the Lumbee. She stated, "I keep my Sage bush out of the way under the grapevine because we believe that if a woman who is on her period [menstruation] touches a Sage bush, she will get sick and die within a short time." Ms. Gertrude Allen, Lumbee, stated that her father, who was a purported expert in healing with plants, stated that Sage was at different potency at certain times of the year. For full potency, he would only gather Sage in the months that contained the letter "r" and only on the full moon. He

was careful to select only the crinkled leaves. A Lumbee healer called Will D. said he recommended that his patients suffering from thrush (a disease that turns the inside of the mouth white) swab their tongues and throats with a tea from the Sage plant. A tea was made from Sage leaves to aid in digestion, and treat the discomfort of measles, dizziness, colds, fever and headaches. An infusion made with honey made a reputedly not-so-tasty gargle for sore and infected throats. One local healer, in cases of skin ulcers, rashes, and dandruff, suggested a strong wash. Sage tea was also suggested as a stimulating tonic to the digestive tract and nervous system. Many Lumbee would rub fresh Sage leaves on the teeth to whiten and clean them. It was added to bath water to tone the skin and serve as an aphrodisiac. The Mohegans would use Sage to treat worms.

Sage Spice see Sage

Saint John the Worker (Hypericum hypericoides)

Saint John the Worker is a shrub that can grow from one to three feet in height. Its leaves are opposite and its four-petaled, yellow flowers are showy and bloom in the late spring to early summer. Saint John the Worker is frequently found in dry woods in the southeastern United States. This plant was called 'yupha tacig ne," or raccoon tree leaves, in the traditional language of the Lumbee. Saint John the Worker is the closely related American cousin in the plant kingdom to the European herb Saint Johnswort (Hypericum perforatum). Saint Johnswort was used by ancient European medical authorities such as Dioscorides and Galen, and later in England by renowned healer Gerard, for treatment of wounds, to provoke urine, and even to treat bladder stones. Saint Johnswort has been promoted by herbal experts around the world as an herb that reportedly encourages feelings of well-being. Mr. Vernon Cooper, a Lumbee healer, made a tonic using Saint John the Worker by combining the male and female varieties (small and larger plants) so that they could be used by either men or women. He suggested that "early stage" of diabetes individuals use this tonic. For "later stages" of diabetes, what Mr. Cooper called "sugar in the bone" or "neuritis," he would occasionally recommend a combination tonic of Saint John the Worker, Wild Cherry bark (Prunus serotina), and Ground Huckleberry (Gaylussacia dumosa). He also used a tonic of the female variety of Saint John the Worker to treat "body trouble in women." The Cherokee make an infusion from St. John the Worker to be sniffed up the nose to treat nosebleed. The Alabama used a tea made from the entire plant to treat dysentery.

Salix nigra see Wild Willow Tree

Salty Berry *see Sumac*

Salvia officinalis *see Sage*

Sambucus nigra *see Elder-berry*

Sampson's Snakeroot (Aristolochia serpentaria); also known as Diamondback Rattlesnake Root
Sampson's Snakeroot is a perennial herb that grows up to eighteen inches tall. The leaves are heart-shaped at the base. The maroon flowers bloom in early summer in wet areas such as stream banks and at the edges of forests. Some Lumbee healers prepared a Sampson Snakeroot tonic or a tea from the roots to treat colic and indigestion, as a diaphoretic, and for obstructed menstruation. Vernon Cooper, a Lumbee healer, said he always used Sampson's Snakeroot in combination with other plants because he believed it was poisonous if taken by itself in large doses.

Sand Plum *see Wild Plum*

Sanguinaria canadensis *see Bloodroot*

Sarracenia purpurea *see Bugle Plant*

Sassafras albidum *see Sassafras Tree*

Sassafras Tree (Sassafras albidum) also known as Sassafrax Tree, Red Sassafras Tree

The mature Sassafras Tree stands from twenty to forty feet in height. This native tree has many slender branches and a smooth orange-brown bark. The three-lobed leaves are perhaps the most distinctive feature. The leaves are broadly oval, alternate, and range from three to seven inches long. The flowers are small and are an inconspicuous greenish-yellow color. The roots are large and woody, their bark being soft, rough, and spongy. Both the bark and wood have a fragrant odor. The bark without its corky layer is brittle and the presence of small crystals cause the inner surface to glisten. Sassafras is one of the most used herbs among the Lumbee. There seemed to be dispute, however, about which variety is the best to use. Most Lumbee used the "red root" (red bark root). One Lumbee said the white root (white bark root) would "run you blind" (cause severe diarrhea). Another healer concurred, especially when a patient was displaying symptoms of leukemia. Sassafras root was collected when needed. Two handfuls were boiled in four pints of water and simmered until only half the liquid remained. A pint of tea, as hot as the child could stand, was given to the Lumbee youth suffering from measles or chicken pox. Several quilts and blankets were placed on top of the child to encourage perspiration when he or she went to bed. Will D., a Lumbee healer, would also suggest sassafras tea for chicken pox. Sassafras was considered a multi-purpose herb, recommended by healers to treat an individual who generally felt ill. Some healers also thought it would make the spots from chicken pox jump out and show themselves. Will D. recommended Sassafras to "take the fever out." Adults or children with colds or flu were treated in the same manner as the children with measles. Sassafras was also given to function as a blood purifier or spring tonic. Sassafras has also been used to prevent diarrhea, sores, pimples, or high or low blood pressure. A generation earlier, many Lumbee children were given several glassfuls of tea for three or four nights in a row every spring and fall. Ms. Lucie Mae Hammonds Locklear, a Lumbee elder, stated, "Us youn-guns' used to go to the ditchbank every spring and gather some Sassafras. We would get some Poplar bark too. We would boil this together." Ms. Locklear believed that the Poplar bark and Sassafras combination would take the sluggishness out of an individual and acted as a wellness enhancer. Ms. Vernon Hazel Locklear also recalls that her mother would send her to the woods to gather some Sassafras for a spring tonic. A "shotgun heart remedy" (combination of herbs to benefit the heart) was made with Garlic, Calamus (Acorus calamus), and Pipsissewa (Chimaphila umbellata). Sassafras was a part of this treatment because Lumbee herbal experts believed this mixture would eliminate any blood contamination. The taste of Sassafras was relished by so many Lumbee that many drank a beverage made from the root as a refreshment. In earlier times, the Lumbee held a taboo against burning sassafras wood and grapevine. This taboo was widely observed among the southeastern tribes, as far north as the Powhatan confederacy peoples of Virginia.

Sassafras varifiolium *see Sassafras Tree*

Sassafrax *see Sassafras Tree*

Saw Palmetto (Serenoa repens)

Saw Palmetto is a small, hardy fan palm whose stem usually remains below ground or runs just along the surface. In some cases, it develops an erect or arching trunk that may lift the whorl of leaves two to eight feet off the ground. The palmate leaves can be two to three feet across and a bluish-green to green in color. In the wild, Saw Palmetto grows in clumps twenty or more feet in diameter. The stems are about two feet long and the leaves are sharply saw-toothed. The white flowers are borne on stalked panicles that emerge from the leaf base. The fruits or berries are round, bluish-black, and about an inch in diameter. Many southeastern tribes used the berries as food and leaves for shelter. Lumbee healers did not make Saw Palmetto into a tea because the medicinal oils of this plant would not dissolve in water. Saw Palmetto dried berries are purported to have a sweet taste and pungent smell. Lumbee healers also used the Saw Palmetto to treat dysmennorhea, asthma, and later years prostate gland enlargement. Welton Lowry, Lumbee elder, states that he uses Saw Palmetto on a regular basis for prostate gland health. The Seminole and Choctaw made baskets, fish drags, dance fans, and rattles from the fibers in the Saw Palmetto plant.

Serenoa repens *see Saw Palmetto*

Serpent's Tongue *see Adder's Tongue*

Shagbark Hickory *see Hickory Tree*

Sharp Leaf Tree *see Holly Bush*

Sheepburr (Xanthium strumarium); also known as Cockleburr, Clotburs
Sheepburr is a nonnative annual herb that grows to five feet tall. It has alternately arranged, hairy-toothed, two- to six-inch long, triangular leaves. The greenish-brown flowers are tiny and the heads are burr-like. This spiny flower blooms in old fields and pastures from late summer to early fall. The recently picked leaves and stems were boiled in a pint of water for twenty minutes and then mixed with the same amount of milk. If a dog had been bitten by a poisonous snake, this compound was given to the canine to drink. One healer said he had only known of this treatment being used on dogs but thought it would also treat people. The Lakota used the medicine from the Sheepburr in ceremonies, and the Koasati tribe used a decoction from the roots to remove afterbirth after a child was born. The Houma tribe used a Sheepburr root decoction to treat a high fever.

Shortleaf Pine *see See Pine Tree*

Shrub Yellow Root (Xanthorhiza simplicissima); also known as Yellow Root
Shrub Yellow Root grows up to two feet tall. One or more stems bear a cluster of bright green leaves at the end. Brownish-purple flowers are found at the end of drooping, loose clusters. Mr. Vernon Cooper, a Lumbee healer, divided plants into male and female varieties. The larger Yellow Root plants had a sizeable root and grew in rich soil. These plants were called males. Mr. Cooper used the male plants to treat men suffering from prostate gland difficulty. He described this suffering as being caused by a blockage in the urine flow with pain in the kidneys being a major symptom. The female plant was thought to appear more like a small twig sprouting from

the ground. Also, the female plant that grew in the North Carolina was considered two to three times as powerful as one grown in New England. So, if a healer took a plant from Massachusetts or Connecticut for treatment, two to three times the amount of plant would have to be used. Mr. Cooper stated, "I've never seen it around here but from Hamlet, N.C., back south there's a lot of it grows there." He recommended the female plants for women with "female tube trouble." Pain around the outer and inner thigh and buttocks, fever, and backache characterized "female tube trouble." A Native American elder from the Prospect community who was a student of Mr. Cooper stated that Yellow Root was the herb that Mr. Cooper used most. She commented that he used Yellow Root as a base for many medicinal concoctions. Some Lumbee healers peeled the root and sliced the pieces in boiling water to make a tea to be drunk for treatment of jaundice. Saint John the Worker (Hypericum hypericoides), Pip (Chimaphila umbellata), and Sarsparilla (Aralia nudicalulis) were combined with a piece of Yellow Root twice the length of the hand and half the diameter of the little finger in a wash to treat skin issues. A piece of Yellow Root was gently simmered (not to a boil) for up to thirty hours to produce a wellness tonic. The tea was left to sit for three to four hours so that the "low wine" could collect on the bottom. The low wine was not taken because it was thought to make anyone who drank it sick. One healer suggested two teaspoons taken four times a day. To treat mouth ulcers and other digestive problems, some Lumbee chewed the root up to twice a day. Yellow root was considered by many healers to be an astringent and tonic. A poultice from the roots was used to treat sore eyes. A root tea was suggested for cramps or nervous trouble. A wash was made for local inflammations. The stem of yellow root was chewed to ease a sore throat and mouth. Mr. Vernon Cooper stated that Yellow Root tea was also used by the Lumbee for gall bladder trouble, jaundice, inward fever, or sluggish kidneys. The Catawba, a sister tribe of the Lumbee, made a decoction from the roots to nurse ulcers on the skin, colds, and jaundice. The Cherokee used ashes burned from Yellow Root greenswitches to treat cancer.

Sida rhombifolia *see Ironweed*

Sidesaddle Flower *see Bugle Plant*

Silk Grass *see Fever Grass*

Silphium compositum *see Rosinweed*

Silver Grass *see Fever Grass*

Sisyrinchium *see Purge Grass*

Slippery Elm Tree (Ulmus fulva Mich); also known as Indian Elm Tree, Red Elm Tree, Sweet Elm Tree

Slippery Elm is a native, deciduous tree that grows from fifty to eighty feet in height. The six- to eight-inch leaves are alternately arranged, oval, dark green, and toothed. These leaves turn a bright yellowish-orange in the autumn. Small, inconspicuous, dark brown flowers with orange tip buds bloom at the tips of branches from March to May. Slippery elm is found near streams, in open areas, and in woods. The Lumbee called Slippery Elm "yap tcu'wi kare," or slimy tree, because they found that when the phloem (sap layer) was put in water a sticky, slimy substance oozed out. Healers believed that this substance was a softening and soothing salve. The fresh inside bark was peeled off and boiled down to make a rich salve or a poultice, then mixed with lard and with Bear Root. The Lumbee healer prepared a salve to be rubbed on rheumatic joints or on the knees or feet where the pain was felt. Some Lumbee thought Slippery Elm to be a mild laxative. The Alabama tribe used a unique combination of gunpowder and a decoction from the bark to treat delayed labor. The Catawba, a sister tribe of the Lumbee, used a bark tea from the Slippery Elm to nurse tuberculosis.

Smilacina racemosa *see False Solomon's Seal*

Snapdragon (Antirrhinum majus)

The Snapdragon has tall, spiked, open florets from six to thirty-six inches high. Snapdragons prefer open sun to partial shade and wet, swampy areas. This plant flowers from mid-spring to early summer. It is not a truly native herb but has become naturalized in many places. Lumbee herbal experts considered the Snapdragon plant to have bitter or stimulant properties. The leaves of this and several allied species have been employed through leaf salves and poultices on cataplasms, tumors, and ulcers.

Sneezeweed *see Bitter Weed*

Solidago odora *see Wild Tansy*

Solidago virgaurea *see Goldenrod*

Solomon's Seal (Polygonatum biflorum)

Solomon's Seal is an erect, perennial herb with an angular stem. It grows from one to three feet in height and is curved like a bow at the top. The alternately arranged, elliptical leaves are large, and the white to greenish-yellow cylindrical flowers bloom from May to June. Solomon's Seal fruit is a blue-black berry. Each summer Solomon's Seal root produces a new stem that dies away. The scar that is left resembles the wax seals once used to close letters. Other tribes used Solomon's Seal as a treatment for bleeding and as an antiemetic. The Lumbee healer would mash the recently picked Solomon's Seal fruits and rub the gooey substance on sores to quicken healing. The Chippewa used Solomon's Seal as a sedative, to ensure a sound night's sleep. The Menominee tribe used a poultice made from the boiled, mashed root to treat sharp pains.

Son Before the Father see Coltsfoot

Sonchus asper see Field Thistle

Sourwood Tree (Oxydendrum arboreum)

The Sourwood is a moderately tall, slender tree that grows to a height of sixty feet, with a diameter of eighteen to twenty inches. It has simple, alternate, deciduous leaves and it often grows with a leaning or arching trunk. The white blossoms, borne on long drooping stalks (racemes), bloom in the late spring and early summer. In the fall, Sourwood leaves turn a rich crimson red color. The Lumbee called this plant "wii tinuse'" or bitter medicine in their traditional language. Many Lumbee would put some of the cut piece of the tree and bark in cool water and let it soak overnight. Some healers would recommend drinking this liquid three times a day to treat menstrual symptoms. A bark tonic was manufactured for dyspepsia and asthma. The bark ooze was employed to treat itch or chewed to nurse mouth ulcers. A tea from the bark and leaves was used to treat problems of the nerves or nervous system. Van T., a Lumbee healer, would recommend that his clients drink a tea made of Cumin seed and Sourwood bark to treat "bad nerves." Van T. believed that "bad nerves" (nervousness, nerve problems, etc.) were at the root of many bodily problems. Sourwood bark was chewed or made into a decoction by the Cherokee to calm the nerves. The Cherokee also used the bark to address itching and diarrhea. The Catawba, a sister tribe of the Lumbee, employed Sourwood bark in a cold decoction to treat excessive menstrual flow and change-of-life sickness (menopause).

Spearmint (Mentha spicata)

Spearmint is a nonnative perennial herb with wrinkled, bright green, and lance shaped leaves. When the fine-toothed spearmint leaves are crushed, they emit a minty odor. The erect, square stem rises to a height of about two feet. Tiny, white to lavender flowers show from June to October. Spearmint is most often found in moist or wet areas. Some Lumbee boiled or chewed raw leaves to treat indigestion. The leaves were also made into a tea to treat fever and upset stomach. Spearmint and Peppermint are sometimes used interchangeably. However, most Lumbee preferred to use Spearmint because its taste was reportedly more pleasant and less strong than Peppermint. Ms. Lucie Mae Hammonds Locklear, a Lumbee elder, recalled that her brother got a wound on his head and it "swelled up great big.... We took him to the doctor and the doctor didn't do him no good. When we got home, momma prayed, 'Lord, let me know what to do.' She went out and gathered some mint and boiled the water out. Then, she made a poultice out of the leaves and put it on my brother's head."

Spigelia marilandica *see* *Indian Pink*

Spiny Leaved Sow Thistle *see* *Field Thistle*

Spotted Bee-balm *see* *Spotted Horsemint*

Spotted Horsemint
(**Monarda punctata**); also known as Oswego Tea, Spotted Bee-balm, Horsemint
Spotted Horsemint is a native, herbaceous to semi-woody, shrubby, and multi-branched perennial. Like most herbaceous mints, it has opposite leaves and square stems. The stems and leaves are hairy. The toothed leaves are lance-shaped and range from one to three inches long. The tiny flowers are arranged in showy heads with two to seven found on each stem. Each flower head rests upon a bright pink to lavender leafy bract. The little corolla is tube-shaped. The principal use of Horsemint was external, and in its pure state was thought to be a vesicant. Lumbee healers were careful to dilute Horsemint with water, soap liniment, or olive oil

(in later times). However, some Lumbee also viewed Horsemint as a diaphoretic, emmenagogue, and diuretic to treat urinary disorders. Horsemint or Oswego tea was applied as a salve to treat backache and chronic rheumatism. A leaf poultice was manufactured for treatment of headache and cold. A leaf and top tea was used by the Lumbee to treat weak bowels and stomach. The Lumbee also used Oswego tea to treat female obstructions. Some Lumbee healers suggested a tea of the leaves and roots be wiped on the head to treat nosebleed. Occasionally, a healer would prepare a hot leaf tea to bring out measles, to treat heart trouble, to treat fever, to encourage restful sleep, to relieve flatulent colic, and to sweat off colds or flu. Horsemint was used also used long ago as a treatment for smallpox. Lumbees called smallpox "the plague." This disease alone killed more than 70 percent of all Native people (hundreds of thousands or millions) living in North Carolina within a short time after European contact. Whole tribes of people including the Sugaree, Pee Dee, and Waxhaw, among many others, were completely annihilated. Some like the ancestors of the Lumbee, fled and sought refuge from this deadly disease in geographically isolated areas. With modern vaccines, smallpox cases are now rare, but there is fear among many civilized nations that a terrorist group or a rogue nation might use this deadly disease once again as a weapon of mass destruction. Witnessing the devastating effects of smallpox in the eastern United States, U.S. army and government officials distributed smallpox infected blankets during the frontier era among some Native American tribes (blankets from people suffering from smallpox) to further decimate the American Indian population in other parts of the country. Lumbees, who were without the aid of modern treatments and vaccines, treated smallpox by going into a sweat lodge after the first sign of skin eruption. A sweat lodge is made of pine branches with an animal skin used for the door flap. The healer heated the stones to a very high temperature in an outside fire, then carried them using animal skins or other methods into the sweat lodge. When the afflicted person entered the lodge, he or she would pour water (mixed at times with Holly leaves, Sage, Horsemint, Peppermint, or Spearmint extractions) over the stones. After he or she "sweated" to the point of near dehydration, the patient would jump naked into the cold water of the river. This method was also used for purification. The Delaware prepared an infusion to bathe the person's face to treat the fever. The Meswaki tribe would make a compound with an infusion of Horsemint leaves snuffed up the nostrils to nurse a headache.

Squaw Vine see Partridge Berry

Star Grass (Aletris Farinosa); also known as Colicroot

Star Grass is a native, spreading, perennial grass that grows in large clumps from three to six feet in height. The sturdy, flat, glossy leaf blade may be as much as one-half inch wide and thirty inches long. The stem is round and usually has a reddish tint. The reddish-purple flowers are inconspicuous and produce shiny teardrop-shape seeds. Star Grass typically turns a pale yellow in the fall. The rhizomes are in active growth from late winter through mid-spring, but the top stays dormant until the soil warms up. In Lumbee traditional language, Star Grass was called "wa'sawi'ti" or cane medicine. The Lumbee soaked the whole plant in water for one day to make a Star Grass drink to treat diarrhea. Roots or "rhizomes" (rootlets) were also recommended to strengthen the stomach and womb, and to relieve menstrual cramps, coughs, rheumatism, jaundice, flatulence, and colic. A poultice of the leaves was recommended to ease an aching back or sore breasts. Will D., a Lumbee healer, would often recommend a tea made from Star Grass to treat dysentery. He said he believed this tea should be taken hot at night. Healers of a Lumbee sister tribe, the Waccamaw-Siouan (men and women) would use Myrtle and Star Grass to treat "athlete's foot" fungus or use the leaves in a tea to allay nausea or soak sore, aching feet.

Stick-Tight *see Mark*

Stillingia syllvatica *see*
  Queen's Delight

Sugarberry (Celtis laevigata
  or Celtis occidentalis); also
  known as Hackberry
Sugarberry is a native, deciduous
tree that grows to sixty feet. Its alternate leaves are elliptical to elon-
gate with a tapering, pointed apex
and teeth along the margins. The
tiny, nondescript flowers bloom
from March to April as the leaves
unfold. The fruits are tiny cherry-
like drupes that are orange-red to
blue-black. The bark is gray with
warty outgrowths. Sugarberry was
called "yap nyu stciwe'" or sweet
tree in the traditional language of
the Lumbee. The fresh (or dried
berries in winter) were eaten by
many Lumbee children as sweet
tidbits that many Lumbee healers
thought would promote good
health. However, they were not
suggested for any particular ailment. The Houma tribe, however,
used a Sugarberry tea to treat
throat ailments. The Comanche
used Sugarberry as food by beat-
ing the berries to a pulp, mixing
them with fat, rolling them into
balls, and roasting this mixture
over a fire.

Sumac (Rhus typhina); also
  known as Salty Berry
The Sumac is a tall shrub or small
tree that usually grows in small
clumps or groups. It can reach a
height of twenty-five to thirty feet.
The leaves are alternately arranged
and pinnate. The fruit is a dense
cluster of deep red dry berries at
the top of the tree. Sumac leaves
also turn a dark crimson color in
the fall. The fruits ripen in the fall
and can be found in the winter.
This shrub or tree is native to the
eastern United States. Sumac
leaves turn a dark red color in the
fall. In the Lumbee traditional language, Sumach was called "yap
wiiti tah-re" or shoe tree. Sumac
berries were boiled by many Lumbee to make a tea and the patient
was instructed to drink a half
teacupful three times a day to aid
in bladder discomfort. A tea was
made from a handful of the roots,
as long as the patient's middle
finger to the bottom of their palm,
placed in two quarts of water, and
boiled until a quart remained.
This decoction was fashioned to
treat kidney and bladder discomfort. The Lumbee healer usually
told his or her client to take two or
three doses per day in between
and at meals and before going to
bed. Sumac was commonly combined with Saint John the Worker
(Hypericum hypericoides) to treat
urinary tract infections, kidney issues, and urine blockage. This
treatment was also given to children who frequently wet the bed.
Hayes Alan Locklear, Lumbee historian and herbalist, states that
children also sucked on the fruits
and spit out the seeds to treat bed
wetting. Apparently, in many cases
the child was expected to repeat
this process with the whole fruit
cluster. The child that continued

to wet the bed was thought to prefer to do this (too lazy to get out of bed) than to have any physiological abnormality. Sumac was combined with Devil's Shoestring (Tephrosia virginiana) to make a tea, even after the advent of modern antibiotics to treat gonorrhea. Some healers used Sumac, like the modern drug Pitocin, to supposedly encourage the onset of labor or help expel afterbirth. Devil's Shoestring, Queen's Delight (Stillingia sylvatica), Beggar's Lice (Bidens frondosa), and Sumac were used to treat pellagra (a disease which was thought to cause the skin to become spotted and peel). Lumbee healers also recommended the berries in an infusion to treat diabetes and febrile disease. Lumbee healers used the bark in a tea or extract to produce catharsis. A tea from bark, roots, and berries was used by the Lumbee to pour over sunburn blisters. The Micmac would use Sumac berries in a tea to nurse a sore throat. The Ute tribe used Sumac berries for food.

Swamp Haw *see Possum Haw*

Sweet Balm *see Lemon Balm*

Sweet Bay *see Bay Tree*

Sweet Elm Tree *see Slippery Elm Tree*

Sweet Flag *see Calamus*

Sweet Goldenrod *see Wild Tansy*

Sweet Gum Tree (**Liquidambar styraciflua**); also known as Gum Tree
The Sweet Gum is a deciduous tree that grows up to one hundred fifty feet. This native tree exhibits star-shaped leaves with finely sawtoothed lobes. The fruit of the Sweet Gum appears to be a spherical, green (turns brown later), thorny burr with a diameter of two to three inches. The trees prefer moist woods and old fields. The bark is gray with narrow, scaly ridges. Sweet Gum is so named because the cut bark releases a sweet, fragrant liquid used today in some perfumes. The Lumbee called Sweet Gum "hasuna're" or gum rosin in the traditional language. The buds, tops, rosin or inner bark were prepared to treat diarrhea or dysentery. Lumbee healers prepared a bark tea from the Sweet Gum tree to treat a nervous patient. A salve was fashioned for wounds, sores, and ulcers. Mr. Earl Carter, a Lumbee healer, uses Sweet Gum leaves to treat cuts. The Lumbee would gather the rosin from a gash made in the tree the previous day or chew a twig to treat pyorrhea or counteract the effects of gingivitis (receding gums). The hardened gum was also used by the Lumbee as chewing gum long ago. The Rappahannock would make a tea from dried bark to treat diarrhea and dysentery. Healers from the Waccamaw-Siouan tribe, a sister tribe of the Lumbee and closest in proximity (thirty miles), would

treat sizeable wounds with Sweet Gum rosin.

Sycamore Tree (Platanus occidentalis); also known as Burr Tremor

The Sycamore is a huge tree with a massive trunk, heavy, spreading branches, and zigzag twigs. Sycamore bark can be peeled off in large, thin flakes and is mottled brown to greenish-white. The leaves are deciduous, alternate, simple, four to eight inches wide, ovate in shape with three to five lobes, and often toothed with star-shaped hairs at the base. The numerous, tiny, greenish-red flowers appear during the spring with the leaves. The fruit consists of one-seeded, narrow, four-angled nutlets surrounded by long, stiff hairs. These great trees are found in wet soils of lakes, swamps, stream-banks, riverbanks, and floodplains. Sycamore was called "yaphi tuwi," or white tree with many burrs, in the traditional language of the Lumbee. A handful of root scrapings were dried, boiled, and then beaten to make a poultice-salve by many Lumbee. It was mixed with grease and applied to burns to draw out the inflammation. One Lumbee healer said the bark had an ingredient that could treat the pain of a menstrual period when made into a tea. Also, many healers would suggest that their clients wash their infected sores with Sycamore bark ooze. A tea was made from the inner bark to treat infant rash and measles. Other uses included: analgesic, antidiarrheal, antirheumatic, blood cleanser, cathartic, emetic, emmenagogue, hemostat, and tonic. Sycamore has been widely used by the Lumbee and some others as a coffee substitute. It has also been used by the Lumbee to aid in childbirth. Many healers would scrape the bark off the Sycamore tree "down the root" to make a tea to treat indigestion.

Symphytum officinale see Comfrey

Tanacetum vulgare see Tansy

Tansy (Tanacetum vulgare)

Tansy or Common Tansy is a non-native herb that grows from one to three feet in height. Its leaves are fernlike and have a spicy aroma. The golden, buttonlike flowers bloom from July through September in showy, flat-topped clusters. Tansy can be found in meadows and fields and along roadsides throughout the United States. Some Lumbee healers suggested this tea to return strength to an individual who was feeling feeble. To treat morning sickness in the first three months of pregnancy, one healer would select a plant approximately one foot tall and boil it in of two cups of water for two hours with Fever Grass (Heterotheca graminfolia) and Sage (Salvis officinalis) to make a tea. The Cherokee used Tansy as a pain reliever (analgesic). The Cheyenne tribe used an infusion of the leaves and blossoms to treat weakness and dizziness.

Taraxacum officinale *see Dandelion*

Teaberry *see Wintergreen*

Teaweed *see Ironweed*

Tephrosia virginiana *see Devil's Shoestring*

Thistle (**Cirsium repandum**); also known as (**Carduus repandus**)

The Thistle is a coarse, short-lived perennial or biennial that can grow up to one foot in height. It has stiff, hairy leaves and stems. The leaves are lobed, spiny and about four inches long. The Thistle has inconspicuous purple flowers and is frequently found in sandy areas and forests. Some Lumbee healers used the roots of the Thistle plant in a poultice to treat the bites of poisonous insects, nonpoisonous spiders, and reptiles. It has also been prepared to treat hemorrhaging, swelling, external infection, and ringworm.

Tickle Coats *see Coat Ticklers*

Tumble Grass *see Coat Ticklers*

Turkey Oak *see Red Oak Tree*

Turkey Vine *see Partridge Berry*

Tussilago farfara *see Coltsfoot*

Typha latifolia *see Cattail*

Ulmus fulva *see Slippery Elm Tree*

Urtica dioica *see Nettle*

Verbascum thapsus *see Mullein*

Viburnum nudum *see Possum Haw*

Viburnum prunifolum *see Black Haw*

Vicia Caroliniana *see Carolina Vetch*

Virginia Pine *see Pine Tree*

Walnut Tree *see Black Walnut Tree*

Water-root *see Blunt Manna Grass*

Wax Myrtle *see Red Myrtle*

White Bloodroot (**Liatris regimontis**); also known as Blazing Star, Button Snakeroot

White Bloodroot is a native perennial herb of eastern North American that can grow up to two feet in height. These plants produce spikes of small colorful flowers. These brilliant purplish-pink flowers bloom in late summer. Mr. Vernon Cooper, a Lumbee healer, would make a decoction of White Bloodroot and Red Shank (Ceanothus americanus) to bathe painful areas.

White Oak Tree *see Oak Tree*

White Plantain (Plantago virginica)

White Plantain is a hardy, perennial, herbaceous plant. It has no stem, only a peduncle. This plant has basal leaves only that can be as wide as four inches. Each shiny leaf is entire, stemmed and distinctly ribbed. Flowers range from green to white with the first blooms appearing in early summer. The small flowers are in a tight slender spike. White Plantain can be found throughout North America in fields and meadows, and along lightly traveled roads and open roadsides. A favorite children's game is to wrap the stem around the top of the head and pop the flower off this plant. This species should not be confused with the banana, also called plantain. This type of banana was wrongly named from the Spanish word meaning "plane tree." Hayes Alan Locklear, Lumbee historian and herbalist, states the Lumbee used Plantain to treat bleeding from a cut. To treat dysentery in children, the healer would make Plantain tea by boiling the entire plant, including the roots. Tribes in the northeast adopted this non-native plant and used the leaves as an eyewash. Male elders from the Kiowa tribe wore White Plantain garlands and wreaths in dances as a symbol of virility and health.

Whiteweed (Antennaria neglecta); also known as Pussytoes, Field Cat's Foot

If one is walking in an open field or meadow in the southeastern United States, one may see short gray stems with little furry balls unfolding at the tops like white kitten's feet. The balls are the tiny compound flower heads of the Whiteweed or Pussytoes. The entire plant may be less than three inches tall. The whitish-green, spoon-shaped leaves lie flat on the ground. Plants may occur individually, but are usually found in clumps. The fruits are only 1/16 inch long. In the Lumbee traditional language, Whiteweed was called "wi'ti hasumi'," flat medicine leaves, or stink turtle. The Lumbee soaked the whole Whiteweed plant in water for one day to make a tea to treat diarrhea. Whiteweed was once employed by the Lumbee as a moth repellent and a head lice preventive, and the gum extracted from the plant stalks served as a chewing gum.

Wicky (Kalmia carolina); also known as Lambkill

Warning: Internal ingestion of Wicky can cause lowered blood pressures, convulsions and death. Wicky can also cause a severe skin irritation.

Wicky is a native, large, evergreen shrub or small tree. It has smooth, elliptical, and alternately arranged leaves that grow in whorls of three. The flowers are showy white or pink with fused petals. These flowers arise in the leaf axils of the upper stems. Wicky grows in low places, open woods, or pocosins in the southeastern United States. A decoction of the top part of the plant and rhizomes was made from three to four pieces no more that two inches long. Wicky was boiled in two pints of water for a few hours. This decoction was poured into a tub of bath water to treat the "mad itch" or scabies. Apparently, not many people were able to stand the bath for more than a few minutes. One healer said it made the skin feel like it was going to catch on fire. Among the elders, jokes about someone taking a Wicky bath were common. Some individuals were said to have run naked around the house and in the yard, attempting to cool off, after a short bath. One healer said it took more than one treatment to be cured, but another healer said he had never used the plant more than one time.

Wild Carrot *see Queen Anne's Lace*

Wild Cherry Tree (Prunus virginiana) or (Prunus serotina); also known as Chokecherry

Warning: Do not eat the leaves and fruit pits; they contain poisonous hydrocyanic acid, which causes difficult breathing, loss of balance and convulsions.

Wild Cherry is a native, deciduous, thicket-forming erect shrub or small tree. Wild Cherry leaves are alternate with glands along the margins of the leaf base. The stems are numerous and slender, either branching from the base or main branches upright and spreading. The height varies from three to twenty feet. The roots are a shallow network of rhizomes with a deep-feeding vertical taproot. Each fruit contains a small stone. Few have gone through life without tasting Wild Cherry cough drops made from the bark of the Wild Cherry tree or a commercially prepared Wild Cherry cough syrup. Lumbee healers used the bark to make a tea to treat diarrhea and lung ailments. The Wild Cherry was also called Chokecherry, because the many Native American tribes thought the raw fruit was so sour it could make someone choke. The raw fruit was thought to cause sweating and as a result help bring down a fever. The bark was also used as an ingredient in a decoction to extract or expel worms. If the extract was applied externally, it was used to treat ulcers and abscesses. Poplar (Liriodendron tulipifera) and Oak (Quercus spp.) and Wild Cherry branches and bark were combined and fashioned into a tea. For kidney and bladder problems, a tablespoon of the tea was recommended to be taken three times a day. One healer collected a seven to ten cherry branches one and one-half inches by six inches. This collection was boiled down in a quart of water until three pints remained. If the family hog was thought to have worms, one-half gallon of fresh cherries was given to the swine (if the hog didn't gain weight, worms were suspected). Many Lumbee women, to stop bleeding between their normal menstrual periods, used a tea made from the fresh sap and sap layer of bark. For women who were having difficulty with their pregnancy, some healers fashioned a wine from the fresh cherries. Ms. Vernon Hazel Locklear, a Lumbee from the Union Chapel community, also commented that her mother would recommend Wild Cherry wine for treatment of diarrhea. Many Lumbee drank Cherry wine as a refreshing beverage. For treatment of fever, Cherry bark was combined with Jacob's Coat (Perilla frutescens) and Poplar to make a tea. Birds and other wildlife are especially fond of the ripe Wild Cherry. In fact, birds sometimes gorge themselves on this fruit so much that they lose the ability to fly. In *The Education of Little Tree* by Forrest Carter, Little Tree, a young Cherokee boy, relates a humorous story about a male cardinal who ate so many berries he passed out. The Cherokee also used the Wild Cherry as a blood tonic to strengthen the circulatory system. The Blackfoot used Wild Cherry juice to nurse a sore throat and diarrhea. The Algonquian tribes used a decoction of cherry bark and Calamus (Acorus calamus) to treat a cough.

Wild Evergreen Grass *see Blunt Manna Grass*

Wild Garlic (Allium vineale)

Wild Garlic is a nonnative perennial herb that is that has alternate, hollow, slender leaves similar to the wild onion. It grows up to two feet tall and the bulb (root) is divided into small bulblets. The lavender or white flower blooms in early summer. Ms. Annie Mae Oxendine, a Lumbee healer, stated that she would drink the juice of the "wild garlet" (Garlic) bulb submerged in vinegar for a week. She thought the juice would treat high blood (hypertension). The Cherokee used Wild Garlic to nurse a stomachache and treat constipation, colds, and dropsy.

Wild Ginger (Asarum canadense); also known as False Heartleaf

Wild Ginger is a low growing plant with heart-shaped or wide, arrow shaped leaves. The flower is just at or below ground level and is in the form of a cluster of brown "jugs." In fact, the Lumbee called Wild Ginger "pi tcu ha hor're," or "pitcher comes" in the native language. The leaves when crushed have the aroma of Ginger. The Lumbee healer prepared a tea with Wild Ginger leaves, roots or blossoms to treat poor digestion, colds, and coughs. Lumbee herbal experts believed that Wild Ginger produced heavy perspiration, which was thought to aid in treatment of fever. Fresh leaves were applied to wounds. Some healers employed the root for treatment of female obstruction, worms, cold, cough, painful menstruation, and heart pain. Wild Ginger was also thought to act as a stimulant, carminative, diuretic, and diaphoretic. The Abnaki would use Wild Ginger in an infusion to nurse a cold.

Wild Lettuce (Lactuca canadensis)

Wild Lettuce is a biennial herb that grows from three to nine feet in height. The stems are reddish to green and contain a milky sap (sometimes called milkweed). The leaves are lobed and alternately arranged (they might have toothed margins). The orange-yellow flowers bloom in fields and woods, and along roadsides in late summer. This plant is a common in the eastern U.S. The milky sap from a recently broken stem was used by the Lumbee to treat sores, pimples, poison ivy, or itching. The mountains of western North Carolina have a different kind of wild lettuce called "Branch Lettuce." The Cherokee used Branch Lettuce as a food. Frederick "Fishhound" Arch (Eastern Band of Cherokee) stated that the Cherokee called Branch Lettuce "Bear Lettuce." As a boy, he gathered the lettuce in the spring. He would wash it thoroughly and his mother would pour hot fatback grease onto the leaves to "kill it" (called "kilt lettuce"). This was one of his mother's favorite foods. Branch Lettuce was found in and along streams and springs in the Appalachian mountains. An African American man named Babe Ray, living in Elk Park, North Carolina, in the mid-twentieth century, is still remembered because of his kindness and gifts of Branch Lettuce to people in Avery County.

Wild Plum (Prunus americana; Prunus angustifolia);

also known as Sand Plum, Chickasaw Plum

The Wild Plum is a native eastern United States deciduous shrub or small tree that can grow from fifteen to twenty-five feet in height. They sometimes grows in thickets. The leaves are alternate and somewhat oval. The leaf is long, narrow, pointed, dark green on top and paler below. The pinkish white flowers appear in early spring and the fruit ripens in late summer. The fruit is an orange-red drupe which is one-half inch in diameter with yellowish, sweet flesh inside. The Wild Plum was called "turii' tcine'" or bitter fruit in the traditional language of the Lumbee. The trunk is short and thorny and is covered by reddish brown bark broken into thin plates. The Lumbee soaked Wild Plum bark for a day in water and mixed the liquid with Horehound and Wild Cherry bark to make a cough syrup. A bark tea was made for treatment of kidney and bladder problems, fever, and dandruff. The Chippewa made a decoction to be used as a disinfectant wash for wounds and to rid the body of worms. The Cheyenne mashed the Wild Plum to treat mouth diseases, and the branches were used in the Sundance ceremony.

Wild Rat's Bane see Pipsissewa

Wild Strawberry (Fragaria vesca); also known as Wood Strawberry

The Wild Strawberry is a native,

low perennial with a scaly rhizome and greenish or very lightly tinged reddish purple flower stem. Wild Strawberry flowers are white with five petals that range from two to ten inches long. The leaves are ovate with straight, prominent veins with no individual leafstalks. The leaf edges are roughly toothed. Wild Strawberry fruit is a small (small compared to its cultivated cousins) red berry with seeds distributed on the surface. The berry usually ripens in June. Wild Strawberry can be found in dry to moist open woods, streambanks, and meadows. Lumbee healers used the Wild Strawberry as a laxative, diuretic, and astringent. The raw fruit was used as a febrifuge and was also prescribed for gravel (kidney or bladder stones). The root was made into a tea to aid in treating diarrhea and dysentery. Some Lumbee herbal experts believed the fresh fruit, combined with a pinch of bicarbonate (baking soda), would remove discoloration of the teeth if the juice was allowed to remain on for about five minutes and then cleansed with warm water. A Lumbee healer known as "Pop M." would use a cut Strawberry to rub over his face immediately after washing his face following a hot day of work in the field. He claimed the juice would remove slight sunburn. For a badly sunburned face, he would rub the juice well into the skin, leave it on for about half an hour, and then wash it off with warm water. The Potawatomi used the root to nurse a stomachache.

Wild Tansy (Solidago odora);

also known as Sweet Goldenrod Wild Tansy is a native perennial that grows from twenty to forty inches tall. It has narrow, dark green, toothless leaves. The small, yellow flowerheads form clusters at the top of the plant. In the early days of the United States, the aromatic, "anise-like" flower of the leaves made Wild Tansy flowers and leaves a popular substitute for commercial teas. The Lumbee called Wild Tansy "ten' siwi," or sweet smelling flower leaves, in the traditional language. Some other tribes would use a Wild Tansy tea to treat urinary and intestinal disorders as well as dropsy. Vernon Cooper, Lumbee healer, would add Wild Tansy to help other medicine teas taste better. The flowers can be boiled to make a yellow dye.

Wild Tobacco see Indian Tobacco

Wild Touch-Me-Not (Impatiens spp.)

The Wild Touch-Me-Not is a native, hardy perennial herb that can grow up to eight inches in height. It has thick stems and deep green leaves. In early spring, pale lilac flowers, which can grow to two and one-half inches across, bloom. This flower can be found most often in peatlike soil or in a bog or swamp habitat. The Wild Touch-Me-Not was called "tupausi'wi su're," or wild flower, in the ancient tongue of the Lumbee. The entire plant was boiled down by the Lumbee healer and mixed with powdered mussel shells and formed into a salve. This salve was rubbed on the painful area to treat stiff joints. The Cherokee used Wild Touch-Me-Not as an ingredient in the green corn medicine (a mixture given for purification before the green corn ceremony). The Iroquois confederacy tribes used "Impatients" as a wash for liver spots on the skin.

Wild Willow Tree (Salix nigra); also known as Black Willow Tree

The Wild Willow is a large, native, deciduous tree with one or more straight or leaning trunks (usually), upright branches, and a narrow or irregular crown. The Willow can range from sixty to one hundred feet in height. The shiny green leaves are one to five inches long, narrowly lanceolate and finely sawtoothed. The Black Willow has dark brown or black bark that is deeply furrowed into scaly forking ridges. The Black Willow is most often found in wet soils such as banks of streams, around lakes, and in flood plains. The fresh leaves and small branches were boiled alone or with Poplar (Liriodendron tulipifera) to fabricate a tea. Three teaspoons of this was taken once a day to reduce fever. The ancestors of the Lumbee would make fish traps or baskets from the willow. At the end of the basket, the tips of the branches were sharpened so big fish could swim in but couldn't get out (little ones could swim out). The Cherokee chewed Willow bark for wind (stamina) in the stickball game.

The Houma made a decoction from the roots to treat a fever.

Wild Yam (Dioscorea villosa)

Wild Yam is a low growing vine that can often be found in open woods and open areas. It is readily identified by its heart-shaped leaves. The lower leaves are often arranged in a whorl. Minute, greenish-yellow flowers are produced from May through June. Wild Yam was called "witeke tcu wa" or wild root plant in the Lumbee traditional language. The Lumbee used Wild Yam as a diuretic, emetic, expectorant, and treatment of urinary pain by making a tea from the boiled root. Many Lumbee women would also drink this tea to relieve the pains of childbirth. The Wild Yam was boiled down to make a salve used to treat pain from rheumatism. The Meswaki tribe used also a root decoction to treat the pains of childbirth.

Willow Herb see Fireweed

Winter cabbage see Collards

Wintergreen (Gaultheria procumbens); also known as Mountain Birch, Teaberry

Wintergreen is a perennial evergreen that grows up to six inches tall. Red fruits or berries follow the bell-shaped, white flowers. Its leaves are leathery, glossy, and a pale green or yellowish green when young. A Wintergreen root tea was used by some Lumbee healers to treat chronic indigestion. Also, the leaves were chewed for dysentery or tender gums. A tea was made from the leaves to nurse colds. The Algonquian peoples used Wintergreen in an infusion to treat colds and headache discomfort.

Wire Grass (Aristida stricta)

Wire Grass is native, perennial herb that grows up to four feet in height. This densely tufted grass has folded, rounded basal leaves. Its tiny flowers bloom in the fall. Wire Grass is a common plant and can be found most often in pinelands and woods in the southeastern United States. After the first frost, Wire Grass was gathered. The whole plant was boiled into a tea and used as a poison antidote. The Lumbee also used Wire Grass and Broomgrass, tied on a stick, to serve as a broom.

Witch Hazel (Hamamelis virginiana)

Witch Hazel is a native, slightly aromatic shrub or small tree with a broad, open crown of spreading branches and small, yellow flowers which bloom in the autumn or winter. Witch Hazel leaves are dull green above and broadly elliptical, pointed, or rounded at the tip. It has light brown bark and produces fruit that is a half-inch-long, light brown, elliptical capsule. It can be found in dry woods to partly shady areas. The Lumbee would often prepare a Witch Hazel bark tea to treat colds. A tea from the bark of this spice wood and Virginia Pine needles were also prepared to treat fevers and sore throat, bathe sores and skinned places, and treat periodic pains. In the past, crushed or bruised leaves were rubbed on scratches. A tea from the bark of Witch Hazel was used to treat tuberculosis. A distillation of the extract of Witch Hazel bark, twigs, and leaves mixed with alcohol and water is widely used today on the skin, mainly as an astringent. Early settlers were taught by Native Americans to make decoctions of different strengths with the leaves, bark, and twigs to nurse hemorrhoids, internal bleeding, and excessive menstrual flow, as well as to function as an eyewash. The Chippewa used the inner bark of the Witch Hazel as an emetic, an agent to make a child vomit, in cases of poisoning.

Wood Strawberry see Wild Strawberry

Woodbine see Honeysuckle

Wood's Mullein (Elephantopus carolinianus); also known as Elephant's Foot

Wood's Mullein is a native perennial herb with flat basal leaves. The pink or purple flowers bloom in late summer to fall. Wood's Mullein is found most frequently in pine forests. A poultice was prepared by Lumbee healers to be held on the chest to treat pneumonia.

Wood Betony (Pedicularis canadensis); also known as Common Lousewort

Wood Betony comes up year after year from a thickish, woody root.

The stems are slender, square and furrowed, and rise to a height of one to two feet. The stems sprout, at wide intervals. The few pairs of oblong and stalkless leaves that are two to three inches long. The majority of these leaves, however, sprout from the root and these are larger and heart-shaped. At the top of the stem are rich purplish-red, two-lipped flowers arranged in dense rings or whorls. The flowers bloom during mid-summer. The Lumbee called Wood Betony "sanu suke'" or red money in the traditional language. A hot Wood Betony root decoction was prepared by Lumbee healers to treat stomachache. The Catawba, a sister tribe of the Lumbee, would also use a decoction from the roots to nurse stomach pain. The Cherokee used Wood Betony to treat bloody discharge from the bowels.

Wormwood (Artemisia absinthium)

Wormwood is a nonnative, shrubby perennial that grows to four feet in height. Its leaves are covered in silky grayish hairs that have downy undersides. This shrub is known to spread quickly and over large areas. The leaves and roots exude a substance that restricts the growth of other plants. The tiny and nearly globular yellow flowerheads bloom in loose clusters at the top of the branch. The leaves and flowers are very bitter and have a characteristic odor. Wormwood was an ingredient in the outlawed alcoholic beverage Absinthe. This liquor has been outlawed in many countries worldwide because of its damaging effects to the nervous system. Ms. Lucie Mae Hammonds Locklear, a Lumbee elder, commented that when she was young, "We used to call Wormwood 'the Bitters.' My brother hated it. If me or any of my brothers or sisters caught a cold or got worms, my momma would make a tea. My brother would run from momma and hide under the bed to keep from taking it." The Mohegans would also prepare an infusion of leaves to treat worms. The Chippewa boiled the plant and dipped a rag in the brew to make a warm compress to apply to a sprain.

Xanthium strumarium see Sheepburr

Yaupon Tree see American Holly

Yellow Birch Tree (Betula lutea)

The Yellow Birch is a large tree maturing to a height of sixty feet and a width of forty feet. It prefers full to partial sun and moist, slightly acidic soils. It has alternate, ovate, doubly serrated and slightly incised leaves with medium to dark green uppersides. In fall, Yellow Birch leaves turn chartreuse in drought striken years and yellow-brown in other years. Flowers expand to three inches around April. Yellow Birch was called "yap koko' ha" or brittle tree breaks in the Lumbee traditional language. Some Lumbee healers would boil Yellow Birch buds down to a syrup and add sulfur to make a salve to apply to ringworm or sores. Various parts of the tree have been applied to medicinal uses by the Lumbee. The young shoots and leaves secrete a resinous substance having acid properties, which, when combined with alkalis, is said by some Lumbee healers to act as a tonic laxative. Lumbee herbal experts claim that the leaves have a peculiar, aromatic, agreeable odor and a bitter taste. Local healers have employed the leaves in the form of infusion (Birch tea) to treat gout, rheumatism, dropsy, and kidney stones. A decoction of the bark has been used for bathing skin eruptions. North Carolina Lumbee healers and herb experts consider the oil to be astringent. One mainly employed the oil for treatment of skin afflictions, especially eczema, but this oil was also used to nurse some internal maladies. The inner bark was also considered to be a bitter astringent, and was used to treat intermittent fevers. Many Native American tribes made a special kind of vinegar from the sap of the Sugar Maple or Birch Tree. The buds and twigs were also allowed to ferment in the sun with the sap, then the liquid was strained through a cloth. A fly on the scene usually told the preparer that the vinegar had fermented. Ms. Lucie Mae Hammonds Lock-

lear, a Lumbee elder, suggested the following treatment for someone who was suffering from gout or a sprain: "To doctor the gout, dig some clay from along the river and mix it with vinegar to make a poultice." Ms. Locklear believed that this poultice would "take the fever out." The vernal sap was also regarded as a diuretic. The Cherokee would chew Birch leaves as a cold treatment or to treat diarrhea.

Yellow Indian Paint *see Goldenseal*

Yellow Jessamine (Gelsemium sempervirens); also known as Carolina Jessamine

Warning: All parts of this plant are considered dangerous. Its use is not recommended. Poisoning can easily occur by the domestic use of this powerful drug even in minute amounts.

Yellow Jessamine is an evergreen perennial vine that can climb up to forty feet. The shiny leaves grow in opposite fashion and are lanceolate in shape. The trumpet shaped, inch-long, yellow flowers bloom from January to May. The attraction of bright yellow flowers and sweet perfume hides the fact that this plant possesses a deadly poison that has been compared to Hemlock. Lumbee healers made a medicine tea for jaundice by boiling approximately 30 mg. of the dried roots and rhizomes in four pints of water. Other tribes used a root tea as a sedative, painkiller, antispasmodic, and a fever-reducing agent. Native peoples also used this plant in a treatment of asthma and whooping cough.

Yellow Root *see also Shrub Yellow Root*

Yellow Root (Berberis vulgaris); also known as Barberry This particular Yellow Root (Berberis) is a thorny, nonnative, deciduous shrub that has yellow wood. It grows up to eight feet in height in tightly compacted soil. Barberry has arched and hanging branches with clusters of pale green, stiff, oval leaves with soft bristly points. The root is yellow and the stems are reddish when young but turn a dirty gray when older. The small, yellow flowers appear from April to May and hang from its branches in clusters. The bright red, oblong berries ripen in August and September. This Yellow Root was called "wii ti wiiya'" or medicine root in the Lumbee traditional language. The Lumbee healer would often boil the stems and roots into a tea to treat an ulcerated stomach and cankers. A piece of the green or the dried root was chewed by some Lumbee to relieve discomfort of the stomach. The virtue (benefit) was thought to lie in its bitterness.

Yellow Snowdrop *see Adder's Tongue*

Yellow Wood *see Graybeard*

Yucca filamentosa *see Bear Grass*

Zea mays *see Indian Corn*

GLOSSARY

Achene—A small, dry, seedlike fruit with a thin wall that does not open.

Acorn—The hard-shelled, one seeded nut of an oak, with a pointed tip and a scaly cup at the base.

Adjuvant—Aiding in action of a medicinal agent or medical treatment.

Alkaloid—Any of a large class of nitrogen-containing organic compounds, found especially in seed plants.

Alterative—Medicine that favorably alters the course of an ailment.

Alternate—Leaves arranged singly along a twig or shoot, and not in whorls or opposite pairs.

Analgesic—That which relieves pain.

Annual—Completing the life cycle from seed to seed production in one year.

Anodyne—An agent that relieves pain or promotes general comfort, usually externally.

Anorexiac—That which limits appetite.

Anthelmintic—Killing or expelling intestinal parasitic worms.

Antibiotic—In modern medicine, a substance that will kill disease-causing microorganisms.

Anticonvulsive—Preventing or controlling convulsions.

Antidiarrheal—Preventing or controlling diarrhea.

Anti-inflammatory—Controlling inflammation, a reaction of the body to injury or infection which is typically marked by swelling, redness, pain, heat, and other symptoms.

Antipyretic—An agent which reduces fever.

Antirheumatic—Easing the discomfort of or preventing rheumatism, a condition that causes inflammation and pain in the joints and muscles.

Antiscourbutic—Preventing the disease scurvy, caused by deficiency of vitamin C.

Antiseptic—Preventing sepsis, or putrefaction that results from bacterial infection; germ-killing.

Antispasmodic—Calming nervous and muscular spasms.

Antitussive—Controlling or preventing cough.

Aperient—An agent that causes a mild laxative effect.

Aphrodisiac—An agent which enhances sexual function.

Aromatic—Having a pleasant or spicy odor, a quality often used in medicinal preparations. A new form of herbal or plant treatment is called aromatherapy.

Astringent—Causing soft tissues to draw together, or pucker. Also, an agent that diminishes either external or internal secretions. Astringents are used externally in herbal medicine to check minor bleeding and internally to control diarrhea.

Axillary—Located or growing in the axil.

Axis—The central stalk of a compound leaf or flower cluster.

Bark—The outer covering of the trunk and branches of a tree, usually corky, papery, or leathery.

Berry—A fleshy fruit with more than one seed.

Biennial—Completing the life cycle in two years.

Blade – The broad, flat part of a leaf.

Blood Purifier—An old term for any substance that was supposed to cleanse the blood of impurities and toxic substances, or in spring tonic, "thin the blood" to restore or maintain good health.

Body trouble—A generic term for problems of the female reproductive system.

Bract—A modified and often scale-like leaf, usually located at the base of a flower, a fruit, or a cluster of flowers or fruits.

Bud—A young and undeveloped leaf, flower, or shoot, usually covered tightly with scales.

Bulb—A modified underground stem having one or more buds enclosed in fleshy modified leaves or scales, which supply nourishment when the bud or buds began a new period of growth. Onions and garlic are examples.

Capsule—A dry, thin-walled fruit containing two or more seeds and splitting along natural grooved lines at maturity.

Carcinogenic—Cancer-causing.

Cardiotonic—Tonic that helps keep the heart functioning normally.

Carminative—An agent which helps release stomach or intestinal gas.

Cathartic—An agent which acts to move the bowels. This term is often used to imply action harsher than that of a laxative.

Catkin—A compact and often drooping cluster of reduced, stalkless, and usually unisexual flowers.

Caustic—Any substance or chemical that causes a burn or burning sensation on the skin.

Colic—Acute abdominal pain, of or relating to the colon.

Complete flower—One having both stamens and pistils or male and female reproductive parts.

Compound leaf—A leaf whose blade is divided into three or more smaller leaflets.

Cone—A conical fruit consisting of seed-bearing, overlapping scales around a central axis.

Conifer—A cone-bearing tree of the

Pine family, usually evergreen.

Contraceptive—An agent which inhibits conception or aids in prevention of pregnancy.

Corm—A bulblike stem, differing usually from a true bulb in that it is solid and sends down a root when a new growing season begins.

Corolla—Collective term for the petals of a flower.

Counterirritant—An agent that causes local inflammation of an area (e.g., the skin) for the purpose of lessening the effects of inflammation in an underlying or adjacent area. Sometimes a counterirritant simply diverts attention from the pain of an inflammation elsewhere.

Crown—The mass of branches, twigs, and leaves at the top of a tree, with particular reference to its shape.

Cultivated—Planted and maintained by man.

Deciduous—Shedding leaves seasonally, and leafless for part of the year.

Decoction—An extract made by putting a plant or its parts in water, bringing the mixture to a boil, and allowing it to boil or simmer for a time. The liquid is then cooled and strained for use. More specifically, a decoction is a tea made of the roots and bark. Sometimes one tablespoon of the cut herb or powdered herb was boiled in approximately one cup of water for thirty minutes. This tea was allowed to stand for thirty minutes.

Demulcent—An agent which soothes an inflammation, especially an inflammation of the mucous membranes. This soothing action may be helpful in relieving coughs.

Dentifrice—An agent which aids in the cleaning of teeth.

Depurative—Another term for blood purifier or cleanser.

Diaphoretic—An agent which increases the amount of perspiration.

Discutient—An agent which aids in removal of tumors or diseased or dead tissue.

Distillation—In herbalism, a liquid made by condensing the vapor from a heated mixture of herbs and water.

Diuretic—An agent which aids in removing liquid from the body or increasing the urine flow.

Dropsy—Another word for edema or swelling due to fluid buildup in the extremities.

Drupe—A fleshy fruit with a central stonelike core containing one or more seeds.

Dysentery—An infection of the lower intestinal tract which produces pain, fever, and severe and sometimes bloody diarrhea.

Dysmenorrhea—Painful menstruation

Dyspepsia—An extremely upset stomach.

Elliptical—Elongately oval, about twice as long as wide, and broadest at the middle; like an ellipse.

Emmenagogue—An agent that regulates and induces normal menstruation.

Elixir—A liquid containing alcohol and a medicinal substance and sweetened, usually with sugar.

Emetic—An agent which causes or produces vomiting.

Emollient—An agent which softens or smoothes the skin or other exposed tissue.

Expectorant—An agent which facilitates the expulsion of phlegm from the respiratory tract by making the mucus less dry or sticky. Expectorants are sometimes given to help alleviate coughs or to ease bronchitis.

Extract—In Lumbee herbal practice, drawing the desired constituents from a plant by physical or chemical means.

Febrifuge—An agent that relieves fever.

Fibrous—A root system having roots all about the same size, with no single dominant root (taproot).

Fleshy fruit—A fruit with juicy or mealy pulp.

Floret—A "little flower"; specifically, the flowers in the finflorescenes (flower clusters) of daisies and other members of the composite family.

Flower—The reproductive structure of a tree or other plant, consisting of at least one pistil or stamen, and often including petals and sepals.

Fruit—The mature, fully developed ovary of a flower, containing one or more seeds.

Fumitory—An agent that relieves an ailment by using the smoke or fumes from burning material.

Fungicide—An agent that kills fungal growths.

Gland-dot—A tiny, dotlike gland or pore, usually secreting a fluid.

Gravel—Kidney or bladder stones.

Grippe—Severe cold that makes the bones ache.

Hemostat—An agent that stops or controls the blood flow.

Herb—A plant with soft, not woody stems, usually dying to the ground during winter.

Herbaceous—Having to do with herbs; specifically, having a non-woody stem that dies back after the growing season.

Herbalist (herb doctor or expert)—A collector or grower of herbs. An herb doctor is one who uses herbs to treat diseases and discomforts.

Homeopathy—A system of medicine that stresses the administration of very small doses of medicines that, when given to a healthy person, would produce symptoms of the disease. The system is based on the principle of "like cures like" (i.e, a fever-producing medication or treatment will combat a fever).

Husk—A usually dry outer covering, often composed of bracts, of a fruit or seed.

Hybrid—A plant or animal of mixed parentage, resulting from the interbreeding of two different species.

Hydragogue—An agent that produces watery stools; a strong laxative.

Inflorescence—A cluster of flowers growing together, rather than singly, on a stalk or stem. Depending on their shape or other characteristics such as the arrangement of flowers, inflorescences are called by many different names including flower-head, panicle, raceme, spike, or umbel.

Infusion—A medicinal fluid made by pouring boiling water on an herb (or herb parts) or adding a plant extract to boiled water; similar to a tea. More specifically, an infusion is a tea made with leaves and blossoms.

Insecticide—That which kills insects.

Intestinal Worm—Any of the various worms that can live as parasites in the human intestines; such an infestation is often called worms.

Irregular flower—A flower with petals of unequal size.

Irritant—An agent that causes inflammation.

Jaundice—Yellowing of the skin and other tissues caused by the presence of bile pigments (liver dysfunction).

Kidney stone—Small, hard stone that may form in the kidneys and cause intense pain. These stones are also called gravel.

Lanceolate—Shaped like a lance, several times longer than wide, pointed at the tip and broadest near the base.

Laxative—An agent that relieves constipation.

Leaf—A primary appendage of most higher plants. Bracts, bulb scales, petals, and sepals are often considered specialized leaves.

Leaflet—Division of a compound leaf; a small leaf.

Linear—Long, narrow, and parallel-sided.

Lobed—With the edge of the leaf deeply but not completely divided.

Mucilage—A gooey, sticky substance derived from seaweed and other plants and often used for its soothing action on skin and its adhesive properties.

Mucilaginous—Sticky, containing mucilage; in Lumbee herbal lore mucilaginous substances are used to soothe inflamed areas of the body.

Native—Occurring naturally in an area and not introduced by man; indigenous.

Needle—The very long and narrow leaf of pines an related trees.

Nervine—A medicinal preparation that is meant to stimulate and "tone up" the nervous system and thus give a feeling of healthy well-being. Also called nerve tonic.

Neuritis—Severe diabetes, or as Vernon Cooper, Lumbee healer, stated "sugar of the bone."

Node—The point on a shoot where a leaf, flower, or bud is attached.

Nutlet—One of several small, nutlike parts of a compound fruit, as in a sycamore; the hard inner core of some fruits, containing a seed and surrounded by softer flesh, as in the Sugarberry (Hackberry).

Nutritive—An agent that has both healing and nutritional properties.

Oblong—With nearly parallel edges.

Opposite—Leaves arranged along a twig or shoot in pairs, with one on each side, and not alternate or in whorls.

Ovate—Oval, with the broader end at the base.

Palmate—With leaflets attached directly to the end of the leafstalk and not arranged in rows along an axis; palmately compound; digitate.

Palmate-veined—With the principal veins arising from the end of the leafstalk and radiating toward the edge of the leaf, and not branching from a single midvein.

Panicle—A branched, compound flower cluster, with the individual clusters forming racemes, especially common in grasses.

Parallel-veined—With the veins running more or less parallel toward the tip of the leaf.

Parasiticide—An agent that kills internal and external parasites.

Paturifacient—An agent that induces the contractions of labor at childbirth.

Pectoral—An agent that affects the chest, lungs, or bronchial passages.

Pedunculicide—An agent which kills body lice.

Perennial—In botany, having a life cycle of more than two years.

Petal—One of a series of flower parts lying within the sepals and next to the stamens and pistil, often large and brightly colored.

Petiole—The leaf stem.

Pinnate—With leaflets arranged in two rows along an axis; pinnately compound.

Pinnate-veined—With the principal veins branching from a single midvein, and not arising from the end of he leafstalk and radiating toward the edge of the leaf.

Pith—The soft, spongy, innermost tissue in a stem.

Plaster—A medication applied externally by placing it over a body part and covering with a cloth or towel.

Plume—A featherlike plant part, as a single tuft of the dandelion seed head.

Pod—A dry, one-celled fruit, splitting along natural grooved lines, with thicker walls than a capsule.

Pollen—Minute grains containing the male germ cells and released by the stamens.

Poultice—A poultice is made of herbs and root, fitted for the disease and members afflicted, chopped small and boiled in water almost to a jelly. More specifically, a poultice is a moist, hot herb pack applied locally. Many healers would add a bit of bean meal, barley meal, or sweet suet. In addition, some healers would also mix the herb with cornmeal, Slippery Elm, or flaxseed to make a thick paste to be spread on a cloth to be applied to the affected area. They would boil the mix and spread it on a cloth and apply the cloth to the aggrieved place to ease pain, break sores, cool inflammations, dissolve hardness, or dissipate swelling.

Powder—In herbal medicine, crushed, dried plants or plant parts

Purgative—A strong laxative or cathartic.

Raceme—An inflorescence (flower cluster) consisting of stalked flowers arranged along the sides of a central stalk or rachis.

Regular flower—A flower with petals all of equal size.

Resin (rosin)—A plant secretion, often aromatic, that is insoluble in water but soluble in ether or alcohol (i.e., pine resin or rosin).

Rhizome—A horizontal, underground stem, often with thickened portions holding stored food for the plant's growth. It can send out both aerial shoots and shoots into the ground.

Root—The part of a plant, usually below ground, that anchors it and absorbs water and dissolved nutrients for the plant's maintenance and growth.

Rubefaciant—A term that means "making redder"; having the action of a counter-irritant.

Salve—Salves and ointments are prepared by boiling the plants in water until only a small amount of liquid remains. The liquid is then strained and combined with hog, deer, or cow fat, or in the present day, a commercial product such as Rosebud Salve or Vaseline Petroleum Jelly.

Saponin—A plant chemical of the glycoside group that produces froth and foam when mixed in water.

Scabies—A highly contagious skin disease that causes extreme itching. A small insect that burrows beneath the skin causes this "seven year" or "mad" itch.

Scrofula—Tuberculosis of the lymph glands.

Sedative—An agent that acts on the central nervous system to produce sleep.

Seed—A fertilized and mature ovule, containing an embryonic (baby) plant.

Shoot—A young, actively growing twig or stem.

Shrub—A woody plant, smaller than a tree, with several stems or trunks arising from a single base; a bush.

Simple leaf—A leaf with a single blade, not compound or composed of leaflets.

Stimulant—An agent that makes a body organ or system work faster.

Sudorfic—An agent that works to increase perspiration.

Tea—A dried substance, usually a plant or plant part, steeped or placed in hot water for drinking. Many medicinal plants are administered as teas, or infusions. (See infusion.)

Thorn—A sharp, rigid projection on a plant; a woody plant bearing thornlike briers or spines such as the Hawthorn of the rose family.

Tincture—A medication that has its medicinal agent dissolved in alcohol. More specifically, a tincture is an extraction of herbs in vinegar or alcohol. Some Lumbee healers in later years used apple cider vinegar.

Tonic—An agent that is used to give strength to a system or that which restores or maintains health in the whole body or its individual organs.

Toothed—With an edge finely divided into short, toothlike projections.

Toxic—Poisonous.

Trifoliate—Having a compound leaf with three leaflets.

Trunk—The major woody stem of a tree.

Tuber—Thickened portion of an underground stem, as the common white potato.

Tubular—With the petals partly united to form a tube.

Umbel—A type of flower cluster with a flattish top, in which the individual stalks radiate from a central point like the ribs of an umbrella.

Vein—One of the riblike vessels in the blade of a leaf.

Vesicant—A counterirritant strong enough in some cases to cause blistering.

Wash—A local liquid medical preparation for external use; lotion.

Weak back—Refers to the range of problems stemming from a weakness of the spine, including backache, lower back pain, sore muscles, and spinal problems.

Whorled—Arranged along a twig or shoot in groups of three or more at each node.

Wing—A thin, flat, dry, shelflike projection on a fruit or seed, or along the side of a twig.

Wood—The hard, fibrous inner tissue of the trunk and branches of a tree or shrub.

Ailments and Herbs Used in Treatment

Cancer (External)
Spotted Wintergreen (Chimaphila), Snapdragon (Antirrhinum magus), Adder's Tongue (Erythronium americanum), Heal-all (Prunella vulgaris), Jimson (Datura stramonium), Poke (Phytolacca americana)

Cancer (Internal)
Mayapple (Podophyllum peltatum), Persimmon (Diospryos virginiana). Queen Anne's Lace (Daucus carota), Goldenseal (Hydrastis canadensis)

Circulatory System (Edema)
Yellow Birch (Betula nigra), Goldenseal (Hydrastis canadensis), Mullein (Verbascum thapsus), Spotted Wintergreen (Chimaphila maculata), Holly Bush (Ilex opaca)

Circulatory System (Heart)
Butterfly Bush (Asclepias tuberosa), Wild Ginger (Asarum canadense), Calamus (Acorus calamus), Hawthorn (Crataegus), Heartleaf (Hexastylis arifolia)

Circulatory System (Hemorrhage)
Goldenseal (Hydrastis canadensis)

Circulatory System (Hypertension and Hypotension)
Red Tag Alder (Alnus rugosa), Queen Anne's Lace (Daucus carota), Hawthorn (Crataegus), Garlic (Allium sativum), Mistletoe (Phoradendron serotinum), Black Gum (Nyssa sylvatica), Wild Garlic (Allium vineale), Onion (Allium cepa)

Digestion (Colic and Flatulence)
Black Gum (Nyssa sylvatica), Star Grass (Panicum), Spotted Horsemint (Monarda punctata), Fennel (Foeniculum vulgare), Queen Anne's Lace (Daucus carota), Calamus (Acorus calamus), Catmint (Nepeta cataria)

Digestion (Diarrhea)
Whiteweed (Antennaria neglecta), Star Grass (Panicum), Blackhaw (Viburnum prunifolium), Dewberry (Rubus hispidus), Black Gum (Nyssa sylvatica), Broom Grass (Andropogon glomeratus), Ball Root (Psoralea pedunculata), Comfrey (Symphytum officianale), Queen Anne's Lace (Daucus carota), Wild Cherry (Prunus virginiana), Wild Strawberry (Fragaria vesca), Sweet Gum (Liquidambar styraciflua), Poke (Phyolacco americana), Holly Bush (Ilex opaca), Oak (Quercus laevis) or (Quercus phellos)

111

Digestion (Dysentery)

Butterfly Bush (Asclepias tuberosa), Persimmon (Diospyros virginiana), Red Oak (Quercus maxima), Comfrey (Symphytum officianale), Fireweed (Epilobium angustifolium), Wintergreen (Gaultheria procumbens), Alumroot (Heuchera americana), Star Grass (Panicum)

Digestion (Emetic) Induce vomiting

Gallberry (Ilex glabra), American Holly or Yaupon (Ilex vomitoria)

Digestion (General Stomach Trouble)

Wild Ginger (Asarum canadense), Wood Betony (Pedicularis canadensis), Pine (Pinus echinata), Sampson's Snakeroot (Aristolochia serpentaria), Horsemint (Monarda punctata), Peach (Prunus persica), Queen Anne's Lace (Daucus carota), Sage (Salvia officinalis), Goldenrod (Solidago virgaurea), Alumroot (Heuchera americana), Catmint (Nepeta cataria), Pipsissewa (Chinaphila umbellate), False Solomon's Seal (Smilacina racemosa)

Digestion (Indigestion)

Sycamore Tree (Platanus occidentalis), Persimmon (Diospyros virginiana), Poplar Tree (Liriodendron tulipifera), Spearmint (Mentha spicata), Peppermint (Mentha piperita), Lemon Balm (Melissa officinalis), Red Oak (Quercus maxima), Wintergreen (Gaultheria procumbens), Queen Anne's Lace (Daucus carota), Goldenseal (Hydrastis canadensis), Carolina Vetch (Vicia caroliniana), Gall of the Earth (Prenanthes trifoliolata), Longleaf Pine (Pinus palustris), Pecan Tree (Carya illinoensis)

Digestion (Laxative)

Mayapple (Podophyllum peltatum), Butterfly Bush (Asclepias tuberosa), Yellow Birch (Betula lutea), Slippery Elm (Ulmus fulva), Butternut (Juglans cinerea), Dandelion (Taraxacum officinale), Purge Grass (Sisyrinchium), Dogwood (Cornus florida)

Digestion (Mouth Sores)

Red Oak (Quercus maxima), Goldenseal (Hydrastis canadensis)

Digestion (Nausea)

Indian Corn (Zea mays)

Digestion (Parasites or Worms)

Poplar Tree (Liriodendron tulipifera), Black Gum (Nyssa sylvatica), Chinaberry (Melia azedarach), Queen Anne's Lace (Daucus carota), Garlic (Allium sativum), Wild Cherry (Prunus virginiana), Indian Pink (Spigelia marilandica), Rue (Ruta graveolens), Jerusalem Oak (Chenopodium ambrosiodides), Poke (Phytolacca americana)

Digestion (Pyorrhea or Bleeding Gums)

Red Tag Alder (Alnus ruaosa), Sweet Gum (Liquidambar styraciflua), False Solomon's Seal (Smilacina racemosa)

Digestion (Stomach and Mouth Ulcer)

Yellow Root (Berberis vulgaris), Sourwood Tree (Oxydendrum arboreum), Calamus (Acorus calamus), Red Myrtle (Myrica cerifera), Poke (Phytolacca americana), Shrub Yellow Root (Xanthoriza simplicissima), Garlic (Allium sativum)

Digestion (Teeth Cleaning)

American Beech Tree (Fagus grandifolia), Sage (Salvia officinalis), Wild Strawberry (Fragaria vesca), Black Gum (Nyssa sylvatica)

Digestion (Teething and Toothache)

Pennyroyal (Hedeoma pulegioidodes), Red Tag Alder (Alnus rugosa), Wintergreen (Gaultheria procumbens), Garlic (Allium sativum), Catmint (Nepeta cataria), Rotten Wood, Field Thistle (Sonchus asper)

Digestion (Thrush) Thrash
Persimmon (Diospyros virginiana), Red Tag Alder (Alnus rugosa), Sage (Salvia officinalis)

Endocrine, Metabolic and Nutritional Disorders (Diabetes and Neuritis) Neuritis is severe diabetes called "sugar of the bone" by the Lumbee
Bear Grass (Yucca filmentosa), Sumac (Rhus typhina), Saint John the Worker (Hypericum hypericoides), Ground Huckleberry (Gaylussacia dumosa), He-huckleberry (Gaylussacia frondosa), Ragweed (Ambrosia artemisiifolia), Old Timey Garlic (Asclepias rubra), Pipsissewa (Chimaphila umbellata), Rabbit Tobacco (Gnaphalium obtusifolium), Bitterweed (Helenium amarum), Longleaf Pine (Pinus palustris), Possum Haw (Viburnum nudum)

Endocrine, Metabolic, and Nutritional Disorders (Gout)
Mullein (Verbascum thapsus)

Eyes
Fennel (Foeniculum vulgare), Goldenseal (Hydrastis canadensis), Eyebright (Euphrasia officinalis)

General Medicine (Blood Purifiers, Tonics, and Circulation Aids)
Pennyroyal (Hedeoma pulegioides), Hawthorn (Crataegus), Daisy (Bellis perennis) Sassafras (Sassafras officinale)

General Wellness Tonics
Purple Coneflower (Echinacea angustifolia), Lemon Balm (Melissa officinalis), Sage (Salvia officinalis), Goldenseal (Hydrastis canadensis), Horehound (Marrubum vulgare), Saint John the Worker (Hypericum hypericoides), Rabbit Tobacco (Gnaphalium obtusifolium), Sassafras (Sassfras albidum), White Bloodroot (Liatris regimentis), Poke (Phytolacca americana), Wild Tansy (Solidago odora), Tansy (Tanacetum vulgare), Shrub Yellow Root (Xanthorhiza simplicissima), Sugarberry (Celtis laevigata), Boneset (Eupatorium perfoliatum), Spearmint (Mentha spicata), Peppermint (Mentha piperita), Fennel (Foeniculum vulgare)

Infections and Parasitic Diseases (Chicken Pox)
Sassafras (Sassafras officinale)

Infections and Parasitic Diseases (Diphtheria)
Goldenrod (Solidago virgaurea)

Infections and Parasitic Diseases (General Infections)
Pipsissewa (Chimaphila umbellata), Oak (Quercus laevis)

Infections and Parasitic Diseases (Malaria)
Magnolia (Magnolia grandiflora), Dogwood (Cornus florida)

Infections and Parasitic Diseases (Measles)
Holly Bush (Ilex opaca), Sage (Salvia officinalis), Sassafras (Sassafras officinale), Indian Corn (Zea mays)

Infections and Parasitic Diseases (Ringworm)
Yellow Birch (Betula lutea), Pipsissewa (Chimaphila umbellata)

Infections and Parasitic Diseases (Scabies)
Wicky (Kalmia carolinina), Indian Corn (Zea mays)

Infections and Parasitic Diseases (Tonsillitus)
Queen Anne's Lace (Daucus carota)

Infections and Parasitic Diseases (Tuberculosis)
Witch Hazel (Hamamelis virginiana), Goldenseal (Hydrastis canadensis)

Infections and Parasitic Diseases (Whooping Cough)
Pennyroyal (Hedeoma pulegioides),

Peach (Prunus persica), Fireweed (Epilobium angusiifolium), Cedar (Juniperus virginiana), Indian Hemp (Apocynum cannabinum)

Injury/Poisons/Toxins (Snake Bites)
Jerusalem Oak (Chenopodium abrosioides), Common Milkweed (Asclepias syriaca), Rattlesnake Root (Agave virginica), Poplar Tree (Liriodendron tulipifera), Purple Coneflower (Echinacea angustifolia), Pennyroyal (Hedeoma pulegioides), Chinaberry (Melia azedarach), Garlic (Allium sativum), Jacob's Coat (Perilla frutenscens), Thistle (Cirsium repandum) (Carduus repandus)

Injury/Poisons/Toxins (Tick Bites)
Jimson (Datura stramonium)

Injury/Poisons/Toxins (Wounds)
Graybeard (Cladrastis lutea), Comfrey (Symphytum officinale)

Muscle, Skeletal, and Joint Disorders (Arthritis or Rheumatism)
Slippery Elm (Ulmus fulva), Hickory Tree (Carya ovata), Red Bud (Cercis canadensis), Yellow Birch (Betula lutea), Wild Yam (Dioscorea villosa), Pipsissewa (Chimaphila umbellata), Poke (Phytolacca americana), Rheumatism Plant (Lycopodium flabelliforme), Indian Hemp (Apocynum cannabinum)

Muscle, Skeletal, and Joint Disorders (Backache)
Blunt Manna Grass (Glyceria obtusa), Beech Tree (Fagus grandifolia), Horsemint (Monarda punctata), Star Grass (Panicum), Carolina Vetch (Vicia caroliniana), Pipsissewa (Chimaphila umbellata), Sampson's Snakeroot (Aristolochia serpentaria), Devil's Shoestring (Tephrosia virginiana), Mark (Bidens frondosa), Ironweed (Sida rhombifolia)

Muscle, Skeletal, and Joint Disorders (Spasms)
Broom Grass (Andropogon glomeratus), Wild Touch-Me-Not (Impatiens spp.), Dogwood (Cornus florida), Mullein (Verbascum thapsus), Poke (Phytolacca americana)

Muscle, Skeletal, and Joint Disorders (Sprains)
Red Shank (Ceanothus americanus), Oak (Quercus laevis), Mullein (Verbascum thapsus)

Muscle, Skeletal, and Joint Disorders (Swellings)
Mullein (Verbascum thapsus), Red Shank (Ceanothus americanus), Oak (Quercis laevis), Rosinweed (Silphium compositum)

Nervous System (Analgesics) Pain Relievers
Pipsissewa (Chimaphila umbellata), Sweet Gum (Liquidambar styraciflua)

Nervous System (Sedative) Relaxation or Sleep Inducement
Sourwood (Oxydendrum arboreum), Peach (Prunus persica), Wild Cherry (Prunus virginiana), Passionflower (Passiflora incarnata)

Reproductive System (Aphrodisiac or Sex Tonic)
Sage (Salvia officinalis), Dog-Fennel (Eupatorium capillifolium), Pepper Grass (Lepidum virginicum)

Reproductive System (Female Sexual Organ and Menstrual Disorders)
Sourwood Tree (Oxydendrum arboreum), Persimmon (Diospyros virginiana), Star Grass (Panicum), Blackhaw (Viburnum prunifolim), Wild Ginger (Asarum canadense), Sampson's Snakeroot (Aristolochia serpentaria), Horsemint (Monarda punctata) Lemon Balm (Melissa officinalis), Pennyroyal (Hedeoma pulegioides), Alumroot (Heuchera americana), Mullein (Verbascum thapsus), Catmint (Nepeta cataria), Passionflower (Passiflora incarnata), Pipsissewa (Chimaphila umbellta),

Queen's Delight (Stillingia sylvatica), Partridge Berry (Mitchella repens), Wild Cherry (Prunus virginiana), Oak (Quercus laevis), Devil's Shoestring (Rephrosia virginiana), Yellow Root (Xanthoriza simplicissima), Sawtooth Palmetto (Serenoa repens)

Reproductive System (Male Sexual Organ and Gland Disorders)
Dog-Fennel (Eupatorium capillifolium), Pepper Grass (Lepidum virginicum), Shrub Yellow Root (Xanthoriza simplicissima), Sawtooth Palmetto (Serenoa repens)

Reproductive System (Pregnancy and Childbirth)
Red Tag Alder (Alnus rugosa), Wild Yam (Dioscorea villosa), Wild Cherry (Prunus virginiana), Sumac (Rhus typhina), Sage (Salvia officinalis), Tansy (Tanacetum vulgare)

Reproductive System (Veneral Disease)
Sumac (Rhus typhina), Queen's Delight (Stillingia sylvatica), Devil's Shoestring (Rephrosia virginiana)

Respiratory System (Allergies)
Bitterweed (Helenium amarum)

Respiratory System (Asthma)
Black Haw (Viburnum prunifolium), Red Oak (Quercus maxima), Fireweed (Epilobium angustifolium), Honeysuckle (Lonicera perclymenum), Nettle (Urtica dioica), Coltsfoot (Tussilago farfara), Mullein (Verbascum thapsus), Indian Tobacco (Lobelia inflata), Wild Tobacco (Nicotiana rustica), Rabbit Tobacco (Gnaphalium obtusifolium), Bitterweed (Helenium amarum), Poke (Phytolacca americana), Indian Hemp (Apocynum cannabinum), Sawtooth Palmetto (Serenoa repens)

Respiratory System (Bronchitis)
Peach (Prunus persica), Comfrey (Symphytum officinale), Wild Cherry (Prunus virginiana)

Respiratory System (Colds)
Pennyroyal (Hedeoma pulegioides), Chinaberry (Melia azedarach), Wild Plum (Prunus americana), Wild Ginger (Asarum canadense), Horsemint (Monarda punctata), Boneset (Eupatorium perfoliatum), Lemon Balm (Melissa officinalis), Wintergreen (Gaultheria procumbens), Spotted Wintergreen (Chimaphila maculata), Garlic (Allium satvium), Mullein (Verbascum thapsus), Catmint (Nepeta cataria), Sage (Salvia officinalis), Queen Anne's Lace (Daucus carota), Horehound (Marrubium vulgare), Rabbit Tobacco (Gnaphalium obtusifolium), Longleaf Pine (Pinus palustris), Sassafras (Sassafras officinale), Purge Grass (Sisyrinchium), Goldenrod (Solidago virgaurea), Indian Corn (Zea mays)

Respiratory System (Cough)
Star Grass (Panicum), Poplar Tree (Liriodendron tulipifera), Comfrey (Symphytum officinale), Elderberry (Sambucus nigra), Honeysuckle (Lonicera periclymenum), Daisy (Bellis perennis), Wild Cherry (Prunus virginiana), Coltsfoot (Tussilago farfara), Wild Plum (Prunus americana)

Respiratory System (Influenza)
Boneset (Eupatorium perfoliatum), Horehound (Marrubium vulgare), Holly Bush (Ilex opaca), Sassafras (Sassafras officinale)

Respiratory System (Pneumonia)
Queen Anne's Lace (Daucus carota), Wood's Mullein (Elephantopus), Longleaf Pine (Pinus palustris), Purge Grass (Sisyrinchium)

Skin (Antiseptic and Cleanser)
Lemon Balm (Melissa officinalis), Beech Tree (Fagus grandifolia), Red Oak (Quercus maxima), Graybeard (Cladrastis lutea), Alumroot (Heuchera americana), Pipsissewa (Chinaphila umbellata), Cattail (Typha latifolia)

Skin (Boils, Sores, Cuts and Burns)
Ball Root (Psoralea pedunculata), Adam and Eve Root (Aplectrum hyemale), Mayapple (Podophyllum peltatum), Witch Hazel (Hamamelis virginiana), Indian Corn (Zea mays), Moss (Cladina subtneuis), Milkweed (Euphorbia maculata), Catmint (Nepeta cataria), Bay Tree (Persea borbonia), Fire Root (Pteridium aquilinum), Oak (Quercus laevis), Comfrey (Symphytum officinale), Rat's Tail (Aloe bardadensis)

Skin (Dandruff)
Sage (Salvia officinalis), Wild Plum (Prunus americana)

Skin (Eczema)
Daisy (Bellis perennis)

Skin (General skin disorders)
Bear Grass (Yucca filamentosa), Witch Hazel (Hamamelis virginiana), Lemon Balm (Melissa officinalis), Beech Tree (Fagus grandifolia), Yellow Birch (Betula lutea), Broom Grass (Andropogon glomeratus), Red Oak (Quercus maxima), Spotted Wintergreen (Chimaphila maculata), Sage (Salvia officinalis), Adder's Tongue (Erythonium americanum), Elderberry (Sambucus canadensis), Wild Cherry (Prunus virginiana), Poplar Tree (Liriodendron tulipifera), Poke (Phytolacca americana), Solomon's Seal (Polygonatum biflorum), Polypodium Fern (Polypodium polypodiodes), Ironweed (Sida rhombifolia), Mullein (Verbascum thapsus), Yellow Root (Xanthoriza simplicissima)

Skin (Hives)
Red Tag Alder (Alnus rugosa)

Skin (Itching)
Sourwood Tree (Oxydendrum arboreum), Holly Bush (Ilex opaca), Wicky (Kalmia carolina), Red Myrtle (Myrica cerifera)

Skin (Jaundice)
Collard (Brassica oleracea), Broom Grass (Andropogon glomeratus), Yellow Root (Xanthorrihiza apifolia), Star Grass (Panicum), Dandelion (Taraxacum officinale), Yellow Jessamine (Gelsemium sempervirens)

Skin (Lotion)
Elderberry (Sambacus nigra)

Skin (Pimples)
Milkweed (Euphorbia maculata), Ironweed (Sida rhombifolia)

Skin (Poison Ivy or Poison Oak)
Red Oak (Quercus maxima), Graybeard (Cladrastis lutea), Milkweed (Euphorbia maculata)

Skin (Rash)
Sage (Salvia officinalis)

Skin (Sunburn)
Sumac (Rhus typhina), Wild Strawberry (Fragaria vesca)

Skin (Swellings and Contusions)
Sycamore (Platanus occidentalis), Peach (Prunus persica), Comfrey (Symphytum officinale), Wild Ginger (Asarum canadense), Queen Anne's Lace (Daucus carota), Daisy (Bellis perennis), Cultivated Tobacco (Nicotiana tabacum), Poke (Phytolacca americana), Elderberry (Sambucus nigra), Mullein (Verbascum thapsus)

Skin (Warts)
Dandelion (Taraxacum officinale)

Symptoms (Chills)
Dogwood (Cornus florida), Red Oak (Quercus maxima)

Symptoms (Fever)
Poplar Tree (Liriodendron tulipifera), Collard (Brassica oleracea), Boneset (Eupatorium perfoliatum), Lemon Balm (Melissa officinalis), Holly Bush (Ilex opaca), Broom Grass (Andropogon glomeratus), Witch Hazel (Hamamelis virginiana), Red Tag Alder (Alnus rugosa), Peach (Prunus

persica), Dogwood (Cornus florida), Sumac (Rhus typhina), Spotted Wintergreen (Chimaphila maculata), Wild Strawberry (Fragaria vesca), Catmint (Nepeta cataria), Heal-all (Prunella vulgaris), Pokeweed (Phytolacco americana), Dog-Fennel (Euptorium capillifolium), Bitterweed (Helenium amarum), Fever Grass (Heterotheca graminfolia), Gourd (Lagenaria siceraria), Jacob's Coat (Perilla frutenscens), Onion (Allium cepa), Longleaf Pine (Pinus palustris), Wild Cherry (Prunus serotina), Wild Willow (Salix nigra), Sassafras (Sassafras officinale), Indian Corn (Zea mays)

Symptoms (Headache)
Lemon Balm (Melissa officinalis), Pennyroyal (Hedeoma pulegioides), Mark (Bidens frondosa)

Symptoms (Pain)
Red Tag Alder (Alnus rugosa), White Bloodroot (Liatris regimentis)

Symptoms (Sore Throat)
Boneset (Euptorium perfoliatum), Witch Hazel (Hamamelis virginiana), Goldenseal (Hydrastis canadensis), Alumroot (Heuchera americana)

Urinary System (Bladder)
Sumac (Rhus typhina), Wild Yam (Dioscorea villosa), Goldenrod (Solidago virgaurea), Wild Plum (Prunus americana)

Urinary System (Kidney)
Pumpkin (Cucurbita pepo), Fireweed (Epilobium angustifolium), Wild Plum (Prunus americana), Dandelion (Taraxacum officinale), Pipsissewa (Chimaphila umbellata), Saint John the Worker (Hypericum hypericoides), Sumac (Rhus typhina), Poplar Tree (Liriodendron tulipifera), Longleaf Pine (Pinus palustris), Wild Cherry (Prunus virginiana), Oak (Quercus laeves), Devil's Shoestring (Rephrosia virginiana), Indian Hemp (Apocynum cannabium)

Urinary System (Kidney Stones or Gravel)
Queen Anne's Lace (Daucus carota), Indian Corn (Zea mays), Coat Ticklers (Ergrostis spectabilis), Saint John the Worker (Hypericum hypericoides), Bugle Plant (Sarracenia purpurea), Pepper Grass (Lepidium virginicum)

Urinary System (Urinary Disorders)
Queen Anne's Lace (Daucus carota), Black Gum (Nyssa sylvatica), Wild Yam (Dioscorea villosa), Elderberry (Sambucus nigra), Honeysuckle (Lonicera perclymenum), Nettle (Urtica dioica), Flax (Linum usitatissimum)

Veterinary (Animal Tonic)
Pipsissewa (Chimaphila umbellata)

Veterinary (Fishing)
Gourd (Lagenaria siceraria), Devil's Shoestring (Tephrosia virginiana), Black Walnut (Juglans nigra)

Veterinary (Intestinal Parasites)
Chinaberry (Melia azedarach), Poke (Phyolacca americana), Wild Cherry (Prunus virginiana), Castor (Ricinua communis)

Veterinary (Laxative)
Chinaberry (Melia azedarach)

Veterinary (Snake Bite)
Jerusalem Oak (Chenopodium ambrosioides), Milkweed (Asclepias spp.), Rattlesnake Root (Agave virginica), Poplar Tree (Liriodendron tulipifera), Purple Coneflower (Echinacea angustifolia), Black Snakeroot (Euphorbia), Sheepburr (Xanthium strumarium)

Voice (Lost Voice)
Red Oak (Quercus maxima)

Appendix A: Interviews with Healers and Elders

Woodrow Cooper

The Oglala Lakota (western Siouan or Sioux band) begin and end all their ceremonies with the traditional phrase "Mitakuye Oyasin" or "All my relations" ("we are all related"). This phrase not only refers to an extended family, tribe, or the brotherhood of mankind, but how we are interconnected and intertwined with each other and to our natural world.

Wales, the grandfather in the book *The Education of Little Tree*, by Forrest Carter, also comments that the word "kin (relation)" has been corrupted down through the years to just mean a blood relative. He asserted that "kin" really means beloved ones or those with whom (or what) we hold a deep understanding. It's an interesting fact that many Lumbee, when acknowledging another Lumbee, will greet them by calling them cuz' (cousin), sis, unc, or pa (for an older man), even though they are not related to that individual.

Mr. Vernon Cooper was blessed with many "kinfolks," related and nonrelated. In the inter-

viewing process, we were able to talk to a few of his blood relations such as Ms. Rosie Lee Cooper, his widow; Mr. Sparks Cooper, his brother; Ms. Margaret Cooper, his sister-in-law; Woodrow Cooper, his nephew; and other non-related kin.

I Can See Far Down the Mountain

I can see far down the mountain,
Where I wandered many years,
Oftentimes hindered in my journey,
With a ghost of doubt and fears!

Broken vows and disappointment,
Thickly sprinkle along my way,
But I have found a richer treasure,
One that does not fade away!

For I am dwelling on the mountain,
That is where I ever will abide,
For I have tasted life's pure river,
And my soul is satisfied!

Well, is this not the land of Beulah,
Blessed, Blessed land of light,
Where the flowers bloom forever,
And the sky is always bright!

Vernon Cooper

Reproduced with permission of Rosie Lee Cooper

Rosie Lee Cooper, who was married to Vernon Cooper for thirty-

119

two years, said that having people come into the house was "a little rough sometimes, but he helped a lot of people." She said she understood that was his calling. She said she would go to the woods to gather medicine or go with him to gather it: "He always wanted someone to go with him to get it." Ms. Rosie added that she is "diabetic and he helped me with that." Before he died, Mr. Vernon began to "grow herbs around in pots to help people, but the herbs have all died now." She commented that he would relax by going fishing; "He loved to go fishing." She also stated that Mr. Vernon never treated himself.

Mr. Sparks Cooper was Mr. Vernon's older brother. "I worked in Hastings and he worked in the woods. So we didn't see each other that much," Mr. Sparks said, "My mother learnt Vernon. He was a pretty good doctor. He dug herbs and made that medicine.... Vernon was in the herb medicine a good while." Mr. Sparks added, "A doctor up in Raleigh tried his best to get Vernon to go work with him. The doctor told him, you've got experience that we don't have." Vernon told him, "'I gotten too old to think about doing that now.' He didn't go, but he had a chance."

Mr. Sparks recalled, "I had some kind of breaking out on my foot. Gerald and I went to Vernon's. Both of us had bad feet. He watched as Vernon boiled those roots, you know, and poured something out in two or three different bottles. He bathed my feet and them scales come off of it and I could walk good. Gerald, the man that was with me, said, 'That man put a spell on you.' He wouldn't let him [Vernon] treat it. He died with bad feet, but mine healed up."

Ms. Margaret, Mr. Sparks' wife, commented, "He could really make stuff to help you, now. I was really hurting in under my breast, up under my shoulder and all in there. I thought I might have cancer in my breast the way it was hurting. I went up there and I couldn't tell you what he put on it, but it burned. It really burned, but all that left out and I ain't been bothered with that since."

Mr. Sparks added, "It would have been nice if someone would have taken that up. He carried a lot of experience to the grave with him. Our older brother, Burris, had pneumonia. Vernon fixed up some medicine and Burris starting coughing all of that yellow stuff up."

Woodrow Cooper was a nephew of Mr. Vernon Cooper, Lumbee healer. Mr. Woodrow also shared a deep understanding and a special friendship with Mr. Vernon. In this interview, Woodrow shares special memories and stories about being healed and his first hand accounts of healings he witnessed.

L.O.—Loretta Oxendine, interviewer

W.C.—Woodrow Cooper, nephew of Vernon Cooper

M.C.—Margaret Cooper, Woodrow Cooper's mother

L.O.—You're a nephew of Mr. Vernon. I was told that you stayed around him a lot.

W.C.—Well, he stayed next door to me right here. He wanted me to help with medicine and all. I wish so many times had a' been, but I weren't. He's made a lot of medicines for me. I've been in the woods and helped him get herbs, but I thought nothing would ever happen to him. He's one of the best doctors I've ever met. Any disease, he had an herb he could go and get. I've been with him in the woods to get them and he would stop and point. That's a Bloodroot and that's the Yellow Root or Devil's Shoestring. I would go dig it up. I never did get interested in it enough to go do it myself, but he could take the doctor's medicine from town and redo it. I've seen him take aspirin and grape juice and redo it for a bad stomach. It got better, just that quick. My oldest child would vomit real bad. She got dehydrated. The doctors couldn't do nothing for her and I took her to him. You could give her water and before you could get the glass back, she would throw it up in the floor. I went over there and he went in the kitchen and came back with a glass with something in it. About that much (points to half of index finger). He gave it to her and told Aunt Rosie Lee to go get her something to eat. She got her something to eat and she kept it down. I mean she was ready to eat. I ask him later, "Unc, what did you give my child?" [He said,] "Well I was going to the kitchen, I ask the Lord what to give her. All he told me was aspirin and grape juice."

L.O.—Just aspirin and grape juice.

W.C.—A small amount of grape juice and aspirin. She had dehydrated and that's all he did for her. Just things like that he could do. I didn't have to carry her back to the doctor. There was no need to. Five minutes after he gave her that, she was better. There was different salves he would make. He would go to town and buy stuff and make his from that, but I didn't know how to mix it up. He wouldn't have to examine you to tell you what was wrong with you. My wife has a hiatal hernia. He didn't know it and I know he didn't know it. One day I came in his house and said, "Unc, how you doin'?" and sat on the couch. She

walked up and asked, "Unc, how are you feelin'?" and she reached out to grab his hand, but he didn't turn her hand aloose. He said, "What are you doin' walking around with all that pain in your body?" She looked at him. He took his two fingers and stuck them right there on that hernia. He said, "You've got a lot of pain right there." The doctors hadn't been long told her that.

My daddy went to him. He couldn't get off the bed. He thought his back was out of whack. My momma would have to take his feet off the bed and put them on the floor. We took him in the car and took him down to Uncle Vernon's and Uncle Vernon examined his back and said, "Son, there's not a thing wrong with your back." Of course, my daddy got upset about that. He said, turn over. We got him turned over on his back. Uncle Vernon said again, "There's nothing wrong with your back." He stuck his fingers in his groin right there. My daddy liked to come up off the bed. It's your glands and not your back, and he rubbed him or done something to him.

L.O.—And, he was all right.

W.C.—Yes, it was affecting him like it was his back. We went in the car and come home. I knew personally some older men who had lost their nature [erectile dysfunction]. I went to the woods with him and he would take Blood Root and Yellow Root, and he called it Devil's Shoestring. It had a long root on it. He could make an herb out of that, that changed their life. Many a person wanted to buy it. He would say, "No, it's a gift from God, I can't sell it." I known him to use it with a lot of older men. I known them to use it and then want to buy it. He would say, "I will doctor you. I will help you, but I can't sell it to you. It's not for sale."

L.O.—So what you are saying is that he wouldn't take any money.

W.C.—If you gave him a gift he would, but if you told him it was something you were paying him for, he wouldn't have it.

L.O.—So, there was no charge.

W.C.—If you said here's a gift for helping me, that's fine, but if you asked him about pay he would say, "I don't charge." I seen him do that so many a time. There's a boy, Lieutenant Governor Green's assistant, was suffering from the effects of Agent Orange; he had come in contact with it in Vietnam. The upper part of his body had black sores all over. Mr. Vernon fixed something for him and I went with him to Raleigh, to the capital, to take it to him. He treated that boy and he had such results from it.

Do you see that worm base over there? As a gift, Uncle Vernon loved to fish, it's made out of cinderblock. That boy sent someone down here to build Mr. Vernon that worm base as a gift for helping him out.

Another thing Uncle Vernon could do is tell your heart. He could tell your mind. I seen him do this because there was a young lady come to him in trouble. She had been cheating on her husband. She was sick. She come to him crying and wanting help. They walked in the back room. She needed something for her nerves. He asked her, "Do you want me to help you?" She said, "Yes, I want you to help me." He replied, "Well, quit cheating on your husband." She looked at him and started crying, and she was going to deny what he said. He said, "You want me to help you, if you do, I'll help you, but you're going to have to do what I tell you to do. This is what you've been doing." She admitted what she had been doing. He actually told her, her heart. There was nothing wrong with her body, it was her mind and what she had been doing. Just by talking to her, by her coming in, he told her what was wrong. He could not only work with herbs, if you went to him with a problem, he could tell you what was wrong. I asked him, "Unc, how did you do that?" He said, "I don't know. The Lord just directed me. It was a gift that God gave me."

He told me that he wanted me to go with him and wanted to learn me. Of course, I weren't interested. I said it to myself. I didn't tell him that, but I was saying that to myself. I ain't interested in that. I don't care about it. I would go with him to get herbs, but I weren't interested in how you put them together.

L.O.—Do you think he could have passed his gift to you?

W.C.—My great-grandmother passed it to him. The gift, he told me many a time, couldn't be passed on, but he would learn me what to do with herbs. But he said, the gift would end with him. He said, I can't pass that on. He had the gift of being able to hold your hand and tell you where you was hurting at, I couldn't get that. She told him and he told me that he was the last one to have that gift. The gift ended in our family. Now, as far as somebody else outside our family, it might have, but I never run across nobody that could do it. I got a problem with my knee right now. The doctor said, I know there's a medical term, but he said water, so I could understand, in between my leg bone and knee bone. I was supposed to have surgery on it today, but if he was living I wouldn't need that surgery.

Me and my brother was playing one day at the tobacco barn and I hit him right on the muscle of his arm. I knocked his muscle from the front of his arm to the side of his arm. I just hit him. I don't know how it did it but his muscle went to the side of his arm. I mean he was disabled and he couldn't go. He was in great pain. My daddy took him over there and he [Vernon] took that muscle and worked with it a little bit and whoop! slid it right back in place. Of course my brother did some yelling. I mean he hollered when he did it, but he slid it right back in place.

My brother got shot with a twelve gauge shotgun in 1964 right in the side here. Shot the top of his hip bone off. He got shot at real close range. He went to Scotland Memorial Hospital. They dressed it, but he just kept on getting worse. They just sent him home. There was nothing else they could do for him, and [he] like to rotted alive. You couldn't hardly go in the room where he was. My daddy went and got Uncle Vernon. He come over there and he went in that hole and took all of that rotten flesh out of that hole. Gobs of rotten flesh they had left in there. He dug all that mess outta there and treated that boy. That was in 1964. Hilton died in 2000. That hole growed back over and he got all right.

There was a lady. I wouldn't care if I could tell you her name [can't remember her name], but I went to her house. I met her and she had a cancer on her leg. As a matter of fact, when she came from Duke, they were going to take her leg off, and she came from Duke and somebody had her come here. You could see the bone in her leg. She came here and Uncle Vernon treated that and scraped that old dead flesh off'n that. I believe he treated her twice. I believe that was in the winter. And one day in the summer, when it was time to pick peas, he said, "Come with me, I want you to ride with me off a piece." He went to that woman's house and she was out in the field picking peas and the skin had growed back over that place. She come out of the pea field, where we was, and let me look at it. She pulled up her garment and the skin was growed back over that place. I might could remember where she lived, but I couldn't remember her name.

The night that Mr. Vernon died, I went over to give him a bath. I gave

him his bath and it was around eight o'clock and L.L. was there sitting with him. [Uncle Vernon] asked her, "Is it one o'clock yet?" She said, "No." He went back to sleep and woke up around eleven o'clock and he asked her, "Is it one o'clock yet?" She said, "No, Mr. Vernon, it's not one o'clock." He went back to sleep. I believe he woke up three times. He woke up at twelve and asked her again and at one o'clock he woke up and told everybody, "Bye." Whenever he woke up around one o'clock, Aunt Rosie Lee walked in the room where he was, and she said she will never forget the way he looked at her and he died around one o'clock. He knowed just about the time he was going to die because he kept waking up and asking. I believe he died, if I'm not making a mistake, about five or ten after one. That was in 1991. He was buried at Sycamore, somewhere around September.

L.O.—Did any of his children or grandchildren pick it up?

W.C.—B.D., if you wanted to know about the herbs. More than anybody, she really studied it with him. She wants to work with them, but she doesn't have the gift he had. It didn't make no difference what you had, he could make something that would change it.

L.O.—He had more than the herbs. He had faith and the Spirit of God with him.

W.C.—When he first moved over here, for several years he didn't have no telephone. Do you know Dr. Brooks?

L.O.—Yes.

W.C.—I know you know Dr. Warriax too. They have called my house and I answered the phone. They would tell me, go over and tell Mr. Cooper that I've got a patient. I don't know what to do for him, but I'm going to send them to him. They called many a time. He would make them something and they would be all right. I've seen him do that. I would be the one to take the call from the secretary from the office. I would go over and tell Uncle Vernon what the doctor's office had said. He'd say, "I'll be waitin' on them." Whatever he would fix must have taken care of it, but they would never call me back about that one. Dr. W. from Wagram also sent patients over to Uncle Vernon.

Have you talked to Uncle Sparks?

L.O.—No, not yet. We'll have to drop by there.

W.C.—I've seen him make medicine out of lightered' (old pine, rich in pine oil, used to light fires). He would take lightered' strips and boil it and get some kind of other herb or two and put with it and make a medicine out it.

L.O.—That would be used for cough syrup if I remember right.

W.C.—I don't what he used it for. Purge Grass. I never knew it until I met him. Purge Grass was the best laxative you could take. You could boil the root of it. A person that was having bowel problems, he could fix it and that would be the end of it. People that had trouble with loose bowels, he could take and boil Gum leaves (Sweet Gum), leaves off'n the Gum tree and he would put a little cinnamon it. You could drink one cup of that stuff and your bowels would check up [stop diarrhea]. Boom! tighten them right up.

M.C.—Put Pepto-Bismol out of business.

W.C.—Pepto-Bismol wasn't in it. But, those Gum leaves would, what he said, "Rough it up" or put a lining on your stomach and get rid of that slickness and would check your stomach right up. He would take those Gum leaves in the spring of the year. The reason I know is because it happened to me. I mean I stayed that way for months. I could never check up. Took it one time and I never had that problem again.

M.C.—Everytime you got sick did you go to him?

W.C.—Unless it was something I could do myself like a headache or something like that. I went to him first.

M.C.—With your children too.

W.C.—Yes. Instead of charging you something, most of the time he would give you something [laughs]. He wouldn't only work at his home. If you asked him, he would visit your home. Locked bowels. Your great-daddy-in-law, T.L., doctors couldn't help him, Uncle Vernon got rid of it for him.

L.O.—Thank you very much for your time.

W.C.—One thing I didn't mention, he could write poems. Oh my land, he had a book of poems when he died. That thick probably. I was riding to Laurinburg with him one time and I said, "Unc, the poem on page blah, blah, blah, what did it say?" He could quote it.

M.C.—What?

W.C.—I would turn over to another page. "Unc, the poem on page blah, blah." He could tell you what it was and couldn't read or write. He would come over here and say, "I want you to write me down something. God's given me a poem. I was on the bed and it just come to me. He would tell it to me and I would write it down. He would get Donna or Ethel [daughters] to type it out for him. He could also quote a whole chapter of scripture word for word.

L.O.—Thank you again for your time.

Daystar Dial

This interview was conducted with Daystar Dial. Ms. Daystar, a member of the Lumbee tribe, was a good friend and apprentice to Mr. Vernon Cooper. She spent many hours talking, observing, and collecting herbs with Mr. Vernon. She is a writer, storyteller, and healer in her own right. One interesting fact that came up in our conversation was her assertion that healers did not choose the plant, but in most cases the plants chose the healer. Mr. Freeman Owle, Cherokee healer and holy man, related a story told by Reverend Robert Bushyhead (Cherokee). Reverend Bushyhead, a respected minister among the Eastern Band of Cherokee Indians, passed away in 2001. He had a lifelong passion for preserving the heritage of his people and was instrumental in reviving the Kituhwa Cherokee dialect. According to Mr. Owle,

> When Robert Bushyhead was a boy, he and his grandmother went out looking for a plant for healing early in the morning. As they walked in the forest, he noticed they passed by this particular herb many times. When it turned afternoon, Reverend Bushyhead pointed out a plant and asked his grandmother, "isn't that the plant that we are looking for?" His grandmother said, "Yes, but that's not the one we need. We will know the right plant when we see it." Toward evening they came up to a small hill, and on top of the hill there was a bush. There was no wind that day, but the bushes' branches were shaking, waving, and swaying and there was a strange light around the plant. His grandmother looked up and told the Robert Bushyhead that was the plant meant for this healing.

Sometimes these plants are called Wisdom plants. Mr. Vernon would "dowse" or get a particular feeling when he came close to the place to find a healing plant. Mr.

Earl "Many Skins" Carter (Pis'swe), Lumbee elder and shaman, said his grandmother would often hold her hands over the plants and wouldn't even know the name of the plant, but would just know if the particular plant was meant for a healing. The Cherokee and other southeastern tribes have a legend that tells how the animals invented poison and disease to get rid of man and how the plant kingdom became a friend of man and offered human beings cures and antidotes to the plagues.

Another interesting topic that came up in our conversation was the fact the Mr. Vernon would not usually take the grandmother or grandfather plant. He would always choose the smaller and more spindly plants. In *The Education of Little Tree* by Forrest Carter, Wales, the grandfather of Little Tree, a young Cherokee boy, explains it in this way: "It is The Way ... Take only what ye need. When ye take the deer, do not take the best. Take the smaller and the slower and then the deer will grow stronger and always give you meat. Pa-koh, the panther, knows and so must ye .... Only Ti-bi, the bee, stores more than he can use ... and so he is robbed by the bear, and coon ... and the Cherokee."

Ms. Dial discusses in the interview how Mr. Cooper was a master practitioner of "pulse diagnosis," a diagnostic technique he learned from his grandmother. Pulse diagnosis is primarily practiced in Eastern medical schools of thought, along with acupuncture. To a skilled practitioner, pulse diagnosis is much more than counting heartbeats. Pulse diagnosis is used to determine the health of various organs. It can be used to discover any advance warning signs of health problems and detecting early symptoms of imbalance. Usually, the radial pulse is felt with the index, middle, and ring finger when the patient is calm. The finger in which the pulse is felt the strongest helps the expert practitioner begin formation of a diagnosis.

A.B.—Interviewer
D.D.—Daystar Dial

A.B.—I wanted to begin by asking you to tell us a little bit about your interests and background.

D.D.—My interests? I enjoy writing. I'm a potter. I love nature. Mother Earth. I love history and antiques. I love reading. My major was in American studies with a minor in writing. I love anything to do with history that has a story. I love the stories.

A.B.—You had told me previously that you were an apprentice with Mr. Cooper. When did you first meet Mr. Vernon?

D.D.—That's interesting. I was just thinking about this since we've spoken. I had dream shortly after my dad passed. I had a dream that I should go and see him. I am a dreamer. I've studied dreams for many years now. I had a dream that he could help me get a message to my dad after he passed. I did, I had to find him. His first words were to me.... He was outside in the smokehouse and I am sure it was in the fall of the year much like it is now. The leaves were falling. He stepped out of the smokehouse and said, "Where have you been? I've been looking for you for fifty years." After he said this, I figured up our ages and he was fifty years and fifty days older than myself. So I am sure he meant that "I have been looking for you for a long time." So I'm sure he recognized me in spirit because he didn't know my name. He didn't know who I was, but he knew that he had been waiting for me.

He was recovering from a major heart attack at the time. He would have been in his late sixties at the time, and I was eighteen years old. He had his first [heart attack] at thirty-six. He had had several heart attacks before I came along. He said that the Lord had spared him to stay around a little bit longer.

This all happened in our first meeting, you know. He told me, "We are going to spend some time together." We were soulmates instantly, so I refer to him as my godfather because of how I was shown to find him. So, that was our first meeting. He was an amazing, amazing man. I found him to be lonely in many ways because of his gift that was so unusual that people did not understand. I would be there with him often when people would call or come. I've been there in the middle of the night when ten or fifteen people [were] waiting to see him from all walks of life from all over the world. So, he felt it was his duty to give back. To give of himself, the gift he received from his grandmother, at the age of eleven years old for him. So, he passed it on.

You mentioned herbs earlier and he used herbs from time to time, but it was really faith healing, his way of working with folks. He had a technique that I had studied by the time I had met him at eighteen years old. I had studied with folks and different healing techniques from around the world, and he had a technique that I had read about but I never met anyone who could do it. It was the technique his grandmother had taught him at eleven years old, and it's called pulse diagnosis. I had read about it in some of my studies. The only place I read that they did that particular practice was in India (east India). Have you heard of Dr. Chopra?

A.B.—Deepak Chopra?

D.D.—Yes, exactly.

A.B.—Yes, but just a little bit.

D.D.—He, Mr. Chopra, was the first one that I heard about that taught this in his school. So, I called his school. I just happened to pick up a copy of *People* magazine previously when he was featured in it his first time. This was in his early years when he hit the scene. The article talked about him and his life and how he was brought up using this particular technique [pulse diagnosis]. I said ah-hah, this sounds familiar. So I called his institute and talked to his secretary. I'm getting ahead of myself. It said in the article, it said they had never met anyone in the West who knew this technique. I called them to let them know my godfather did, but he was very sick at the time. Deepak Chopra was on tour and she [his secretary] was very glad to hear that because they had never met anyone who knew this technique and wanted Mr. Vernon to meet him. So we talked and she said he would be on tour for the next four months, but I am sure he will want to meet him as soon as he can. Before his tour was over, Mr. Vernon passed, but like I said, it was called pulse diagnosis.

But it's taught now in many Eastern schools of thought along with acupuncture. That was his technique, but folks didn't know what he was doing. He could tap into the pulse and tell you where the problems were. I met one female doctor since then at a friend's house in Chapel Hill [North Carolina], and she was from the east, from India. She had been interested in traditional healing like Deepak, and there was a medicine man in her community as she was growing up. She had told him she wanted to become a doctor when she became of age. She went to visit him and asked if he would teach her. He said, "Oh, sure." She asked, "How long would this take?" He replied, "Every day for two years." She knew she didn't have that much time because she was getting ready for college. That's how in-depth the study is and it is a very sensitive technique. I have studied it somewhat but I'm not particularly interested in that particular style or practice of healing, but it's very rare. Very rare.

A.B.—So, how long did you study with Mr. Cooper?

D.D.—I was with him from the age of eighteen until he passed ten years ago. I was thirty-five when he passed. So we were connected that entire time. Let me tell you this, the first time I met him, I told you that story, but what he told me was to come back and we'll do something. But, when I went back to see him again he had moved [laughs]. I told him, "You didn't tell me you had moved." He said, "I didn't, did I." He said later if I needed to find him I would, and I did. He lived in the Hawkeye community the first day I met him. He was up there living at the school. He was the caretaker of the school before integration [Hoke and Robeson counties had three separate school systems; black, white, and Indian]. He lived within walking distance of the school, within a quarter of a mile. He was having a home built at the time. When I went back, he had moved. The new house was the house he died in. He was quite a nomad. He had moved at least a dozen or so times in his lifetime. He traveled all over the state. He would say, I've slept here and slept there. All over the place. He would often say he didn't like his folks knowing too much of his business.

A.B.—Did he move mostly around Hoke and Robeson counties?

D.D.—No, he lived in Moore County for a while, close to the Lee County line. I know, because I think about it when I go through there. Lobelia, the herb lobelia [Indian Tobacco (Lobelia inflata) or Asthma Weed], he lived on a road up there called Lobelia. That could be all the way over in Lee County. His folks originally came up from the Pee Dee River in South Carolina (Marlboro County).

A.B.—A lot of Lumbee families came up from that area.

D.D.—Exactly!

A.B.—Many Quicks, Chavis, Locklears, etc. came from there.

D.D.—I passed through Chavistown just last week, between Cheraw and Bennettsville. I had never heard of it before.

A.B.—How would Mr. Cooper use his faith and his personal walk with his Creator as part of healing?

D.D.—That's pretty broad. Let me tell you this story and maybe I can get to it. I would often go after he had seen folks all day. His hands would be all knotted up. He would tell me what he had done, who he'd worked on, and did this and did that. Apparently, the pain would go up into his hands. I asked him, "Why do you chose to keep it?" He thought that was the way he was supposed to do it. Because at the time I was studying and doing, I believed you didn't have to keep it. So, often I would work on his hands to try to get some of that misery out of his hands and give him some relief. He thought for some reason he was supposed to suffer in that respect. I find often in Christianity, which I don't seem to find in other religions, the aspect of guilt and suffering. So, he felt that was the way to do it. I don't know if he ever entertained the thought of not doing [it] that way. That's the way he had been taught. That's the way he continued to live life. It kept him in a lot of pain.

A.B.—So he would take in the other person's pain?

D.D.—Exactly! He would do hands-on healing. He would have a way of moving it out. Just like it was an object that he could move out. My own personal observation is that so many people would come and see him that professional doctors had given up on. So, I would often see people desperate. I have seen how powerfully desperation can move mountains. I have myself chose to look at other people's mistakes or experiences to learn on my own instead of waiting for trouble to move me. So, I would often see folks to come and see him as their last straw. I do see it as an agreement. Mind, body, spirit. There has to be a balancing act there that makes that work. So, one gives of himself or herself over. Like giving yourself over to God. It's a kind of miracle [that] happens when the pain leaves. One chooses to give it up. It's ....

A.B.—It's, in a way, a personal choice and they have to let the pain go to be healed?

D.D.—Yeah, but I'm not sure they knew it consciously. They were desperate. The power of desperation. I have heard of Lumbees coming to church who have drank all their life, thirty years, and give their lives over to God. Gave themselves up, over, and never desired it again. I told some professional medical friends about this, and they commented, "Wow, that's amazing. Never went to A.A.?" I said, "No, they never heard of A.A." So, it's power of giving it up, letting it go and the power of asking. Often in my teaching, I say, "Whatever you want in life, ask for it." Because it's a symbol of humility. There's power in that. Some people call it the false self because the only thing that separates us from God, in my personal belief, is the ego.

Amazing Grace in our Native Lumbee Language

Amazing grace how sweet the sound
Eswa imosahay tane' it'cwahe ki' yu

that saved a wretch like me. I once
heya' uyi' dopa' yi'mabara wi'here ni'. Di' dupe'

was lost but now I am found was
ni de'tcerede mi ka' nacia ya'nire ni

blind but now I see.
yitu'hare mi ka' di' da'nire.

A.B.—Pride?

D.D.—Pride. Some people ask,

what's the difference between pride and ego? I have pride in my heritage. I have pride in the work I do. To me, they are just somewhat different. But, I chose not to have an ego with it. I choose not to have an ego with it. Because I have seen also what we have been taught, too, as Native people, from Europeans.

A.B.—That's interesting because a lot of present day Western philosophy places a high value on personal achievement, emphasis on self rather than on the group, and praising yourself in front of others about your accomplishments. Many Native people I have worked with preferred to emphasize group accomplishment and working together rather than individual competitiveness and personal accolades.

D.D.—Exactly.

A.B.—Many Native healers held special ceremonies when collecting herbs such as gathering the material on a certain side of the plant, or [they] would bury a portion of the herb taken. Did Mr. Vernon hold any special ceremonies such as this?

D.D.—He would not take what I consider to be the grandmother or the grandfather of the plant kingdom. So, he would often take the babies and not the grandmother or the grandmother to which the little ones owed their life.

A.B.—Mr. Freeman Owle, Cherokee healer, believes that the plants choose the healer or patient and not vice versa. Did Mr. Vernon believe this?

D.D.—He had this gift I have observed. A lot of times he didn't have words for things. He had this gift for "dowsing." We would be walking or even riding along and he would say let's pull over there. I would ask him why and he would say, "We need to be over there." He was known for his gift of "dowsing." He did it with his body and found treasures all over the place.

A.B.—What is dowsing?

D.D.—Dowsing is when people take a meter or whatever they are using to find treasures. He would sometimes use a stick, but most often he could feel it in his shoes. We would just be riding along and he would say, "I can find something over there." His body was like a rod. Some people call it "divining."

A.B.—What would Mr. Vernon suggest for specific ailments such as external cancer?

D.D.—As far as herbs are concerned?

A.B.—Yes.

D.D.—The details of most of the herbs he used, I couldn't tell you, but just remember much of his healing dealt with faith more than the concoction or anything. In faith, when one comes seeking, a transformation happens.

A.B.—It sounds kind of like the placebo effect.

D.D.—Absolutely!

A.B.—Did Mr. Vernon do smudging (smearing of Sage and Sweet Grass leaves on objects and individuals) to drive away evil omens or spirits and cleansing?

D.D.—He did not do a particular smudge. He dealt with a lot of people with things, for things, that were going on. He really didn't do many smudges or burning of anything, but he always had the person do a particular thing, but I can't tell you what he had them doing.

A.B.—Did study with or know any other Lumbee healers?

D.D.—No, in his capacity, he was, he was quite amazing. One particular person that awakened my thoughts to this particular path was Mary Bell, wife of Pastor James Bell of the Saddletree community. She was a healer and pretty amazing. I grew up with her and she would often come and visit my folks. The first time I met her was when I was eight or ten. I always had problems with nosebleeds in the hot summertime. She was visiting one Saturday or Sunday to eat lunch with us. I had been running in and out of the house playing and getting ready for lunch. When I walked in my nose started bleeding, pretty much. Mom had called me in to put some ice in the glasses. She said, "Come over here baby and lie down on the couch." She always called me baby. She came over and mumbled something. I couldn't understand what she said, but she said, "You'll never be bothered with it again." My nose never bled again because of Ms. Mary's prayers. I knew of her walking the halls of Lumberton hospital, praying for people and them going home. She had healed them. So she was my first experience with healing. I remember the teacher asking me what I wanted to do right after that. I told her I wanted to be a healer. I could get feel the energy from Ms. Bell when she would walk in. Ms. Bell would often talk about her sister. She was a twin and her twin died at birth. She said she never understood why the Lord spared her to live and her sister died. I'll never forget her and she died of cancer shortly after that.

A.B.—Would some people in the community be suspicious of Mr. Vernon and Ms. Bell, calling them root-workers or such?

D.D.—I know they would with Mr. Vernon, but I don't think they did with Ms. Bell because she was a minister's wife. People didn't come particularly to see her but she would go out and minister to folks. When Mr. Vernon had moved, I asked some folks down the street where I could find Mr. Vernon and they asked, "That old witch doctor?" Many would come, and it would just anger me, because they would ask, "Don't tell so and so you saw me here." That bothered me. He would give of himself, asking them for nothing.

A.B.—Do you practice the healing arts?

D.D.—People often call on me and I do what I can.

A.B.—Mr. Vernon "blew fire" for some ailments. Do you do that?

D.D.—I have done that. My dad could do that too. My dad did that. He would whisper some healing words to himself. When I had the store, I had some clients for a couple of years. That was a major stepping stone of my direction. It turned out to be a center for folks in need rather than a business. I learned a lot of what I needed to be doing with my path. I saw a lot of folks, in and out, that would come through. You work through their hearts. You work from both ends. It's a sharing. Often times, I have this body barometer. If my right side begins to get stiff, it means I'm not giving enough of my self away. I'm not sharing enough. So, it never fails, when I'm not sharing enough, my entire right side stiffens up. That's my signal.

A.B.—That's a mind-body connection!

D.D.—Exactly, never fails!

A.B.—Have you had apprentices in the past to study the healing arts from you?

D.D.—I have shared with folks. I don't want to put myself up. I find myself not wanting to be responsible [laughing]. That's a lot of responsibility. I would assist someone in need. Some people will ask if I will come to speak for an engagement. I'm not lazy, but I do tend to connect with those I need to be with. That never fails. My ego doesn't need that stroking. I really try to be humble.

A.B.—Did Mr. Vernon have any connections with Lumbee healers or healers from other tribes such as the Waccamaw-Siouan, Coharie, or Meherrin?

D.D.—Not that I know of. I think I would have known. I don't think so. He had his hands full. Often I would try to get him to go fishing to give him a break. That was his life's work. People would come see him from the time he was young if they could find him. That was the deal, if you could find him.

A.B.—Did you ever meet a Native American healer called Two Trees?

D.D.—Yes, at Old Fort [North Carolina]. I went through there to see him one time. I had a friend who studied with him. He said he was quite an amazing man, but I didn't have any time to spend with him. I understand his daughter is trying to carry on his work.

Native American Elder from the Prospect Indian Community

Mr. Vernon said, "These days people seek knowledge, not wisdom. Knowledge is of the past and wisdom is of the future." (Wisdom-Keepers) Ms. L.L. is a Native American elder from the Prospect Indian community (Motto: Cradle of Indian prosperity). Ms. L.L. would often fish or go to find herbs with Mr. Cooper. Ms. L.L. also assisted Mr. Vernon on many occasions with healing individuals. She explains how Mr. Vernon would help people of all races any time of the day or night, and relates her belief how faith is the missing ingredient in science. She was a good friend of Mr. Cooper, and shares stories and personal accounts how he used his faith instead of knowledge to help individuals. It was this faith that made Mr. Vernon an incredible man and healer. Mr. Vernon, she commented, stood at the end of a long line of faith healers.

L.L.—Native American elder
L.O.—Loretta Oxendine, interviewer

L.O.—Ms. L.L. is here with me and she is going to share some things about Mr. Cooper. Ms. L.L. would you....

L.L.—We went places. I wanted to know about spirituality and everything. I didn't believe these things could happen. He told me, I could show you things, but you wouldn't want to see them. And I remember we went off and what I would call booger hunting, but we went to this place. I could see these women, they were stirring a pot. They were just as natural to me as you are sitting there, and I was telling him about it. We were having a conversation. Well, Mr. J.S. was with us and he asked, "What are you looking at?" He was looking everywhere and said, "I ain't seen nothing" and Mr. Cooper said, "See, you can see things." Well, it was almost unbelievable, but it made me start thinking there really are things.

But when "K" my daughter was small, she was sick, and she had been to the doctor everywhere. She weighed ten pounds seven and one half ounces when born and when she was two, she only weighed eighteen pounds. They had given her up because they didn't know what. I was leaving Chapel Hill with her and it was like someone spoke and said go to Mr. Cooper's. So, I went there, and he said, "I knew you were coming." I said, "How did you know because I didn't call you?" He said, "I just knew you were coming." Mr. Vernon said, "You know that child could have been healed a long time ago if you would have had faith." I looked at him like ... I had known him several years, but it took that much time to trust. But, I took her there, and he laid her up in the bed, and he took some stuff. I don't know what it was, but he rubbed her, rubbed her legs. She had a bone infection that kept going from place to place. He gave the Bible and some scripture and told me to read that scripture while he did what he was doing, and he said, "You'll never have no more trouble with her." Today, she dances, she's healthy, she's never had no more. She was seeing a GI specialist at Chapel Hill and she had had the bone infection that had been going on and on, and she's never had no more trouble. They checked her for two years, every six months, and there was no sign of it anymore. Never had no more problem. Now, getting back to him, he would call me to go with him, and I would usually take him fishing. We would go to certain places and I would gather herbs for him. The main herb that he used was Yellow Root.

L.O.—How did you know which herbs to gather?

L.L.—He showed it to me, and I finally came familiar enough with Yellow Root that I knew what is was when I found it. But, he was always real particular that you left it to look like it hadn't been tampered with because people would dig it all up. Lion's Tongue, he showed me that and I would figure out what it was. I would gather that for him. Those are the main ones that I gathered. Now, the Yellow Root, he used that as a base in a lot of medicines. It was real good for something he made for diabetes, and for anything that was wrong with your mouth. Like, soreness in your mouth. You could take the Yellow Root and just make a tea with it. It was real yellow and you could swish your mouth and if you had any loose teeth or soreness, it would get rid of it. We could used to just chew on the Yellow Root for a cold. It was used as a base for a lot of medicines.

L.O.—Could you tell me again how he felt about being a healer for all people?

L.L.—He stated that being able to heal was a gift. He had a gift of healing. He used it for Indian people, white people, and black people. All people. There was no stopping point. He was using a gift that God give him to heal people in general. He told me at one time, he tried to get away from it. He tried to not use the gift, but he realized…. He got to the point that he couldn't even move, and he realized that was like a whipping for not using what he was supposed to use. So, no matter where he was, people found him. He would say, "How did they find me?" Well, he realized he had to use that gift to be able to maintain or function in life. I saw some x-rays of his. There was an x-ray that showed a hole all of the way through his femur [long thigh bone]. He was down and he couldn't walk. They said it was cancer, and I also saw an x-ray taken a while after that, but that next x-ray showed the hole was gone. The first x-ray, he said, showed a hole that was there when he was trying to run away what the Lord had told him to do. He was trying to not use his gift, and he knew that he must do what he was told to do or he would perish.

L.O.—So that was his purpose in life—to be a healer.

L.L.—He often said if the Lord called him while he was helping somebody, he couldn't think of a better way to go because he would be doing what he was supposed to be doing. He said that quite often. There was something else I wanted to say. There was a lady from Chapel Hill who came and did her dissertation on Mr. Cooper. She came and stayed for six weeks. I don't remember her name, but there's a copy of her book at Chapel Hill. She did it on healing, but she stayed there and followed him around. So, I am sure there's documentation of it somewhere. I remember reading it. She talked about how all times of the night people would come and how did he know these things. She was not a believer in the beginning, but by the time she finished those six weeks she was a believer in things happening. There was a study done at Duke and they found when he put his hands together to pray, the power made the light from a laser beam waver.

L.O.—They were doing a test?

L.L.—Right. They were talking about how much spiritual power [was] there when he put his hands together. His hands—I've seen him rub babies that had a fever and the fever would go into his hands. His hands would peel like a potato, but the child's fever would be gone. The child would be at rest. Ms. P.M. could tell you the same thing. She would take her children there. She could tell you stories. She's seen the same thing happen. He had the most comforting, warm hands. You can think about it and still feel that. The warmth and the comfort there, but I have seen a lot of people come there, all different races and he would work with them and give them medicine.

L.O.—Have you tried to make any medicine like he did?

L.L.—No, the reason is, what he had was a gift and it would stop with him in his family. I know that they was things that he said. There were only a few things he said I asked to keep. He would start saying poetry and he would say, "Girl, go get your pencil, I want you to write." I would write them down. There were two poems I asked could I keep a copy of, but I didn't. C.P. had a lot of his poetry and would share it. I don't know if she still has copies. The medicine. He had a way of telling you things and you would go out and someone would ask you what he said and you couldn't tell them to save your life. I don't know if it was meant that you couldn't be able to do that, or what. It was strange to me that could happen. I knew what he said, but I could always repeat it for some reason. There were certain things you could talk all about, but there was cer-

tain things you couldn't … like C.P. wanting to get him on videotape and he told her no and she could never get him on tape [the machine wouldn't work].

Welton Lowry

Mr. Vernon Cooper, Lumbee healer, considered the present age dangerous, because people were only existing rather than living. He felt as if people were becoming more distant from spiritual realities. Modern medicine is discovering that treating the body alone is not sufficient to encourage good health. Mind, body, and spirit all need nurturing.

One of the newest business enterprises in Pembroke, N.C. (the heart of Lumbee land), addresses this need. The Healing Lodge is part of the American Indian Lay Health Advisor Project of Native American Interfaith Ministry. Their goal is that a comprehensive health promotion be focused on the community level through church outreach. Not only do they promote awareness about diseases such as diabetes and cancer (Native Americans, as a group, suffer one of the highest rates of diabetes in the United States), but focus on issues such as substance abuse, sexual abuse, mental health, divorce counseling, and battered women's assistance, among other needs.

In *The Education of Little Tree* by Forrest Carter, Little Tree, the young Cherokee boy in the story, explained it this way: "Grandma says everybody has two minds. One of the minds has to do with the necessaries for body living…. But she said we had another mind that had nothing atall to do with such. She said it was the spirit mind...."

Mr. Welton Lowry has been a respected elder in the Lumbee community for many years. He has dedicated his life to nurturing the spirit and mind of Native American people in southeastern North Carolina. Mr. Welton was born to Mrs. Flora Locklear Lowry and Billy W. Lowry on September 26, 1912. Mr. Lowry attended the college now known as the University of North Carolina at Pembroke (UNCP), East Carolina University.

Mr. Welton first went to work as a schoolteacher and administrator with the Waccamaw-Siouan people of Bladen County. Through his endeavors, a new school called the "Wide Awake School" was built. He did this to motivate the "awakening of a group of Indian people" to promote a greater understanding of the value of education.

After leaving Bladen County in 1940, Mr. Welton joined the Air Force. He and Mr. Herbert Oxendine made the *Charlotte Observer* news as being the first Native American flying cadets in the Air Force. After World War II, Mr. Lowry became principal at Piney Grove School in 1945. He worked there for fifteen years, until 1959. He received his master of arts degree from George Peabody College in Nashville, Tennessee, in 1951. Mr. Welton also worked at Union Chapel, Pembroke Graded School (Elementary), and Pembroke High School before retiring from the educational field in 1976.

In 1962, Mr. Welton began his work as a minister at West End Baptist Mission in Lumberton. This mission church was sponsored by Reedy Branch Baptist Church until it became a chartered church of the Burnt Swamp Association. Burnt Swamp consists of more than forty-nine Native American churches in eastern North Carolina. He worked as a minister for West End Church for twenty-seven years. The sanctuary was named the Lowry-Hunt Sanctuary to honor the oldest member of the church and Mr. Welton in 1984. He has received numerous awards for his dedication to education (including the Leo Reano–NEA award for individuals who are instrumental in providing opportunities for Native American students) and the ministry.

Mr. Welton has also become an expert in herbal medicine after years of study. He states that he has taken herbs for his health for many years. He states two of his favorite herbs are Saw Palmetto, to encourage prostate gland health, and Hawthorn, to promote heart and blood vessel health. One of Mr. Welton's latest claims to fame is an herbal arthritis and muscle cream that he makes himself. He gives the small, amber colored bottles labeled "Rub Away: made by Welton Lowry" to friends. The bottle has a drawing of a Native American in a Plains style Native American headdress on the corner. He said one ingredient in the arthritis rub is Wintergreen, but he was reluctant to discuss any other elements.

A.L.—Amy Locklear, interviewer
W.L.—Welton Lowry

A.L.—I am here with Mr. Welton Lowry. Mr. Welton, could you tell me a little bit about your background?

W.L.—I was born where the campus [UNCP] is now. My daddy ran a farm. I finished here three different times, one time in high school in the same building as Old Main [a beloved landmark]. Then I went back to what they called a two year normal [Indian Normal School]. That gave me a "B" certificate to teach. Then they added on a three year, and in a year or two they went to a four year college. I took care of that. I had to leave and go to Tennessee to do my graduate work at George Peabody College. If you see that silver cup [points up to the mantel above the fireplace] … they have an award they present every hundred years to a person who is one of their students who followed in the footsteps of George Peabody. Look up there and tell me what does it say?

A.L.—This award is presented to Welton Lowry, 1995.

W.L.—I think that's the international one because I went with students from different nations that could speak English. I received an honorary doctor's degree here [UNCP] along with Senator Terry Sanford, but this is what I think is my greatest award. I received the National Education Association [award]; they paid my way to California for an NEA meeting and gave me an award [Leo Reano]. I started reading and studying a few years ago about herbs, vitamins, and minerals. We had a lady here that was a midwife. When a doctor in the county couldn't handle a case, whatever it was, they would go get this lady. Her name was Ms. Cat Lowry [Aunt Cat Lowry]. Dr. Roscoe McMillan, most popular doctor from Red Springs, told me she grew her herbs in her garden. When he had a case he couldn't handle, he would go to her home. He would tell someone to go get Cat. Not Ms. Lowry, but Cat. He would say, "Go get Cat." If she came out with a bag on her back, he said, he knew he had it whipped. I never will forget him telling me that. If they find the right herb, they will find a cancer cure. This body was made from the earth. All the minerals that are in the herbs are in the body. That's the reason why doctors suggest calcium if someone has fallen and broken a bone. Herbs is the natural cure if you know what to use. For instance, Sassafras, you ever heard of it?

A.L.—Yes.

W.L.—See that long stick over there at the door? A friend brought it to me. That's Sassafras. I don't know if you can smell it. Would you know it if you would smell it? Would you know it if you would see it in the woods? There's quite a few hills around Mt. Olive Baptist Church. The Lumbee used Sassafras in the spring, after the winter, to tune up their bodies. Just like you have a car tuned up after so long. That's Sassafras. Sage is another good, soothing medicine. Hawthorn is one of your best medicines for high blood pressure, but it takes two weeks to a month to work. One of the safer and more popular herbs is Dandelion. It's naturally high in potassium and a diuretic. If you have gallstones or a bladder disease you should not use Dandelion. I use Goldenseal as an immune system enhancer. In the old days, people around here would boil Goldenseal root into a tea to help lung infections, for the skin, and digestive system. One of the best medicines for your eyes is Bilberry or Huckleberry or Strawberry. I take a Bilberry every day. I've also bought over one thousand dollars in books about herbs. I wanted to see how other peoples used herbs.

A.L.—And how old are you?

W.L.—I'm ninety. Ninety years old.

A.L.—And you still read without glasses?

W.L.—I started with natural medicine many years ago. If you want to be healthy and look twenty-five years younger and feel twenty-five years younger, take herbs. One lady came up to me recently and asked how old

I was. I said, "Ninety." She exclaimed, "Ninety?" I shocked her. If you can learn herbs, that's good. There was an Indian who visited. He was from a reservation and was a captain in the Marine Corps. We were riding by Riverside Golf Course and he said, "Fella, there's enough herbs there to cure every disease in Robeson County." He was seeing herbs that I hadn't thought about. I still usually buy mine. Speaking of healing, I helped get the first chaplain at Lumberton hospital. The medical officials finally realized there was spiritual power in healing. The reason I went into this is I went to a medical meeting in Raleigh at a medical clinic. They had me come speak on spiritual medicine. I was a pastor at that time. They had a man there in Raleigh with herbs. He had a board about the size of this couch with a leaf of this and a leaf of that and this stalk and that stalk. He talked for a good while, but here's what surprised me. He said, "Gentleman, we have doctors now finishing medical schools and going to Indian reservations to spend a year with the medicine man." You ever heard of a medicine man? He said, "I'm going to tell you something, I believe that in twenty years from today you can go to some doctors and instead of the doctor writing you a prescription, they will tell you to go by the grocery store." What he said is coming true now. A good grocery store will have herbs, fruits, and vegetables.

A.L.—I understand you have a special arthritis cream you prepare with herbs. Can you share a little about how you prepare it?

W.L.—You got a sore spot?

A.L.—On my hand.

W.L.—I want you to use it like you would wash your hands.

A.L.—[Rubs it in hands.] It took the swelling out of it. That's a whole lot better. I haven't got that knot right there. It smells strong.

W.L.—It's natural. It has Wintergreen in it.

A.L.—Can you tell me how you prepared it?

W.L.—No, ma'am.

A.L.—It's a secret?

W.L.—It's a secret!

A.L.—It's more of liquid. Do you think herbal medicine and traditional healing has a place in modern medicine?

W.L.—I think when they find out there are no side effects from a lot of herbs. Your pain tablets has side effects. Just about all medicine they sell has side effects. That Viagra they sell must not be natural. People have died with it, but they have another one that is just as good. It's got a lot of herbs. There three or four herbs that works together. It has its place, but it doesn't have the money. The doctors are wanting money. The reason is when they discover something and test it they have to spend a million dollars advertising it. So they have to charge for it. Isn't Viagra like ten dollars a pill?

A.L.—I don't know.

W.L.—There's a difference in herbs and drugs. Side effects makes the difference. You may get relief right sudden with a pain tablet, but it will affect something else about you. I've read that taking aspirin too long can affect your eyesight and can cause bleeding of the blood vessels of the stomach. That Mullein is good for pain relief. I'm supposed to have some of that around here somewhere. When I was younger, we had forgotten a lot about herbs. We had turned to drugs. We did use Catnip, Sassafras, and Mullein and others. When I worked in Columbus County [Waccamaw-Siouan], I did a lot of research talking to herb people about Sage, Sassafras, and there was a grass they would dig up and ship it. They would go in the woods and dig it up with shovels and sell it. They were shipping it. You can't find it much anymore.

Dr. Joseph Bell

Joseph T. Bell, M.D., Lumbee Indian, is the medical director for Pembroke Pediatrics. Dr. Bell has worked as medical director for Robeson Health Care Corporation, as pediatrician for the Choctaw Nation Indian Hospital in Talihina, Oklahoma, and as assistant director for the medical education development program at UNC–Chapel Hill (he is a graduate of UNC-CH medical school). Dr. Bell is founder and director of the Native American Pediatrics Education Project, a member and past president of the Association of American Indian Physicians, and a certified member of the American Academy of Pediatrics.

J.B.—Dr. Joseph Bell
A.L.—Amy Locklear, interviewer

A.L.—Dr. Bell, could you tell me about your background?

J.B.—I'm from here in Pembroke, grew up here and went to school here and I graduated from Pembroke High School. Both of my parents are Lumbee. I went to the University of North Carolina for undergraduate school; I have a pharmacy degree, and then I went to medical school in Chapel Hill. I graduated from medical school about seventeen years ago. I did my training in Greensboro Pediatrics. I worked out in Indian Health Services in Oklahoma for four years and I've been back here about ten years. I'm a pediatrician and medical director of this clinic.

A.L.—When you worked out in Oklahoma, did you ever meet any traditional healers or herbal healers?

J.B.—Herbalists, yes I did. Yeah, I had the opportunity to meet a few traditional healers and herbalists and sometimes that was with interacting with patients. Sometimes it was interaction like in places where you might be speaking about health issues. They might have somebody who's talking about traditional medicine, somebody talking about western medicine, you know, contact that way.

A.L.—Did you work with any of these healers professionally in your practice? What were some specific healing techniques [touching or chanting] that they used?

J.B.—I did a few times, I done it mainly here, though. I've worked with herbalists here as opposed to Oklahoma. There where some rituals, some ritual healing. Some of the traditional healers did ceremonial practices, a lot related to song or, you know, ceremonies involving tobacco like smudging ceremonies and things like that.

A.L.—Being a former head of the American Indian Physicians Association, what is this organization's attitude toward traditional or herbal healing?

J.B.—Our feeling is that the blend of Western medicine and traditional medicine is probably the best approach. So we're very pro–traditional medicine.

A.L.—What is your personal attitude toward traditional Native American healing or using herbs in healing?

J.B.—Same, because it has a very good place in Indian culture. In this area especially, herbal medicine, I think it's very positive.

A.L.—When you were growing up, were you aware of any traditional healers in the community? What are some of the things they did?

J.B.—No, I don't remember that when I was growing up. I may have heard faintly about maybe somebody who practiced traditional medicine but I never was exposed to that personally. Maybe just heard about that. My family was pretty non-traditional.

A.L.—In your practice today do

you work with any healers? What healers are you aware of out in the community?

J.B.—Yeah, I do I work with some herbalists.

A.L.—Do you practice any traditional forms of Lumbee or Native American healing in or outside your practice? What forms of traditional healing are you aware that the Lumbee use today?

J.B.—Mainly through referrals, not personally. Mainly herbal remedies, there are a very few good herbalists I know of and I refer to, and they use herbal remedies for different types of ailments or diagnoses. I mean, you do hear about some traditional practices for like burns or kids who in my practice have thrush [or] asthma, I think it would be traditional treatment. Those are usually treatments that are referred or practiced by somebody else, not me. I'm not recommending those to somebody. I mean, I support that but I don't prescribe that.

A.L.—Do you feel that there is a place for herbal and traditional healing in modern medicine?

J.B.—Absolutely.

A.L.—When you visited the Catawba people as a physician, how would you gauge their level of interest in herbal or traditional healing methods?

J.B.—I don't think that there is a whole bunch of traditional healers at Catawba, but there is a few, so the interest I think is there, but it's not great. I don't think everybody practices traditional medicine.

A.L.—Do you feel that other Native American physicians are making an effort to incorporate alternative forms of medicine into their practice? How are they are doing this?

J.B.—Probably some are and some aren't, I think it just depends on the individual. I mean if you have an interest it's not hard to find out who in the community can be helpful as far as different traditional methods of healing. It's not that hard to do, especially if you are from here. That's kind of how I hooked up with people I feel I can refer to, you hear about them and talk to them and kind of get an idea of their beliefs and what kind of traditional healing they're doing and if you feel comfortable, you send patients that way.

A.L.—What do you feel is the biggest threat to the health of Native American children and adults in Robeson County and throughout the country? Why?

J.B.—It's probably substance abuse and mental health issues [that] are the biggest, I mean that is what we probably struggle with the most. Those are two problems I see escalating through time; it is not getting better [but] is kind of worsening, alcohol use, drug use, which leads to physical abuse of kids, sexual abuse of kids. They almost go hand in hand. I think that is something that we really have to work on for a long time to come.

A.L.—Does the Indian Health Service have a position on herbal or traditional healing?

J.B.—Yes, they have some folks they consult with that are traditional healers, which I think, that is real encouraging. I think that there is a big push in the Indian Health Services over the last few years to actually be able to pay traditional healers as consults, which is real neat. Especially in areas where traditional medicine is very strong, that can be a big jump to therapy, for a patient to have the blend of Western medicine and traditional medicine.

A.L.—When did you decide to become a doctor?

J.B.—When I was high school, I think. I always had this interest in life sciences and biology, things like that. I always liked working with children, so this is kind of a natural blend for me; it's kind of like a calling. I feel like it's a calling, so I would probably say it was in high school.

A.L.—When did you decide you wanted to work with a Native American population?

J.B.—Same, I mean I never thought I would not, and as I started going through training, it was stronger and stronger in my mind, so if I couldn't practice with Native people I wouldn't practice. That is about as strong as I can put it.

Vernon Hazel Locklear

It was often discussed among the Pembroke Lumbee community how Vernon Hazel Locklear's smile was "like a dose of medicine" because her joy and zest for life could almost brighten the gloomiest of days and lift anyone's spirit. Ms. Locklear (aunt) is a respected elder of the Pembroke community. She is a relative of the Lumbee folk hero Henry Berry Lowry. As with many Lumbee families, when Ms. Vernon was young, her family collected herbs from the nearby woods and other areas for medicine. She remembers collecting Heartleaf for her grandfather, Orlin Lowry, and Sassafras and Blackberries for a spring tonic, among other herbs. Ms. Vernon graduated from Union Chapel High School in 1945 and earned her bachelor of science degree in elementary education from the college now known as the University of North Carolina at Pembroke in 1949. In 1951 she married Sanford Locklear and settled in Pembroke. She taught 1st and 2nd grade children at Piney Grove, Magnolia, Pembroke, and Union Chapel Elementary schools in the Robeson County School system for over thirty-five years. Ms. Vernon died shortly before publication of this book.

V.L.—**Vernon Hazel Locklear**
A.L.—**Amy Locklear, interviewer**

A.L.—I am here with Vernon Hazel Locklear. Could you tell about your background?

V.L.—My name is Vernon Hazel Locklear and I'm seventy-five years old. As a young child I grew up in a time when there was not very much going to the doctor. We had our own remedies. Our remedies were herbs and different things. We used them when we were sick because we didn't go to the doctor. I can remember my grandfather very well, and my grandmother. My grandmother would have us to walk through the woods to look for Heartleaf and she used that for my grandfather's heart. He had a bad heart, so she would take the leaves and boil them and make a tea and he would drink it. I also remember when I was a child my mother [would] go up the side of the ditches, in the woods, and find Sassafras. Sassafras was an herb. It was a good tasting herb, but my mother made it more inviting by adding a little sugar to it and that would cause the measles to break out on us. When one of the children started taking measles, and they where hard to get them to break out, she would use sassafras. I also remember my grandmother making Blackberry wine and it was used for all of us when we changed our diet in the spring, eating the first greens that were in the garden. She made that wine. When we would have diarrhea and have it bad, she would use that wine and we would drink it and it would stop the diarrhea.

A.L.—How did you learn about the herbs used for healing and which ones to collect?

V.L.—Basically, from my grandmother and mother. They taught me which ones to collect and how they looked. They would always describe what we were supposed to be looking for. If it was a new herb, one we didn't know that much about, they would describe how it looked and we would walk the ditch banks and be in the woods looking for these different herbs.

A.L.—What kinds of herbs did your family use? Where would you find them? Were they hard to find?

V.L.—When the children had worms, stomach worms, my mother would take the berries from a Chinaberry Tree and boil that and made a medicine that would help diarrhea. The Chinaberry Tree was in most yards. Back when I was a child you didn't have to go in the woods to look for it, it was in the yards.

A.L.—The ones in the woods, where they hard to find?

V.L.—Well, they didn't grow that many in the woods. So you might could find some in one spot, and the next spot would be quite a distance from that place where you found it the first time.

A.L.—Did you go out by yourself or with a group to find the herbs?

V.L.—I usually went with my mother and if it were something that was growing near the house, my grandmother would go. Usually we would have to go to the woods and along the ditchbanks, places like that, to find the different herbs. No, we knew what we were going after and it could have taken a long time to find it, to get where it was; herbs just didn't grow out over the place. There were different places that the different herbs would be.

A.L.—Were there any healers or people who used herbs for traditional healing in the community when you were growing up? Who were they? Did your family go there to treat any ailment or disease?

V.L.—When I was growing up there was a man and he was Mr. Oxendine and he came and used herbs. He brought the medicine and gave it to whoever needed it. I just remember one who did that. Now, he would always go from house to house and find out who was sick. If he didn't bring the herb with him, he would go get it and bring it back.

A.L.—How were these people thought of in the community? Is this kind of healing practiced today as far as you know?

V.L.—They were highly recognized because they knew what to fix. It seems that more women had influenza back then, and my grandmother would mix some things together; I don't remember the things she mixed together. She made an ointment from these things. She often went to houses where the woman there was sick with influenza. She would get under the cover and put that ointment on the woman. To keep the woman from getting cold, that is why my grandmother would crawl under the cover, and she would be putting that ointment on her. Starting with her face and arms and she would go all the way down rubbing. A lot of those women who had influenza, they didn't die, but some of them did die from that. If it was a woman who had a baby, she was more prone to die than a lady who did not have a baby. No, my grandmother wasn't considered a healer; it was just herbs she knew. She could fix stuff for the people. I don't think it is practiced today. I remember we children had colds a lot in the wintertime and my mother would go in the woods and she would get Pine top, a little limb out of the Pine Tree. She would bring it home and there was a wood that had a lot of fat in it and she would sit that piece of wood on fire and that would drip in the Pine top. It would make a tea and we drank that for colds.

A.L.—Can you think of any stories [or] events, in the past, in which a healer or herbs were used to help treat someone?

V.L.—I remember one time when I was a little girl and I stepped on a nail. I loved to go barefooted. It was in the spring and it was warm and I was barefooted and I stepped on this nail or the nail scratched my foot. My grandmother took kerosene and I don't remember what the other herb she used, and she put that on my foot and wrapped my foot in white cloth. Until this day I have a scar from that nail scratching my foot. For a long time I had a problem walking, but there was no going to the doctor because we didn't have any money to go the doctor. A lot of people didn't go to the doctor, but when it was a case where a herb could not be used and [it] needed a little something more potent, then they would send for the doctor.

A.L.—Did your husband's parents gather herbs for use in healing?

V.L.—I don't know, I didn't know his family until we had met and I was introduced to his family. I don't know if they had herbs, I'm pretty sure they did, but what they were and how they were used, I don't know that.

A.L.—Do you think the herbal medicine worked? Why is it not used as much today?

V.L.—I think it did. Well, I think people has gotten away from using herbs because it is easier to go to the doctor now than it is to walk up and down the ditchbanks and in the woods and look for different herbs that we used back then, even though I heard herbs that were used back then are in some of the medicine today. I don't what that would be. I just heard that from someone who was talking. They said the medicine we have today has a lot of herbs in it.

A.L.—As I was talking with my other interviews they said a lot of time with healing you had to have faith. Would you think that would be the main ingredient in healing?

V.L.—Yes, yes my grandparents were very religious and they did have to have a lot of faith.

A.L.—So in order for these herbs to be powerful and to heal, the person would have to have faith.

V.L.—Faith was a very important factor in the healing that came from the herbs.

A.L.—Can you think of any other stories, etc. dealing with your family, community, healing, etc.?

V.L.—I can't remember that well, but if we had a sickness we would just let it run its course.

A.L.—What do you know about blowing fire or talking the fire out?

V.L.—I have heard people talk about that. They have that gift, but I have never actually seen anyone talk out the fire. My family was not blessed with that gift. With my grandmother gone, we kind of got away from using the herbs and anyway, our living was improving and it was so much easier to go to the doctor than using herbs. She knew what to get; the Heartleaf, Sassafras or the berries for the wine.

Henry and Leitha Chavis

In *The Only Land I Know*, by Adolph Dial (Lumbee born) and Daniel Eliades, an unusual Lumbee treatment for arthritis was reported. The authors state that many Lumbee would attempt to have bees or wasps sting them in the area of arthritic pain. Modern science is now investigating the beneficial effects of bee or wasp stings on arthritis. It is interesting how many "folk remedies" or treatments have become of interest to modern science.

In this interview, Henry and Leitha Chavis, originally from the McIntyre community between Deep Branch and Pembroke, discuss growing up in Robeson County and the folk, herbal, and traditional treatments their families used. Ms. Leitha's grandmother was a traveling healer. She tells how people came from far away with horse and wagon to pick up her grandmother, Aggie

Brewer, and take her to their homes to treat a sick adults or children.

In our discussion, Leitha's distant cousin, Reverend Zimmie (Z.R.) Chavis, was mentioned. Reverend Zimmie recorded the words "Epta Tewa Newasin" from his grandmother. These words, in the Lumbee traditional language, meant "Creator, we love you." Reverend Zimmie's grandson, Freddie Chavis (husband of Pandora Chavis) called Reverend Zimmie a "praying healer man." Mr. Freddie Chavis comments, "People would say that if Mr. Zimmie prayed for you, you would get well even if he wasn't there." Mr. Freddie also recalls that his grandfather would walk from Pembroke to Rennert, a distance of twenty miles, along the railroad track to minister. Mr. Freddie states, "I had warts come up on my ear and the side of my face and my grandfather wet his fingers in his mouth and touched the warts. In a few days they were gone." Freddie, Henry, and Leitha all recalled that Sassafras was the most often used herb in their households as they were growing up.

Mr. and Mrs. Chavis have lived in Drexel, North Carolina, a central Blue Ridge Mountain foothills community in Burke County, since 1962. The remains of this fort, built for the Spanish by the Cheraw, was recently unearthed in the Upper Creek area of Burke County (Berry site). This fort, erected by a Spanish conquistadors and their Portuguese Captain Juan Pardo, was destroyed by the Cheraw within eighteen months of being built. Mr. Henry and Ms. Leitha continue to keep in close contact with their friends and family in Robeson County.

H.C.—Mr. Henry Chavis
L.C.—Mrs. Leitha Chavis
A.B.—Arvis Boughman, interviewer

A.B.—I am here with Henry and Leitha Chavis. Could you tell about your backgrounds?

H.C.—We moved up here in 1962 because there was little work in Robeson County.

L.C.—When I was sixteen we got married. He was twenty-one. He knew better, but I didn't.

H.C.—You said yes, didn't you? I had an uncle that lived up here. He's passed on now. His name was Gilbert Chavis. He lived in Connelly Springs [a community twelve miles to the east of Drexel]. My uncle married one of A. A. Lockee's daughters [Mr. Lockee was a Lumbee Indian originally from Pembroke]. The Lockee name was originally Locklear. Mr. A. A. became a well known pastor in Burke County.

L.C.—You know he had two sets of children—about twenty something in all.

A.B.—No, I didn't know that. What was your grandmother's name, Ms. Leitha?

L.C.—Aggie Brewer. I know your family knows them because she was from the Brewers down there at Saddletree.

A.B.—Mr. Henry, did your folks ever do any herb gathering?

H.C.—No, not that I know of.

A.B.—Did you know anyone in the community that did that?

H.C.—No.

A.B.—Ms. Leitha, didn't your grandmother do some healing in the community?

L.C.—Yes, I remember her doing that.

H.C.—I've known my dad to make Sassafras tea. Dig roots and boil it. He used it as a tonic.

L.C.—Seems like that Sassafras, when kids started taking measles, they would drink that stuff and make the measles pop out.

A.B.—Ms. Leitha, you had mentioned that you used to go and look for herbs with your grandmother. How did you find out what the herbs looked like?

L.C.—I did go with her. Me and her would be digging in the woods or along the ditchbank and she would tell me what to look for. I remember many times we went out and dug those roots and made medicine out of them. Back then, kids went barefooted all the time. They would go out and run in the yard and the fields and in the mud. Their feet would get red and irritated. I know you've heard of the foot itch or ground itch. You know, you get raw and infected in between your toes tromping all around in that stuff. Probably around the mule stables. She would get peach twigs and boil them and we would stick our feet in that tea. She also made a molasses cough syrup out of it. That was the raunchiest tasting stuff. I know there was something else in it. It seems like it was baking soda.

A.B.—Ms. Leitha, you had also mentioned a grass or grain that your grandmother would use. What was that?

L.C.—I remember that Pepper Grass, that Pepper Weed. Daddy, you remember that?

H.C.—Yeah, it had a seed in it.

L.C.—Yeah, she would boil and stuff and make a tea for gravel [kidney stones] and it was hot. That's probably why they called it Pepper Seed.

H.C.—A wild weed was what it was.

A.B.—You had mentioned that your grandmother would go to treat someone and stay a week or sometimes more. Would she stay at people's houses?

L.C.—I've known people to come get her on the mule and wagon. She wasn't a granny lady. She didn't de-

liver babies, but she had her little black bag.

A.B.—Would she stay a week doctoring one person?

L.C.—Yes.

H.C.—Back then, people just believed in that.

L.C.—When people back then got sick, they went to bed. She would go and stay and take care of them until they got back on their feet.

A.B.—What would she do to take care of them?

L.C.—She would make poultices and some kind of liniment [salve] and she would rub them. It just depended on what was wrong with them. If they had a fever or something, she made some kind of onion poultice.

H.C.—I've known people that had a fever to take collard leaves and put them on their forehead. My brother, when he had pneumonia and was real small, the collard leaves worked for him.

A.B.—From what you saw from your grandmother, do you think what she did worked?

L.C.—Evidently, because everybody seemed to have a lot of faith and confidence in her. They would drive those old mule wagons for miles to come get her and have to stay at least a week because it was so far away. She went around Mount Olive, Prospect, Pembroke, and Maxton.

A.B.—Did anyone in your family decide to become a healer like your grandmother?

L.C.—No, but my daddy's daddy was the community vet. People would come from miles around if there was something wrong with their animals. Now, daddy dabbled in that some. He was pretty good at it.

A.B.—What would he do to treat the animals?

L.C.—He would fix concoctions and medicine. I seen him put a twitch in a horse's lip and pour the medicine down it.

A.B.—Was it like a clothespin?

H.C.—No, it was like a long stick and I remember that he would tie a rope around that thing and take the horse's lip and put that lip in there and twist it.

L.C.—To make him open his mouth where you could pour the medicine down his throat.

H.C.—There's other ways you could do it too.

L.C.—That's the only way I remember.

H.C.—You also could throw a rope around a limb [and] pull their head up to where they had to swallow it.

L.C.—I also remember Chinaberry. If the horse would step on a nail they would make a salve and rub him down with that.

A.B.—How did people in the community feel about people who treated [with] or used herbs?

L.C.—That's all people knew because you didn't go to the doctor unless you were about dead. That's all they had to rely on because they didn't have money to go to a doctor.

A.B.—Did they talk about someone who knew how to blow fire or talk the fire out?

L.C.—No, they didn't talk about them. They tried to find where a good one was at. Now you were talking about talking the fire out of somebody. Let me tell you about a good one. I know you've heard of him, Mr. Zimmie Chavis. He lived over at St. Anna. I think it was the same year we moved up here. I went in the kitchen and perked a pot of coffee. I had baked a cake that night, and that evening I perked some coffee. I put in on the stove and boiled it. I thought I was in the kitchen by myself. I poured Henry that cup of coffee and turned around and put the pot on the stove. When turned back, I saw that cup of coffee coming in my oldest daughter's face. I mean it was in her face. I guess the

good Lord had to be with me to do it. I don't know why I thought about it, but I grabbed her clothes and I was so excited that I just ripped them all the way down because it was hot and burning her. If I had pulled it up over her face, her whole face would have gotten burned real bad. Her face was swollen so bad that her eyes was closed. We took her to the doctor that night and the next morning. Later that morning, I took her to momma. She said, "Let's go to Mr. Zimmie's." When we took her over there, Ann was standing up in the seat between us, her face was just one big blister. We took her in the house, and Mr. Zimmie prayed for her, put ointment on her, blowed on it, and he said, "In a week's time you won't be able to tell that this baby's been burned." We started backing out of the yard and Jim Chavis, Mr. Zimmie's son, stopped us and we talked with him. I weren't paying any attention to Ann there standing beside me in the seat, but Mr. Jim said, "Look at that baby's face." The water was dripping off of her chin like you had poured water on her head. By the time we got back home, it was still burned, but all that swelling had gone down.

H.C.—It didn't even leave a scar!

A.B.—Isn't that something?

L.C.—We took her to the doctor again the next morning and he said, "What in the world have you done with this baby? If I wouldn't have saw this, I wouldn't have believed it." He said, "Whatever ya'll have done, keep it up." She had just started walking. You talk about blowing fire or talking fire, Mr. Zimmie could. Mr. Zimmie's wife, Agnes, was a midwife. She delivered babies. She delivered one of momma's babies, I think it was my brother. They had two hospitals in Lumberton. Baker's was the one you went [to] if you had to have surgery, but Lumberton was fifteen miles away.

H.C.—Folks wouldn't believe in that today.

L.C.—When you see it with your own eyes, it makes a believer out of you.

A.B.—Is Mr. Zimmie the only one you knew that could do that?

L.C.—No, Mr. Freeman. What was his name, Daddy?

H.C.—I can't recall his first name.

L.C.—About my grandmother, she wasn't expecting nothing in return for what she did. People weren't able to pay her except in vegetables in the summer. You know how people used to share stuff around.

A.B.—Did she ever say that was her gift?

L.C.—No, she just enjoyed helping people. It probably was a gift, though. We all had to depend on each other back then. If someone in the community got sick, we would all get together and say, "All right, on Tuesday [i. e.)] we're going to go clean out his crop out for him." We all farmed back then.

H.C.—It's not like that today. I have two neighbors here. I know their first names but I don't their last name.

Mary Sue Locklear

Mr. Vernon Cooper, in addition to many other Lumbee healers, would "blow fire" or add heat to the system to rid the body of an ailment in addition to talking to, praying over, singing, or blowing the medicine or "healing breath" over the affected area. Healers in the Lumbee's sister tribe, the Catawba, would also blow the medicine from a reed or some hollowed out object onto the wound or affected region. Mr. Hayes Alan Locklear states that some Lumbee healers will "blow fire" while others will "talk the fire out" or say chants or healing words

over the affected area to take the fever or pain away. One modern healer who uses herbs and "talks the fire out" is Mary Sue Locklear, wife of Reverend George Locklear.

In an interview with Wendy Brown for *The Atlanta Journal and Constitution*, Ms. Mary states that she was raised looking for herbs and roots in the woods with her mother. As the fourth of twenty-one children, Ms. Mary comments that she often walked through the forest and weeds as a child looking for Red Tag Alder for her mother (to purify the blood). Ms Mary explains, "When I was small, my mother would send me out for it. She would describe the shape of the leaves." She also said, "It's for yellow jaundice in babies." In this same interview, Ms. Mary searched through a great many plastic bags which contained herbal cures. She also asked her granddaughter, depicting the shape of the herb with her hands, to go collect an herb in the garden.

Ms. Mary's treatments were derived from advice from her mother, area elders, books, and a hit-and-miss method. Ms. Mary seemed especially proud of the cough drops she made to treat sore throats. Another of her treatments was using okra blossoms or potato peelings to treat infections and Catnip (Catmint) tea to treat a cold. According to Ms. Mary, Goldenseal, Sassafras, Catnip, and Yellow Root are key ingredients in many herbal remedies.

Ms. Mary also makes and uses a special lye soap. She states, "I started making it for the teenage girls at church.... I can use it to wash my dishes and take a bath in it." She makes it "only during a full or new moon" (*Atlanta Journal and Constitution*). She believed that if it were made any other time, the soap would not be the right consistency.

Ms. Mary Locklear has an exhibit based on her work with herbs and healing at the North Carolina Museum of Natural History in Raleigh, in a section dedicated to the history of medicine in North Carolina. The museum display shows a picture of Ms. Mary, specimens of the herbs she uses, and a tape interview of how she uses faith in healing.

A.L.—Amy Locklear, interviewer
M.L.—Mary Sue Locklear

A.L.—I am here with Ms. Mary Sue Locklear. I understand that you talk the fire out. What is it meant by blowing fire and talking the fire out?

M.L.—Before I do this I always, if it's a grown-up, I ask them if they have faith and if they believe in it. A child automatically looks for help, they automatically believe. My mom taught me when I was small. You just repeat part of the Lord's Prayer, "Our Father who art in heaven, hallowed be thy name, come out fire in the name of Jesus." You repeat it as you're blowing on the burn and you can feel the heat from that burn coming in your face. If it were a big burn, your face would burn. It's all because of having faith, if you don't believe in it, it won't work for you. My mom has been to the hospitals and I have been to the hospitals and people that call, they have the faith whether their child or whoever it was did or didn't, they have enough faith for them, too. I've been to Chapel Hill and I've been to Cape Fear and I've been to Lumberton and several people have come here and bring children. When I was working, for twenty years they would send the children to the cafeteria where I worked, "Mrs. Mary, the child got burned." The child didn't know what I was doing but

it got relief and it didn't bother it any more.

A.L.—So it's just for burns?

M.L.—The particular thing is having faith and believing for what prayer asking the Lord to take the fire out. I had one child to come out there one morning and had a blister on its little arm as big as my finger. It had got the curling iron a hold. It was crying and crying and when I got through, they said it never bothered it anymore. So you see, my baby sister can do thrash. Thrash is when the baby's mouth gets real raw inside and sore where they can't nurse, can't take their milk or anything. By her not seeing her natural father, our dad died before she was born, so she had the gift automatically to blow thrash and all she did was just blow in the mouth. It's just a gift and my mom taught to me mix up Sage, if you got green Sage it would be better, with honey and alum and you mop the baby's mouth out with it and it heals it up. You give it a laxative to work the fever on out of its system, get it to run on out; the baby would be fine.

There are lots of little things that … if we had upset stomachs, mom would fix up flour, vinegar, and sugar and water. We did not know what Pepto-Bismol was, and it worked [for] us. So in recent years I've been telling people about it. This one lady, she had been taking prescription stuff and seemed like everything she said weren't working and I told her that one morning and it choked her bowels right up. Just two home remedies that's been handed down from generation to generation. If we didn't have this knowledge back then, I don't know what we would've done because we sure didn't have the money to go to the doctor with. I did have to go to the doctor once, I slightly remember, I got poisoned. The medication the doctor had left with my mother, the wind blew off of the shelf of the fireplace and I ate it. Liked to died. I can remember the doctor giving me raw eggs putting in me, and I remember that morning the wind blowing, but beyond that I don't know anything. Ever since then I have had a bad stomach, I guess it came from that. There's a lot of stuff out there, there's still a lot I don't even know.

My mother taught me from twelve. She started at least twelve or thirteen years old going out looking for herbs. She would describe it, the leaf, how it looked, the shape of it, the color of it and whereabouts to find it in the swamp or the bay. I would never forget the time I was going out looking for what they call Red Root, or it's called Red Alder or Bloodroot, and it grows in the bay down in the swamp, and it don't get very big. They have a long, single root, and they don't get much bigger than your finger, just as red as it can be. The root will purify your blood, help build your blood, and the bark was for yellow jaundice. My sister had yellow jaundice. That's one of the first roots I ever gathered, and mom told me what to do and I went to find it. I went three times before I could ever find it. I would bring things back to the house. [She'd say,] "This is not it." She used that bark and made a tea from it and gave it to the baby, and the coloration came back to her skin. So now they quarantine them, she didn't have to do that.

A.L.—What is the most important thing for the patient to do or have if they want to be healed?

M.L.—Faith, they have to have faith to be healed.

A.L.—Would you share a little how you make your herbal cough drops?

M.L.—If you're making a cough drop you can use a recipe like you were making hard candy. Instead of putting flavoring in it you would use herb flavor oil. Like if you would want to make eucalyptus, if you wanted mint or any of those type herbs that is good for a cold or sore throat, you would use the oil if that is your kind of flavor.

A.L.—I know you use Red Tag Alder often. What other herbs do you use and how do you use them?

M.L.—I've made cough syrup, I make vapor rub, hand cream, lip balm, a facial, a shampoo, hair conditioners, salves for any rash of any kind so far has took care of it, and also one for the burn.

A.L.—Do you sell them?

M.L.—Yes, it helps to get my money back in order to go purchase stuff to make it with.

A.L.—Do you consider healing to be a gift? If so, when did you find out you had the gift?

M.L.—Yes, any time God gives you something, it is a gift. Probably not until after my children where up some size. When they were all small I used a lot of those little home remedies, but you know I didn't think much about it because I'd be to busy taking care of them and the house and everything else and trying to work on the farm. It just didn't dawn on me until my oldest granddaughter was little. I was raising her at that time and I sort [of had] gotten interested in them again. I started back making the soap and people had started coming and people started interviewing me and it just went and started growing and growing and growing. That was way back in some part in the eighties, when I got started back into them again.

A.L.—What are the steps you go through when you blow fire or talk the fire out?

M.L.—You take the person, whatever part of its body and you just blow and you're repeating those words as I'm blowing and you repeat over and over and over until you feel within yourself that it's enough. Now this one particular elderly man that I did up in Cape Fear, he had the bandages all on him. Hot tar had fell on him, poured on him, and I did it. I didn't take any bandages off, I just had the faith, he had faith and I blew, it healed and when he sees me he says, "You see that miracle hand?" The doctors told him he would never use it, but he uses it. My son used to be a roofer and he had hot tar on his flesh where it had spilled on him and he used the salve. It healed up and he doesn't have a scar. His buddy wouldn't use it and went to the drugstore and got him some salve or something or other and he has a scar.

A.L.—Are there other healers in the area? How is what they do the same or different than how you are used to healing?

M.L.—Not that I know of. The other herbal person that lived was up in Hoke County, I was never blessed to meet him. They called him Mr. Cooper. I've heard a lot about him, but I never got to meet him.

A.L.—I have heard that you make great lye soap. Could you explain the steps in making this soap?

M.L.—Just the old fashion way of making what they call lye soap. No, it isn't the kind they used to boil in washpots. An elder taught me how to make it from cold water; I don't have to boil it. I use lard and lye and water and make it up and skin it, pour it in molds to make different sizes, shapes, where I used to put it in pans and just cut it out in blocks. It's easier to handle if I put it in the molds and it looks better too. What you have to do with hard soap is you make it on the new moon. When you're making soft soap you make it on the full moon. There is a difference in it, and if you make it on the quarter, your soap is gonna shrink. It shrinks just like that moon. That's when they love to dry up lard, when the moon is changing.

A.L.—How has healing changed since you were a child?

M.L.—I think it has made me a better person to appreciate what I was

taught and didn't have to rely on others for a lot of help. It's good to rely on people sometime, but sometime people don't want to have time for you no more. So I was blessed to be taught this as I was growing up. I listened. Now my other brothers and sisters didn't. I'm the only one that listened to what mom had to say. My mother gathered herbs with her grandmother, not her mother. See, there is only certain ones that seems to be interested in it, but some people gathered stuff for sale. I think some of the stuff people gathered was ginseng. It's been gathered so much because people thought they could make a lot of money out of it. So they just overdone and destroyed it and now there's not any here.

A.L.—Are you teaching anyone else about healing?

M.L.—Well, whenever I'm called to do presentations or workshops with educational people or doctors. I visit the schools a lot during November, which is Indian Heritage month. I have done that. I already have what I know in a book form. I'm just waiting for someone to get it to market. I've also collected or gathered herbs to go to a museum in Raleigh. The Museum of Natural History. It's up on the third floor if you want to go check it out. They have a sweat lodge in there.

A.L.—What about your children, are they interested in traditional or herbal healing?

M.L.—They're interested to a point, but not interested enough to sit down and learn about it. My granddaughter is in college in Pembroke now. She did an article on it. I tried to help her with it. To take time to sit and do it, no. I have a son that likes to go out and gather herbs. He likes Sassafras tea. He says it gives him energy. I made up four gallons last weekend. It's also a blood purifier, blood tonic, and [for] colds. I couldn't begin to tell you all it's good for. When I was growing up my momma told me to get it when the baby had red measles. You drank that tea and it would help break the measles out. So you could get shet [rid] of the fever and the sores would dry up. I love to just drink it. It helps you sleep, too.

A.L.—Sassafras tea? I need some of that.

M.L.—Get brown vinegar. You can take you a couple of tablespoons with vinegar. One with honey and a cup of hot water and drink it before you go to bed. That will help you sleep. It really works. There was this lady that used to go to our church. She was taking medication to go to sleep. It wasn't working. She asked me, "Sis, what can I do to get some sleep?" I told her. The next Sunday she overslept, because she was late for church.

A.L.—What do you think is the most frequent complaint of people that visit you?

M.L.—Well, right now it's hair loss. I've had hair loss. I have a whole lot more hair now, but a year ago I was bald, up here and around here (pointing to her the top and sides of her head). I wore a hairpiece or wig for a long time. I knew what herbs you could get to grow hair. I just hadn't proved it. So, one morning I had the herbs here and had never worked with them. All the sudden, the Lord placed it in my mind. I got right up and started measuring and made up a shampoo. I started washing my hair everyday with it, and my hair grew back. There's lots of people using it now, and it's helping them too. I also prepared a hair rinse to go with it. I use most of the same materials I put in the shampoo, but the base of it is vinegar.

A.L.—Do you use a lot of vinegar?

M.L.—No, not a lot. Just enough in it to keep it from spoiling. You see, the vinegar has minerals and potassium in it. White vinegar has been stripped. All it's good for is cooking and canning. Your brown vinegar still has all the minerals.

A.L.—So everything you make, you use the brown vinegar?

M.L.—If I'm using vinegar, yes. But, that's the only thing I put vinegar in is the hair rinse. In cough syrup, I tried honey, which is a natural, but it made it bitter. So now I use brown sugar. It worked. For colds, bronchitis, and pneumonia, I put some herbs together and made a cough syrup. I made it also because I was bothered with asthma. I still have it, but not like I used to. It just stops the wheezing and cut up the congestion where you can spit it out.

A.L.—What do you use to treat high blood pressure?

M.L.—You can eat baked potatoes as long as you don't put all that stuff on it. Herbs you can take for high blood pressure are Garlic or Hawthorn. Basically, all your vegetables that have potassium and magnesium. All of this will lower blood pressure. I have made out some sheets for suggestions for people who have high cholesterol or suffer from diabetes. What they should and shouldn't eat. The one thing that works, I mean really works, is Dandelion. You know that grows in the yard. You can eat Dandelions. It's edible. You get it, you parboil it maybe twice. Throw the water out, or you can save that water and use it as a tea to drink for diabetes. You can cook those greens till they're tender with bacon or whatever seasoning you want. When they're done, you stir egg whites in it. Just egg white. It kills the bitter taste. Dandelion is loaded with potassium and minerals. People want to shet [rid] of it and throw it away, and the root is a substitute for coffee. A very valuable weed. This lady, I started a doin' this stuff with her. I suggested she start drinking the Dandelion tea and after a little while she came off insulin. If you take Goldenseal with Dandelion it will block the sugar not taken care of by your body. Goldenseal can also build your immune system.

A.L.—Do you think people feel [about you or] treat you differently or talk about you because they don't understand your gift?

M.L.—Sure, people used too. They called me a witch because they do not know or understand. You mentioned herbs. Some people have the tendency to think of rootworkers or rootpeople. It's not. It's not. I only use herbs for healing. The Lord knows what it is and that's all that's important.

A.L.—Are there any particular stories you could share about someone being healed or a personal healing story?

M.L.—There's a lot of things. Like my grandchildren. One grandchild told his sister, "Don't tell grandmama I'm sick. Don't tell grandmama I'm sick." They knew I would give them some medicine to take, but then down the line they found this medicine worked. Especially the granddaughter I have in college. She ran out of her asthma medicine. It was on a weekend. So she had no choice but to take grandmama's medicine. It's good her daddy carried some home with him and found out how well it really did work. I can tell people what to do, but they don't choose to do it. I can't make them do it. If they ask my advice, I give it. But, whether they take it, that's up to them.

A lot of people around here have a problem with their blood sugar. People bring their children to me that have been burned. Many people also have problems with blood pressure. Some people come with arthritis. Arthritis has a lot to do with what people eats. They eat the wrong combinations of food. White bread and white sugar is very bad for arthritis. If they eat more vegetables and less of certain types of meat, it's not as bad.

Also, not taking care of their bodies in their younger life. Children go out without nothing on their arms. I say, oh gosh, how they're abusing their bodies, not taking care of it. In later years, it's going to hurt them. They'll be eat up with arthritis, exposing their body to the weather, especially in the wintertime. Arthritis is a bad, crippling disease. Painful. It mainly affects the joints. This is what you call [points to wrist] a copper magnet. That's what that is. It works. It works. If I didn't have it on, I would have so much pain [points to wrist] right in there. I don't have to take arthritis medicine. It might work for a week, but basically it doesn't do me any good. I've been blessed so far. I've got it in my back from lifting. You ruin your back in certain ways. You don't know how to lift. My pain is from picking cucumbers. That's a back killing job.

A.L.—Have you had a chance to work with any local physicians?

M.L.—I've done consultations with two physicians in High Point. I've also done a consultation with the health department here.

A.L.—Tell me more about the exhibit based on you at N.C. Museum of Natural History in Raleigh, N,C.?

M.L.—I think it was in 1997, we gathered the herbs that are in there now. They said as long as the museum was there, they [the herbs] would be there. I was chosen because I had done some presentations at the civic center in Raleigh. It just went from word of mouth. They were asking around, who would you recommend? My name was given. The day they did the tape, we were sitting up here in the house, and it was the hottest day of the year. It was in July 1997. We had to close all the windows and we had to cut all the fans off. We didn't have air conditioning back then. We couldn't have no noise while they were making that tape. I would have preferred to do it under a shade tree or in the woods, but they gathered all of that together and give me a copy of it. That was really good to see that. They got it on video that is constantly going and also on computer. They also have some herbs on display.

Earl Carter (Lumbee) and Keith Brown (Catawba)

This interview with Mr. Earl Carter and Mr. Keith Brown took place on the Catawba reservation near Rock Hill, South Carolina. Mr. Earl is in his early sixties and has been practicing medicine for the past twelve years. He states that he began practicing traditional medicine after he had a heart attack. Mr. Earl, also called "Many Skins" or "Pis'swe" in the native language, is "keeper of the sacred fire" (one who uses his knowledge for the benefit of the tribe), healer, and honored elder of the Lumbee tribe. He states that modern medicine doesn't treat the body and spirit, it only treats the symptoms and tries to mask the real problem with various drugs. A true healer will listen to the soul or spirit of the patient.

Mr. Earl believes his art is a gift given to him by the Creator and passed down to him by his grandmother, Polly Strickland. Hayes Alan Locklear tells about how he and Mr. Earl were raising shelters for a spiritual gathering at the Lumbee Cultural Center. Mr. Locklear states, "We were putting up the shelters and a tent stake cut my leg real bad and it started bleeding. Mr. Earl looked around, took a few steps, and pulled up a cluster of plants that was growing there in the clearing and pressed them on my leg. In just a few seconds, the bleeding stopped. The wound also healed quickly." Mr. Earl told the interviewer that he had been sick for over a year. He was not able to walk for a long time because of Lyme disease. He comments, "There's nothing in traditional medicine that will cure this disease, so I supplemented my diet with Vitamin C."

Mr. Keith Brown, Catawba elder, is the great-grandson of Ms. Margaret Brown, Catawba wisdom-keeper and one of the last native speakers. He is the events and activities coordinator for the tribe at the Catawba Cultural Center (Catawba Cultural Preservation Project). Mr. Brown and his family carry on the Catawba tradition of creating fine pottery. He specializes in creating pots in the form of a bear, Catawba chief head, medicine pipe, and other ceremonial vessels with traditional designs decorating the outside. His Catawba name is "Ne ne enu" or "Little Bear." Mr. Brown has extensive knowledge of Catawba pottery and history.

At the time of my visit, Mr. Earl stated he had been "cooped up for so long that he needed to get out." Today, he was visiting his friends on the Catawba reservation. He and Mr. Keith Brown gave me a tour of the cultural center and grounds and took me to a traditional long house and a family dwelling they had built together. The side frame of the family dwelling and long house was made of saplings with plates of oak bark secured to outside frames. The bark was gathered in early summer. The long house is rectangular shape on the bottom and formed like an upside down "u" shape on the top. The top frames were constructed of Bamboo. Mr. Earl stated this was done to provide sturdiness and save a lot of little trees. Mr. Brown commented that in the past, the Lumbee and Catawba would have used mostly rivercane. Mr. Earl said he had "cane break" growing beside his home. This grove cooled the breezes coming from that direction in the summertime. But bamboo is so plentiful and grows so quickly, they used that to build the dwellings.

For the roofing, broom straw was woven into thick, dense mats. Earl Carter stated that the broom grass was gathered in the fall, after the first frost, for the roofing and bedding material. Keith Brown added that they also used Cattails as roofing and bedding material. The roof was left open in the middle of the family dwelling to allow the smoke from the central fire to be drawn upward. Mr. Earl said the Lumbee would also use Broom Straw for burial ceremonies. Inside the family dwelling, there was a rock-lined pit where fires were built. Mr. Brown tried to start a fire with what he called "lightered" (old rich pine), but the wood was too wet. Also inside the family dwelling, there were three bed frames made of Poplar saplings. The posts made the bed sit off of the ground. The bedding was made of Broomsedge, but Mr. Earl said it could have been fashioned from animal skins also.

Most of our conversation took place inside the Catawba Cultural Center exhibit hall. One interesting point Mr. Brown brought up was how the Catawba holy man would often blow the medicine (blow fire) from rivercane or reed to cover the patient or blow the medicine up his or her nose to also impart part of his spirit to the person in need.

A.B.—Arvis Boughman, interviewer
E.C.—Mr. Earl Carter
K.B.—Mr. Keith Brown
A.B.—I'm here with Mr. Earl Carter and Mr. Keith Brown. Mr. Earl, how did you get into healing? Who were the healers in your family?

E.C.—My great-grandmother, and it come down to my grandmother. Emmaline was my great-grandmother and Polly was my other one. They were both Stricklands.

A.B.—Did you take trips out to the woods with your grandmother or did they describe the herbs for you to go collect?

E.C.—We would take a lot of trips gathering. Back then there wasn't too much tore up like it is now. We would go into fields and woods. We would get a lot of medicine from pine trees. She and I would gather the Longleaf Pine, but we don't have much of that any more.

A.B.—Mr. Brown, did your family search for herbs?

K.B.—When I was coming up there weren't many people looking around for herbs. I remember my grandmother and I would go walking through the woods and gather up some stuff. My grandmother was a Harris. She had a special cough remedy.

A.B.—Do you have an herb that you prefer to use more than others?

E.C.—It does depend on the situation, but Raspberry is my favorite herb, the natural fresh leaves. A lot of people now can't take herbs. There all kinds of different herbs, and the herbs that are good for me wouldn't be good for you or him either one.

A.B.—How do you know if an herb might work for one person and not another person?

E.C.—Well, you really don't know. If I have a feeling, I will try it. It's like trial and error, but the herbs I use won't hurt you. They are all natural. Some people like to make their own medicine. What ails me might not ail you. A lot of people today come in with more of an ache these days. A lot of people that believe it, it's not convenient for them to go out and practice it. Modern medicine is readily available and people don't know where the herbs are at or what kind of pure form it is. Sometimes when I am walking along I will get a real strong feeling in a certain spot. I usually find an herb there that can help heal a person. I sometimes will get that feeling not knowing you will need it, but soon after, a person will come that needs that particular herb. But, sometimes I will still pass by it because after a just a little while the herb loses its potency and healing power.

A.B.—So, you prefer to use fresh or recently gathered herbs?

E.C.—Yes. Herbs are something you take, but you got to believe it.

A.B.—Do you find that the herbs that you find in the wild are better than the ones grown in a garden?

E.C.—Yes. They are a whole lot better. They're a whole lot stronger.

A.B.—Do you think it's the strength of the soil that affects the potency of the herb?

E.C.—I don't know if it's the strength of the soil or the Creator. The herbs are getting depleted anyway. That's one reason we need to take a lot of herbs with our foods. Food fills us up, but it doesn't help us right. Prayer really helps. I've had people praying for me all over the country.

A.B.—Prayer really does work wonders.

E.C.—If I ask you to pray for me, it's a sharing experience. A healer has to have strong faith in the Creator and a belief that the Creator is almighty and can heal us. It takes strong faith and respect for the herbs and the way. I heard it said that a sincere prayer is more powerful than an atomic bomb.

A.B.—Mr. Brown, do you think in your tribe that the faith was more important than the actual medicine used?

K.B.—Not particularly more. We believe you have to have a good balance of the herb and the faith. But even if you didn't have an herb, but still had faith, you could be healed. But if you had the herb and didn't have the faith, you would come up way short.

E.C.—It's like when we were talking about Ms. Barbara Locklear. Without her faith in the Creator and the belief she would get well, we would have wasted our time.

A.B.—Didn't you use Sweet Grass and Sage? [See Sage entry for short account of this story]?

E.C.—Yes, that's what I used that time. I also carry some stones here in my pocket.

A.B.—Are they special stones?

E.C.—I don't know whether you would call them special or not, but one I got is a cave pearl. They won't even let you get them out anymore. I use it in healing sometimes.

A.B.—Do you feel faith is more important than the herb?

E.C.—Yes, yes it is. A whole lot.... You know the herb you need is sometimes related to a vitamin deficiency, like vitamin A. You can't really get it or use it like your body is supposed to out of medicine. Can't get nothing out of medicine [modern medicine] that doesn't destroy something else.

A.B.—So you say a lot of medicines today are not good for the body because they are not fresh and they add so many chemicals?

E.C.—I think we use many medicines today, that are prescribed, but are not needed. Sometimes the medicine does what they are prescribed for, but it seems that every time someone goes to the doctor's or physician's office they are going to prescribe something for them. They seem to be prescription happy. I think a lot of times people will think they need something but they have talked themselves into believing they are sick. A lot of times, with my problems, I have woken up expecting to feel bad. The few times I have been to the doctor and he prescribed something, I have only taken it up until I felt better because after awhile, it loses its effect. This is how a lot of people get addicted to a drug. Many times if I feel bad, I make a little concoction and take [it] or take an aspirin and I feel better.

A.B.—Mr. Brown, in the Catawba tribe are there still people that practice traditional medicine?

K.B.—I wouldn't say practice as much as they know and have studied traditional medicine. Diane George can identify the plants and their medicinal uses. A lot of people know of the medicine but not enough people don't take the time to find the herb. Like Mr. Earl said, with many plants, you have to collect them at a certain time and can't keep them but a whole long time. Some plants you only collect when its flowering or when it's roots are dormant.

E.C.—Collecting herbs also have a lot to do with the signs.

A.B.—Do you have any information you can share about when you gather plants?

E.C.—You already have someone of that information such as phases of the moon, etc. A lot of this information is sacred and can't be shared. I will say, this that certain herbs are better or more potent under certain signs. Different parts of the plant will be used for different things. The flowering tops might be used for one thing and the root might be gathered at a different time and used for something totally different.

K.B.—I agree with Mr. Earl. Different herbs and different medicine will be more potent and better at certain times. A lot of times it depends on what you are using it for. This plant's flowers may be good for one thing and in the fall when the flower is gone use the root for something else. We didn't want to gather it all. In places where it was growing, they leave plenty—take very minimal from an area.

A.B.—Mr. Brown, a lot of Lumbee still practice the art of blowing fire or talking the fire out. I'm aware that the Catawba would often do the same thing with a reed hollowed out. Can you share anything about this practice?

K.B.—I don't know of one particular person that practices that in our tribe now. My grandma Emma used to be good at doing that.

A.B.—Is that what you called it—blowing fire or talking the fire out?

K.B.—Yes, talking the fire out. It's not done much anymore, but the Catawba people had a lot of faith in the medicine people or medicine man. He or she had to be a very special chosen person. This person would mix up a concoction and they would often blow the strength or power of the person and blow it on them, up the nose, or in the mouth.

A.B.—Mr. Earl, some Lumbee and maybe Catawba healers when they layed their hands on an afflicted person, the illness would actually go up into their hands and in their arms. Have you ever had an experience like this?

E.C.—Well, you're not going to write this down are you? [Laughs.] Like I said, it's the people that you're talking to. It's the situation and what's around you that time. Its like one time I was at some kinfolks' house and there was a little girl running around. One of the adults told her you better calm down and mind [be careful] or the asthma is going to take you and get you again. Right about then the asthma struck her and she was out of breath. I took her around back, did a little ceremony, brought her back, and she was all right. The mother asked, "What did you do to my child?" I didn't do nothing to her in a way, but in another way it took the faith of a little child.

A.B.—You placed your hands on her.

E.C.—Yes. More than anything it was her faith that made her well. Some people watch me lay hands on someone and ask, "Why don't you do that for me?" It wouldn't work. Sometimes it takes laying on hands, other times it takes herbs and prayer.

A.B.—Do you feel like the traditional type of medicine is fading out?

E.C.—No, it's not fading out. It's just that nobody's doing it anymore or no one knows how to do it. They don't know how to do it and why it's done. You won't find many who will take up that chore and believe in it. It's fading out that way. The Great Spirit works through a real healer. Some have the gift and they don't use it. I've been asked before if I would take an apprentice. Most of them don't understand how much of a responsibility I feel for what the Creator has blessed me with. If it's used in the wrong way, it could be used for bad. That's why I have to be careful about what I share.

A.B.—Do you consider what you have to be a gift?

E.C.—Yes.

A.B.—Was it a gift that was passed down?

E.C.—Yes, it was passed down.

A.B.—Do you feel like you are the last one and it won't be passed down after you?

E.C.—Yes. You can write it down, but something would be missing. It's like Mr. Vernon. There's a lady down home [Robeson County], she wrote down what Mr. Vernon said and did

for a long time. She would just cry and cry because she couldn't do it. It wasn't meant for her to do. It was wrote right down in there. It just wasn't made for her to do it. You just sit around and talk to people some time, and they will say, "I had a headache when I started talking to you and now it's gone, what did you do?" I didn't do nothing. It's the power of suggestion. It can make you sick or make you well, either one. That's a big part of medicine. Often the herb is just something you take.

A.B.—Do you feel it's important to get to know the person to heal them?

E.C.—No, not really. If you're in a crowd of people and you feel like the energy is dragging down, you'll find a person or see someone that needs healing.

A.B.—Are there any other stories you can think of that relate to healing?

E.C.—No, there are so many of them.

A.B.—Can you remember the first person you [healed]?

E.C.—When I began, I was fifty years old. It was the furtherest thing away from my mind when I had my heart attack. I ask the Creator then what he wanted me to do. So, I go here and go there. I could have started before my heart attack, but it's such a big responsibility. Some people come up and ask if they can do what I do. Some of them could, but you have to stay pure and stay straight. I pray each day, Great Spirit, keep me in the right path, the straight way today. When we have a 'sweat,' we pray this prayer three times a day. You can't play games with it, and you have to be humble. Not bragging saying, "I can do this or do that." We had a sweat lodge down home [Robeson County]. Those boys were in the sweat lodge and it was thundering and lightning in the background. They began to say, "It's going to mess us up. It's going to rain us out." When they asked, "What are we going to do if its rains?" I said a little prayer to the Creator and the rain went right around us. When those boys got out, it hadn't rained a bit.

A.B.—[At this time Mr. Brown places some Sage leaves in a small Catawba pottery pot and lets the leaves smolder.] Isn't that Sage?

K.B.—Yes, it has a calming effect. Just recently, we had a sweat lodge around here. Mr. Earl and I are usually the ones that start the fire and get it going. We went down there and it was raining, and we went and sat in the truck a little while. We took a step of faith and went back down there to start the fire and by the time we had began to start the fire, it had stopped raining. We took that as a sign of faith that the Creator was going to bless our ceremony.

A.B.—When you have a sweat lodge ceremony, do you use any kind of mint on the stones?

K.B.—We do use Sage leaves on the rocks and cedar.

A.B.—Do you take a swim in the river or a cold bath after the sweat?

E.C.—Yes, a five gallon bath of water [laughs].

A.B.—A five gallon bucket, huh?

K.B.—The last sweat we had, it was around thirty-two degrees. We thought that water was going to take our breath, but we felt pretty warm after we dried off.

A.B.—Mr. Brown, your great-grandmother, Margaret Brown, once stated that the Lumbee were once part of your tribe but left to avoid the smallpox plague. Do you believe this statement?

K.B.—I never have thought about it much. I've heard stories about how after a sign of smallpox, our people would go into the sweat lodge. They would sweat them and then they threw them into the river. They would just about kill them. A large number of our people just left in the middle of the night and went somewhere. They thought they could sneak out in the dark, without telling anybody, and get away from this thing, this sickness. You know the Catawbas used to travel a lot between here and Virginia (salt was a popular trading item). The country that the Lumbees are in is right in the middle of where they would go. It's logical to think that they hid out in these swampy areas so the people who brought this sickness couldn't get to them. You mentioned Grandma Margaret. Well, the little people took her brother and led him off into the forest. He was gone for about a week. When they finally found him, the little people had left him out there in the swamp sitting on a stump. Her brother said they had sucked the blood from his arm. This is the way it began, they took the blood out of his arm and made him a medicine man. The old people used to talk about seeing spirits of people, hearing things, or thinking you hear things. There is a story in our tribe of a little boy who was real special. The little people had been watching him and they captured him, led him out, and took him way back in the woods. They brought him in front of the three tribal elders. The first elder wanted to give the boy a gift. He offered him a knife. The little boy refused to take it. The second elder of the little people offered him some poisonous plants. He refused to take those plants, too. The third one offered him some medicine plants, some good herbs he could use for healing. That's what he took. He decided to take that. They taught him how to use the different plants and medicines. They brought him back to his people. That's how a lot of people were chosen, when they were young, by the spirits. Sometimes they accepted it and sometimes they don't accept it until late in life. I think it is always there.

I can only recall one instance with myself. A long time ago, I must have been about seven or eight years old, we lived over here and had to go to the spring to get water. We played all day, we had a good day, it seems like it was an exceptionally good time. We didn't go to the spring to get water. It came dark and momma said, "You gotta go to the spring to get that water." We went down that hill, just over hill, over at that old spring that hasn't been used in years. It was down a real steep hill down to the spring. My older brother and sister went with me down there in the woods. It wasn't but about a quarter of a mile from the house, but it was down this hill. They stopped and said, "You go down it." I said, "I don't want to go down that hill." But I ended up going down that hill in the dark with a bucket to get the water. It seems like about the time I got down there, a light came up over and shined right down on the spring. I still remember that. It could have been the full moon coming up about that time, but it was like an answer to a prayer. I need to ask my older sister about that. Ask her, do you remember the time.

A.B.—The Lumbee used to believe in little people, too. In fact, mothers would sweep their children's footprints away in the sand before night so the little people would not steal them away that night. The Lumbee also believed that anyone born with a special birthmark over his eye was gifted with the ability to hear and see spirits. Have you ever heard of that, Mr. Earl?

E.C.—Oh, yeah!

K.B.—The mothers would also be careful to take their children's clothes off the line before night in fear that the little people would play in their clothes and cause their children to have fitful dreams or nightmares.

A.B.—The Lumbee used to call them boogers.

K.B.—Yeah, we used to call them that, or little people.

E.C.—You still working on the language some?

A.B.—Yeah, some. You know many of our ancestors, the Cheraw and eastern Siouan people, lived with the Catawba for over ten years, and there is maybe a different vowel sound or accent variation difference between the Cheraw and Catawba language.

K.B.—The Harrises that live here, there are a lot of Harrises, they say they come from Cheraw. A lot of Harrises are still here. My cousin, Billy Harris, looked a lot like Mr. Earl.

A.B.—They have a glossary of some of the Cheraw language at Lumbee Legal Services.

K.B.—A lot of linguists are trying to write stuff down that have never been written down. Whether they get it right or not is up in the air, unless you get a good native person, I think. We have a linguist on our staff who is more German descent. She has done a lot of research. What we need is more conversational language.

A.B.—It's not enough to know the words, you have to know how to communicate.

K.B.—To me, the leaders of the Indian people are the ones who practice and preserve the ceremonies, language, and culture.

E.C.—You know we have a spiritual gathering in March. You need to get ready. That's when they have the sacred fire ceremony.

A.B.—Thank you. I will remember. Mr. Brown, does the Catawba have anything like spiritual gatherings?

K.B.—No, we never have anything much going on around here. I guess the last little gathering we had here was the sweat lodge. I'm about the only one that's doing it. Some of them do it a little bit, but they quit. Most of the people that come are Lums [Lumbees]. They come over here and sweat some and I've been over there to sweat with them.

Pete "Spotted Turtle" Clark

Vernon Cooper said, "Everything I know, I learned by listening and watching.... Doctors study what man has learned. I pray to understand what man has forgotten" (WisdomKeepers, p. 58).

Mr. Pete is a unique individual who, among a few others, is responsible for a renewing of interest in traditional Lumbee culture. This renewal started in earnest during the early twentieth century with the Red Man's Lodge Movement, a quest to rekindle interest in the Lumbees' Eastern Siouan traditional language, religious practices, dances, healing techniques, and culture. This awakening has also been carried forward by modern day groups such as the youth group Seventh Generation (name taken from the Oglala Lakota prophecy made during the ghost dance period [late 1800's] that the seventh generation would bring back the traditional ways).

Mr. Pete is a respected elder of the Union Chapel Lumbee community. An elder instructs or counsels individuals, offers suggestions, leads by example, and gives a name in the traditional language to infants. He states that he learned his knowledge of healing from his father, Bartow Clark. Mr. Pete, his son Ray Littleturtle, stepdaughter Kat Littleturtle (a Cherokee), grandson Tony Clark, and step-granddaughter Angelica "Saru" Clark make up TurtleVision Inc., an enterprise that presents traditional music, stories, and dances from the past to schools, community groups, and powwows. However, as representatives from a living culture, they also share modern aspects of Lumbee culture.

L.O.—Loretta Oxendine, interviewer
P.C.—Mr. Pete "Spotted Turtle" Clark

L.O.—I'm here with Mr. Pete Clark.

P.C.—I have a box which I keep ... a little box in which I keep some traditional healing treatments.

L.O.—Mr. Pete, could you tell me something about how you or your family used herbs growing up?

P.C.—Well, for malarial fever, we used Sweet Gum bark. It cures malarial fever. You could make a tea out of that.

L.O.—Do you have any other herbs you would like to share with us?

P.C.—Actually, all the trees are good for you. When I was in the Navy in boot camp, there was a boy from Ohio. He asked, "Do you know anything about herb medicine?" I said, Yeah, I had to know it. My dad was medicine man of the tribe. I was in Virginia. They had different bushes than we had. We would go out and dig up roots for every disease we could think of. He had a suitcase packed full of dried roots and herbs. I didn't know what they was. I got a letter from him saying that his folks said that was some of the best medicine they had ever had. I knew exactly what he was saying. You can believe me. You can make a tea out of just about any root or herb if you believe it. This is a value of life. It teaches you mind over matter. What some of the Indian people did is they found some root that tasted better than some other. That's what they used. Any root or herb, the Creator put here on earth. If you know how to use it, it can be good for you.

L.O.—You said your dad was a medicine man.

P.C.—No, he wasn't, but that's what I told folks.

L.O.—But you had learned about herbs from your dad. What was his name?

P.C.—Bartow. I also got a brother named Bartow.

L.O.—I didn't realize that was your brother, Mr. Bartow.

P.C.—Yeah!

L.O.—Mr. Bartow, Jr. Do you have something there you wanted to read?

P.C.—This is some remedies we used. Black Sage tea to remove objects from your eye. Carry buckeyes for rheumatism.

L.O.—I don't think I've heard about that one. A buckeye was like a bean, wasn't it.

P.C.—Yes.

L.O.—A big bean!

P.C.—The Chestnut was good for rheumatism.

L.O.—You say a Buckeye is another name for Chestnut. OK.

P.C.—Goldenseal for nosebleed.

L.O.—You can also put it in your hair.

P.C.—A mixture of bakin' soda and catnip tea will remove a cold.

L.O.—That's interesting.

P.C.—For arthritis, eat a warm teaspoon of honey each day.

L.O.—That's what I used to do.

P.C.—For colic and colds, use the Mustard plant.

L.O.—Was anything put in with the Mustard?

P.C.—As far as I know, just a regular Mustard plant. [Mr. Pete begins reading from cards.] We also used Calmy and baking soda for colic. Calamus was also used for cough. It could also put you to sleep. The Lumbee used boiled Sage leaves for sore throats. Drink Sassafras tea in the spring for the blood. Have sassafras smoke blown in your ear for earache. Apply inner Oak bark to a fever blister.

L.O.—I'd forgotten that.

P.C.—Cobwebs will stop bleeding. Speaking of bleeding, when I was young, if you stuck a nail in your foot, we put a piece of fat meat on the nail. It would completely cure it for us. If we believed it, it seemed to cure it—going back to the truth of mind over matter. Some people would put the tallow or fat meat on the wound, but it seemed to work on the nail.

L.O.—That's amazing. Do you think we have any herbal healers today?

P.C.—Mr. Earl Carter is a healer.

L.O.—He is?

P.C.—He could tell you more than I could.

L.O.—I didn't know that. I knew he was keeper of the fire.

P.C.—He makes medicine. He knows how to make medicine out of the mints. He also used to make a cream. I don't have any of it now.

Hayes Alan Locklear

In the book, *In beauty may I walk... Words of Peace and Wisdom by Native Americans,* Francis Laflesche (Osage) says, "All life is Wakan [sacred]. So also is everything which exhibits power, whether in action, as the winds and drifting clouds, or in passive endurance, as the boulder by the wayside. For even the commonest sticks and stones have a spiritual essence which must be reverenced as a manifestation of the all-pervading mysterious power that fills the universe." It is a basic truth held by all Native American peoples that we are all interconnected with each other, our natural world, and our Earth. We cannot destroy or alter anything within our living world without it affecting us also.

Mr. Hayes Alan Locklear, tribal historian, healer, herbalist, and tribal clothing designer, alluded to the fact in this discussion that every action one takes in life does have an equal and opposite reaction (a spiritual as well as a physical law). This is as a result of our kinship or interconnectedness we all share.

Hayes Alan said he picked up his herbal knowledge from relatives as a child, but he didn't seriously practice the healing arts until much later in life. Mr. Locklear comments that his paternal grandmother practiced traditional healing, she was a medicine woman, and she treated people with herbs and was a midwife. He states that his great-grandmother and her father were healers also.

Hayes operated a florist and Native American gift shop called Mother Earth Creations for more than ten years. Mr. Locklear's store also serves as an art gallery for local and nationally known Native American potters, basket weavers, and artists. Directly across the street, Hayes' cousin stocks Goldenseal, Sassafras, Catnip, Chickweed, and other herbs in the Native Herbs and Natural Foods store. Hayes Locklear and Kat Littleturtle were the first ones to incorporate a traditional symbol of the Lumbee, the Lumbee Star or Pine Cone design, into a male and female regalia worn proudly by Lumbees at powwows, spiritual gatherings, Miss Lumbee beauty pageants, and other tribal events.

A.L.—Amy Locklear, interviewer
H.L.—Hayes Alan Locklear

A.L.—Can you tell me about your background?

H.L.—I am a native of the Union Chapel community. I've lived there all my life. I started learning about herbs when I was a little boy from my aunts and uncles and family members. I started doing research when I was in eighth grade. That's when I really started getting involved in Indian history and culture. Every research paper I had to do from high school through college I did on Lumbee history and culture, which included herbs. I have collected forty or fifty herbal remedies that are used among the Lumbee people.

A.L.—Can you name a few of them?

H.L.—Yes. There's Mullein, which kind of looks like tobacco. It's used from sprains and bruises and you can also smoke it for bronchitis and asthma. You can also make a cough medicine or a tea from it. The Ratsy Vein [Pipsissewa], which is used for high blood pressure. Heartleaf is used for heart trouble. Green Sage tea is used to get rid of pin worms. Goldenseal is used as an antibiotic. Goldenrod is used for kidney troubles. Salty berry [Sumac] for bed wetting. Tobacco is used for bee stings or things of that nature. You put the juice on that.

A.L.—My daddy used to do that all the time.

H.L.—There's one that's called Wax Myrtle that's used for whooping cough. Garlic is an excellent herb and an antibiotic also.

A.L.—You learned all this from your family?

H.L.—From my family. My momma's sisters, their husbands, and her in-laws. I talked to a lot of old people when I was young that were in their eighties, and that was thirty something years ago. Most of the people I was talking to were born in the late eighteen hundreds. Sassafras is used for cold, flus, or blood purification. Poplar bark is good for stomach trouble. Cherry bark and some other things mixed together make a good cough medicine. You can take bramble briars and make a burn medicine. Rabbit Tobacco is used in a tea for colds and flu. There's a lot of them. I have a lot of them written down, and I can get you a copy later on. I started learning how to recognize these plants in nature when I was young. The ones I can't find, I will usually buy at the herb store. You can get them year 'round then and not just in a certain time of year.

A.L.—Do you use herbs daily?

H.L.—I don't fix herbs for myself because we're not supposed to heal ourselves. I only do it for other people. Some people will call me up and say I've got so and so, what can you fix for me? Or they will ask, I need something for this, what can I use? I sold medicine one time and I only charged for what I had to buy. I've felt guilty ever since. I'll never do that again. I will never charge another one because I look at it like a gift from my ancestors and the Creator. I don't look at it as a way to make money. That's not what it's for. I don't knock people who do. That's just my personal feeling. I've learned how to gather some wild things, but there's a lot that I don't recognize. Like Plantain is used for bleeding. If you get cut, you can put that on it, but there's two other plants that look just about like it. You've got to know exactly what you're doing and which one to gather, too. You might give a person an herb to cure one thing and they might be allergic to it and it would make something else wrong. So you've got to know the whole person.

A.L.—It sounds complicated.

H.L.—It's very complicated. It's like regular medicine. People have allergies. They're allergic to plants. You have to be very, very careful. Especially those you don't know.

A.L.—Do you teach about plants and herbs?

H.L.—I used to, through RCC [Robeson Community College]. I did some herb classes and classes on plant natural dyes and foods. I also did some classes on Indian arts and crafts. They call me just about every year wanting me to go back, but this business keeps me so busy I don't get a chance to do it as much. Usually, people come by doing research papers or whatever and they'll interview me. I can pass it on that way. I've written down the herb, how we used it, parts used, and where I learned it from or the person that told me. So in fifty years if I am living or I'm gone, people can take my work and say, "Well, he learned this from so and so, and this is what you do." That's the kind of thing I am trying to do for future generations. There's not a lot of young kids coming up that want to learn, and that's the reason I'm tickled to death to talk with you. It's very interesting. You learn so much not only about the herbs when you study traditional medicine, but the whole cycle of life. All Indian people believed that everything is in a circle. You start at one point in childhood, adulthood, old age, and you come back and have to be cared for like a child. To heal a person of sickness, you can't just heal one thing. You have to heal the whole person. The whole body, the spirit, to make things better and well. When you go out and gather herbs, you just don't go out there and pluck up what you need, or I don't. I always thank the Creator for it and always leave an offering like tobacco, or a penny, or a nickel.

A.L.—So you go through a ritual when you gather the herbs?

H.L.—Pretty much, because we couldn't have it if it wasn't for the Creator giving us the gift and the knowledge. When I prepare herbs for people, I always pray over the medicine also.

A.L.—A healing prayer?

H.L.—I pray in the name of Jesus to make this work and heal this person.

A.L.—Do you consider yourself more of a healer or an herbalist?

H.L.—I'm more of an herbalist, I guess.

A.L.—You've heard about some of the healers around here, haven't you?

H.L.—Oh yes, I know quite a few. Some heal in a lot of different ways. Some just do one thing. I have a friend who blows fire and can also cure thrash [thrush]. My aunt could do that and she passed away and passed it on to her daughter-in-law. Her daughter-in-law then gave it to me.

A.L.—So you know how to blow fire?

H.L.—Not blowing fire. I know how to cure thrash. My grandfather could do that. My dad's dad could blow fire, because when I was baby I got scalded by hot water. He blew the fire out and I don't even have a scar.

A.L.—I talked with Ms. Mary Sue Locklear and she said she blew fire. She was telling me about some of the miracles. She said she wouldn't work unless the person she was working with had faith.

H.L.—Ms. Mary is a wonderful person. I learned a lot from Ms. Mary Sue also. It's like when you go to a doctor and he gives you medicine. If you don't have faith in that doctor you might doubt the medicine he has prescribed for you. Faith will heal the body quicker than anything else. A lot of time that herb just cleanses the body and makes the body work to cure that problem, whereas a lot of medicines today just cover up the symptoms. They don't really heal. It's like when you get a cold, you get an antihistamine to keep your nose from running. It doesn't cure the cold.

A.L.—How do you go about curing thrash?

H.L.—Well, I can't tell you. If you tell it, it doesn't work anymore. A lot of these things you have to keep private until you're ready to pass it on to somebody. Then when you tell that person, they're able to do it, but if they tell it, they can't do it anymore. Some healers claim they don't have to know the person. Just their name and when they were born, but the person has to have faith. If they don't believe in what's going on, they won't be healed. But, if I fix something for someone else and have some left, I will take it then. But, just to sit down and make something for me, it won't work. I've tried it.

A.L.—So you can't treat yourself?

H.L.—I've talked to healers and medicine people. They told me that's the reason it doesn't work because we're not supposed to heal our self. I believe in Jesus. He didn't ever heal himself. He wasn't sent here for him, he was sent here for us. I believe these things come through God. I know they do. For every disease that came about, he created a cure. It's in the plant kingdom. You just got to find them. Most of the healing parts of the plant [are] the root or the bark. Of course, it depends on the plant you are using. You also use the leaves at times. Many times you peel the outer bark off and just use the inner bark. That's were most of the healing properties are anyway, in that inner bark of the plant or tree. The inner bark carries all the nutrients to the tree. You know if you cut that, the tree will die. You can use sap from trees also. Like Pine Trees. It has sap that is a very good astringent, which is an antibiotic for cuts or things of that nature. Sweet Gum leaves can be used to break a fever. One side of the leaf is cold and one side is hot. You should put the cold side against your body and it will pull the fever out. You can also crush the leaves up and put it on that cut and it will stop the bleeding just like that.

A.L.—I need to get some of that. Yeah!

H.L.—We were talking about Ms. Mary Sue. She freezes a lot of herbs. She gathers them in the summertime and she freezes them, so she'll actually have that fresh herb.

A.L.—Well sir, she didn't tell me that. Thank you very much for your time.

APPENDIX B:
ARTICLES

Medicine Man

By Mark Price. Copyright 1989. *The Fayetteville Times*. Reprinted with permission

WAGRAM—Vernon Cooper was barely 10 at the time, but he remembers well that night 73 years ago when his great-grandmother stirred from her deathbed long enough to grant him "the healin' power."

Even then, herbal doctors were scarce among North Carolina's Indians. Particularly the kind who could heal by touch, as Betsy Cooper was rumored to do.

She'd mixed enough home remedies in her 89 years to cure every Lumbee within 100 miles. Yet when her old heart started giving out, no amount of bloodroot tonic or hog foot ointment could help.

"This family's been allotted the power for 400 years," she is remembered to have said by her great-grandson. "It was given to me by my father, and given to him by his father. When I die, it goes to you. When you die, it dies, too. You're the last. It ain't meant to go no further."

And so she died, leaving her young apprentice with a legacy that decades later brings people to his modest house near Wagram—folks complaining of headaches, nervous stomachs, rashes and shortness of breath.

Most, like Cooper, are Indians of limited means. They offer pocket change or vegetables in return for centuries-old herbal cures of boiled sheep's fat, rat's bane and opossum haw.

Then there's the touch.

Cooper says that , like his great-grandmother, he has the power to diagnose and heal by touch. He calls it "rubbin'."

"When I get my hand over a pain, I can feel it. I feel the pain like they feel it. I can feel it being drawn out like a 'lectrical charge. The more it comes out, the less they hurt," says Cooper, clad for business in bifocals, a pair of overalls and a cowboy hat.

"The Lord anointed me to do it, but I had a stroke a few years ago and it's not working like it did before. Now my hands peel if anybody has a high fever. Sometimes they swell, too," he says.

Even in a community where

herbal cures are as common as corn bread recipes, the 82-year-old retired farmer is rumored to have forgotten more about plants and herbs then most ever learn.

Among the Lumbees, Cooper is considered to be the last of the tribe's bonafide medicine men. Some even go so far as to say he's got a little of the supernatural in him. "It's like he can see in your body," says Maryland-based anthropologist Rebecca Seib, who was mystified when Cooper correctly diagnosed an enlarged ovary simply by holding her hand.

"I was stunned. This man is a miracle," she says. "I went not as a patient, but as an anthropologist working on the Lumbee application for federal recognition. He held my hand, closed his eyes, then told me about my enlarged ovary as if he were looking right inside me."

Thanks to such testimonials, Cooper and his wife Rosey Lee are visited daily by indigent neighbors and desperate strangers. They arrive at all hours, parking under his plum trees and loitering in his chair-lined living room, where signs plead with parents to keep youngsters out of the kitchen cabinets.

During the short three weeks in 1979 that he kept a tally, Cooper says he treated more than 300 people. It hasn't slowed much since, even though his health is failing and the house is nearly impossible to find.

"If they come to my door and have need, I help them. But I don't know if I can do it much longer. I'll be 83, if I can make it to July. I'm weak," says Cooper, who talks as slowly as he walks.

"I'm hoping I'll die on the job. I would love to have my hands on someone and just as the pain left them, the Lord would take me. That might sound foolish, but I think I would enjoy death better that way."

Cooper has conversed with the Lord on this matter many times. In fact, he claims to converse with the Lord on just about everything going on in his office, including diagnosing and treating patients. He has to, having never learned to read or write his own remedies.

Even with this celestial touch, however, the cures are odd smelling and almost always bad tasting.

Shortness of breath, for example, commands a tonic made of pungent smelling asafetida (plant resin), the gum from a sweet gum tree, some bitter tasting red bloodroot (an herb) and an ounce or two of liquor. A Coke chaser is recommended, along with holding one's nose.

For sugar diabetes, a tea is brewed with opossum haw (a bush) and the triple threat of red bloodroot, yellow bloodroot and white bloodroot. You drink four ounces a day for 20 days.

Cooper has similar tonics and ointments for nervousness, heart trouble, rashes, headaches and even skin cancer—all made from things like boiled pig's foot juice, beef foot juice, lion's tongue (an herb) and Big and Little Saint John (also herbs).

Most are stored in recycled baby food jars in Cooper's bedroom, along with store-bought necessities like Spirits of Turpentine, Extract of Myrrh and something called "Indian Snake Oil," which is good for corns, toothaches, chest colds and sore throats.

"Every herb has a mate, like male and female," Cooper says, trying to explain his collection. "No one herb will work by itself. You must mix it with others to complete it."

Anthropologists have determined that 400 years ago, Indian medicine men may have known 300 to 400 plants and their specific uses. This life-saving knowledge was often passed in families from generation to generation.

As a boy, Vernon Cooper learned by tending his great-grandmother's herb garden and accompanying her on trips in search of rare herbs. The old woman lived with the family and had regular 4 P.M. to 10 P.M. doctoring hours, Cooper recalls.

Payment often came in the form of meat, butter or milk, which were much needed by a struggling tenant farm family with seven children to feed.

"The best thing she ever taught me was to trust the Lord, because you got to believe for the medicine to work. She also told me that there's a lot of cases where words would mean more than medicine. I've seen many a person I didn't do nothing for, except talk and do a little rubbin'," Cooper admits.

His great-grandmother also predicted that he'd take the power with him to the grave, as the last of the family's medicine men. Cooper says she was as infallible in this prediction as she was in her medicine. The father of two has never found a worthy apprentice.

"She didn't tell me how the family got the power to begin with, or why it was only to last 400 years," Cooper says.

"I had hoped to find somebody prepared to fit into the age we're living in now. You see what we were doing 200 years ago, in a lot of cases, is no good now. The medicine is as good as it ever was, but these days people have less confidence. They don't believe what they can't understand."

A Healing Bond

By Diane Lore. Used with permission of *The State*.

Long ago, when man was new, life was good. Man would hunt the animals and cut the plants for his needs but no more than that.

But later, man got greedy. He started to kill the animals and waste their lives. The animals, disgusted with man's behavior, called a council to punish the humans. It was agreed that they would send illness among humans and kill them for their crimes.

But the plants had pity on man. When they heard the animals conspiring against humans, they also made a pact: For every illness the animals would cause, the plants would create a cure.
—Indian legend told by John George, member of the Catawba Tribe

CATAWBA RESERVATION, ROCK HILL—The medicine cabinet is a sweltering field, filled with goldenrod, mullein, blackberries and the rolling click of cicadas.

John George, 49, and Earl Carter, 54, moved slowly through the field, eyeing the plants and weighing their valve against arthritis, hay fever and pain. Carter stops and says a small prayer. He reaches into a plastic bag and pulls out a pinch of tobacco to offer to a blackberry bush. Then he thanks it, clips it and places its leaves in his pale wooden peach basket. Carter, also known as "Many Skins," is a medicine man, a shaman, a "keeper of sacred fire," who uses his knowledge of herbs and spirituality to keep his people well.

It is a knowledge that takes years to acquire and a journey that Indians believe only a few can take. But for Carter, who lives in Waxhaw, N.C.—about 20 miles south of Charlotte—it's critically important to pass his wisdom on, in this case to John George, chosen by the tribe for the duty.

Shamanism—like other forms of alternative medicine—is getting a second look by those who believe in the healing bond between mind and body, nature and science.

It's the focus of this month's cover story in Alternative Therapies a journal that examines the scientific validity of what's considered fringe medical treatments.

"I think one of the most surprising things is that some people really do get well," said Peggy Ann Wright, author of the article, "The Interconnectivity of Mind, Brain and Behavior in Altered States of Consciousness: Focus on Shamanism."

"In some cases, it really seems to work," Wright said. "Rather than being charlatans, there are people who seem to really have an effect on the health of others—and it seems to be deeper than just a placebo effect."

That's no surprise to George and Carter. Carter, who never refers to himself as a shaman, says modern medicine often misses the mark.

"They don't look at the whole person," he said. "They only treat the symptom. They don't cure it, they just cover it up with this drug or that drug.

A shaman listens to the soul of the patient, Carter says. When he treats a patient, for example, he moves within a hand's distance from the patient. During that intimate moment, Carter says, something intangible happens: He realizes what's wrong with the patient and the patient starts to feel better. Often patients will inhale a mixture of herbs from the tortoise shell vial around Carter's neck, getting, he says, exactly what they need to heal.

"They stand in my realm and something just happens in that instant," he said. "Often I don't even tell people what I do, but they come and start telling me about their problems. It's like they just know."

In the family. Carter is a member of the Lumbee tribe. Always the tribe's chosen medicine man, he continued a tradition he learned from his grandmother. "I remember watching her in the field, she wouldn't even know what the name of some of the plants were, but she would just stand over them with her hand over them," he said. "And sometimes she would just say to me, "Get some of that. We need some of that.""

Following tradition, Carter should have passed his knowledge on to a granddaughter in remembrance of his grandmother. But he doesn't have one. For years, he did not have anyone to teach.

But then Carter heard through the grapevine about George, who has had premonitions and encounters with ghosts or spirits all his life. George also was learning the art of herbs, studying their edible and medicinal qualities. Perhaps, Carter thought, George could be the link between tradition and the future.

But their first meetings were less than ideal: George was an alcoholic.

"I told him he was going to have to stop it all if he wanted to do this," Carter said. "It wasn't going to work if he was using any kind of drugs." George stopped drinking eight months ago. Since then, he has been meeting with Carter at least once a week. Carter, along with teaching George about the wild plants and their medicinal purposes, has started giving George detailed instruction about certain ceremonies that are the foundation of American Indian spirituality.

"I realized this was my purpose. I realized that everything in my life was leading up to this," George said.

Mind and body. Carter said it might take years for George to learn all he knows. One reason is because strict knowledge of plants is not enough, Carter said.

Book knowledge is great, he said, but books only outline plants' purposes and how they can be recognized. People need to know when to gather the plants, which parts can be used and how they should be applied.

Carter remembered, for example, a doctor calling him for advice.

The doctor had a patient who had been chopping down bushes and got smacked in the face with a poison ivy plant. The plant not only got on the patient's face, but also in his throat. Nothing had worked to cure the problem.

Carter told the doctor to use more poison ivy. "Poison ivy? The doctor thought I was crazy," Carter said. "But I told him how to boil it and make a tea out of it. I told him the patient would get better. And he did. Within a week."

Carter also used plants to make a cream for a scar on his wife's leg—caused after she had a knee replacement. "The doctor said, 'How did you get it to heal this fast?' I just told him I had what was needed."

And Carter says modern medicine is still fairly unwilling to view healing as a mind and body experience, either for the patient or the physician.

For example, a key component of shamanism is the medicine man's ability to enter an altered state of consciousness, according to Wright.

That's not so strange: Most people are familiar with hypnosis, meditation and visualization of help patients deal with pain or other physical ailments. But usually, it's the healed, not the healer, who enters the altered state. That's not the case with shamans.

"Whatever the reason, there does seem to be a correlation between the neurophysiology (of the shaman) and the act of healing," Wright said. "Even though it's a very hazy picture and all the pieces are not there yet, a pattern is emerging."

That pattern, she said, seems to be linked with certain sections of the brain, brain waves and genetic factors.

"Whatever it is, it is not chaotic or random," Wright said. "An outline is there."

George and Carter already knew that.

"We know some people who are skeptical. I don't blame them a bit."

George said, "But I know the power of the plants, the mind, spirit and soul. And I don't question it.

BIBLIOGRAPHY

General

Barton, Lew. "Me-Told Tales Along the Lumbee." *North Carolina Folklore* 19.4 (November 1971): 173-76.

Brown, Wendy. "Home remedies—and a pinch of faith—cure ills in N.C." *Atlanta Journal and Constitution* (Georgia) 15 January, 1995: Sec. M, p. 6.

Carter, Forrest. *The Education of Little Tree*. Albuquerque: University of New Mexico Press, 1976.

Croom, Edward M., Jr. "Herbal Medicine Among the Lumbee Indians." *Herbal and Magical Medicine: Traditional Healing Today*. Ed. James Kirkland. Durham: Duke University Press, 1992. [137] -69.

Croom, Edward M., Jr. *Medicinal Plants of the Lumbee Indians*. M.A. Thesis, University Microfilms International, Ann Arbor, Michigan, 1983.

Dial, Adoph L., and David K. Eliades. *The Only Land I Know: A History of the Lumbee Indians*. San Francisco: Indian Historian Press, 1975.

Exley, Helen, ed. *In beauty may I walk... Words of Peace and Wisdom by Native Americans*. New York: Exley Publications LLC, 1997.

"Lucie Mae Hammonds Locklear (and others), Lumbee Herbologists: "Informal Conversations" Videotape. Lumberton: Title IV Compensatory Indian Education Program, Public Schools of Robeson County, 7 Dec. 1989. [IERC] Indian Education Resource Center.

Native American Ethnobotany Database: Foods, Drugs, Dyes, and Fibers of Native North American Peoples. University of Michigan, Dearborn. Information made available by Dr. Dan Moerman, Professor of Anthropology (http://www.umd.umich.edu/cgi-bin/herb/).

North Carolina's Medicinal Plants: How Native Plants Are Used For Their Medicinal Properties, by Ingrid P. Fricks (http://www.uncwil.edu/bio/fricks2.html).

Okuda-Jacobs, Angelina. *Planting Health, Culture, and Sovereignty: Traditional Horticulture of the Lumbee Nation of North Carolina*. M.S. Thesis, Land Resources, University of Wisconsin, 2000, p. 38.

Snow, L. F. "Catawba Medicines and Curative Practices." *Journal of American Folklore* 52 (1944): 37-50.

Steedly, Mary Margaret. *The Evidence of Things Not Seen: Faith and Tradition in a Lumbee Healing Practice.* M.A. Thesis, University of North Carolina at Chapel Hill, 1979.

Vestal, Paul K., Jr. "Herb Workers in Scotland and Robeson Counties."

North Carolina Folklore Journal 21.4 (Nov. 1973): 166–170.

Wall, Steven, and Harvey Arden. *WisdomKeepers, Meetings with Native American Spiritual Elders.* Hillboro, Oregon: Beyond Words Publishing, 1990.

Lumbee History

Arnett, Ethel S. *The Saura and Keyauwee in the Land that Became Guilford, Randolph, and Rockingham.* Greensboro, N.C.: Media Inc., Printers and Publishers, 1975.

Dial, Adolph L., and David K. Eliades. *The Only Land I Know: A History of the Lumbee Indians.* San Francisco: Indian Historian Press, 1975.

1885 *Laws of North Carolina* ch. 51, "An Act to Provide for Separate Schools for Croatan Indians in Robeson County." 10 Feb. 1885.

1887 *North Carolina Session Laws* ch. 400, "An Act to Establish a Normal School in the County of Robeson." 7 March 1887.

Eighteenth-Century N.C. (http://www.nchistory.dcr.state.nc.us/museums/ed__time__line__18th__pt2.html).

84th Congress. 2nd Session. P. L. 84-570. "An Act Relating to the Lumbee Indians of North Carolina. 70 Stat. 254. Dated 7 June 1956, Rpt. in *U. S. Code Congressional and Administrative News,* 84th Cong., 2nd Session (1956), vol. 1.

Evans, W. McKee. *To Die Game: The Story of the Lowry Band, Indian Guerillas of Reconstruction.* Baton Rouge: Louisiana State University Press, 1971.

Knick, Stan. "How Long Have the Lumbees Been Here?" *Robesonian* 16 Jan. 1992: 4A.

The Lumbee Homepage (http://www.lumbe.org/chr___history.html).

N.C. Constitution, Amendments of 1835, article 1, sec. 3, clause 3. Rpt. in *North Carolina Government, 1585-1979* (Raleigh, 1981), p. 820.

1953 *North Carolina Session Laws* ch. 874, "An Act Relating to the Lumbee Indians of North Carolina." 20 April 1953.

Rights, Douglas. "The Trading Path of the Indians." *North Carolina Historical Review* (October 1931) 8: 403–426

Swanton, John R. *The Indian Tribes of the Southeastern United States.* (Smithsonian Institution. Bureau of American Ethnology. Bulletin 137) Washington: Government Printing Office, 1946. Pp. 112, 145, 178, 183.

73rd Cong. 1st Session. H. R. 5365. "A Bill Providing for the Recognition and Enrollment as Cheraw Indians of Certain Indians in the State of North Carolina." Introd. by Clark, 1 May 1933.

South Carolina Indians, The Cheraw (http://www.sciway.net/hist/indians/cheraw.html).

Speck, Frank G. *Catawba Texts.* New York: Columbia University Press, 1934.

Timelines of History (http://www.members.theglobe.com./algis/1725-1749html).

INDEX